The Short Oxford History
of the British Isles

General Editor: Paul Langford

# After Rome

Edited by Thomas Charles-Edwards

**OXFORD**
UNIVERSITY PRESS

# OXFORD
UNIVERSITY PRESS

Great Clarendon Street, Oxford OX2 6DP

Oxford University Press is a department of the University of Oxford.
It furthers the University's objective of excellence in research, scholarship,
and education by publishing worldwide in

Oxford New York

Auckland   Cape Town   Dar es Salaam   Hong Kong   Karachi
Kuala Lumpur   Madrid   Melbourne   Mexico City   Nairobi
New Delhi   Shanghai   Taipei   Toronto
With offices in
Argentina   Austria   Brazil   Chile   Czech Republic   France   Greece
Guatemala   Hungary   Italy   Japan   South Korea   Poland   Portugal
Singapore   Switzerland   Thailand   Turkey   Ukraine   Vietnam

Oxford is a registered trade mark of Oxford University Press
in the UK and in certain other countries

Published in the United States
by Oxford University Press Inc., New York

ISBN 978-0-19-924982-4

Printed in the United Kingdom by
Lightning Source UK Ltd., Milton Keynes

The Short Oxford History of the British Isles

General Editor: Paul Langford

# After Rome

Edited by Thomas Charles-Edwards

# General Editor's Preface

It is a truism that historical writing is itself culturally determined, reflecting intellectual fashions, political preoccupations, and moral values at the time it is written. In the case of British history this has resulted in a great diversity of perspectives on both the content of what is narrated and the geopolitical framework in which it is placed. In recent times the process of redefinition has positively accelerated under the pressure of contemporary change. Some of it has come from within Britain during a period of recurrent racial tension in England and reviving nationalism in Scotland, Wales, and Northern Ireland. But much of it also comes from beyond. There has been a powerful surge of interest in the politics of national identity in response to the break-up of some of the world's great empires, both colonial and Continental. The search for new sovereignties, not least in Europe itself, has contributed to a questioning of long-standing political boundaries. Such shifting of the tectonic plates of history is to be expected but for Britain especially, with what is perceived (not very accurately) to be a long period of relative stability lasting from the late seventeenth century to the mid-twentieth century, it has had a particular resonance.

Much controversy and still more confusion arise from the lack of clarity about the subject matter that figures in Insular historiography. Historians of England are often accused of ignoring the history of Britain as a whole, while using the terms as if they are synonymous. Historians of Britain are similarly charged with taking Ireland's inclusion for granted without engaging directly with it. And for those who believe they are writing more specifically the history of Ireland, of Wales, or of Scotland, there is the unending tension between so-called metropolis and periphery, and the dilemmas offered by wider contexts, not only British and Irish but European and indeed extra-European. Some of these difficulties arise from the fluctuating fortunes and changing boundaries of the British state as organized from London. But even if the rulers of what is now called England had never taken an interest in dominion beyond its borders, the economic and cultural relationships between the various parts of the British Isles would still have generated many historiographical problems.

This series is based on the premiss that whatever the complexities and ambiguities created by this state of affairs, it makes sense to offer an overview, conducted by leading scholars whose research is on the leading edge of their discipline. That overview extends to the whole of the British Isles. The expression is not uncontroversial, especially to many in Ireland, for whom the very word 'British' implies an unacceptable politics of dominion. Yet there is no other formulation that can encapsulate the shared experience of 'these islands', to use another term much employed in Ireland and increasingly heard in Britain, but rather unhelpful to other inhabitants of the planet.

In short we use the words 'British Isles' solely and simply as a geographical expression. No set agenda is implied. It would indeed be difficult to identify one that could stand scrutiny. What constitutes a concept such as 'British history' or 'four nations history' remains the subject of acute disagreement, and varies much depending on the period under discussion. The editors and contributors of this series have been asked only to convey the findings of the most authoritative scholarship, and to flavour them with their own interpretative originality and distinctiveness. In the process we hope to provide not only a stimulating digest of more than two thousand years of history, but also a sense of the intense vitality that continues to mark historical research into the past of all parts of Britain and Ireland.

*Lincoln College*          PAUL LANGFORD
*Oxford*

# Contents

# List of illustrations

# List of maps

# Acknowledgements

Springmount Bog Tablet
© National Museum of Ireland

Aberlemno Churchyard, battle scene
© RCAHMS

Lagore motif piece
© National Museum of Ireland

Ipswich-ware pottery
© *The Society for Medieval Archaeology*

The Lindisfarne Gospels. St Matthew
British Library, Cotton MS Nero D.IV, fo. 25v

The Ruthwell Cross. Christ recognized by beasts in the desert
Photo: Tom Middlemas

The Ruthwell Cross. Inhabited vine-scroll: the Tree of Life
Photo: Tom Middlemas

The Codex Amiatinus. The *armarium* of the Scriptures
Florence, Biblioteca Medicea Laurenziana MS Amiatinus I, fo. V

The Book of Durrow, *Incipit* of Mark's Gospel
Dublin, Trinity College MS A.4.5 (57), fo. 86
Courtesy Trinity College, Dublin

The Book of Durrow. Symbol of Matthew
Dublin, Trinity College MS A.4.5 (57), fol. 21v
Courtesy Trinity College, Dublin

Armenian Gospel book. Evangelist portraits.
Courtesy Baltimore, Walters Art Gallery MS W.537, fo. 114v

The Lindisfarne Gospels, Canon Table I: material common to all
    four Gospels
British Library, Cotton MS Nero D.IV

The Book of Kells. Canon Tables VI–VIII. Symbols paired Mtt-Mk,
    Mtt-Jn, Mk-Lk, Lk-Jn

Dublin, Trinity College MS A.I.6 (58), fo. 5
Courtesy Trinity College, Dublin

The Book of Armagh. Four-symbols page facing Matthew's Gospel
Dublin, Trinity College MS 52, fo. 32v
Courtesy Trinity College, Dublin

The Trier Gospels. Four-symbols page facing the preface *Plures fuisse*.
Trier, Domschatz, Cod.61, fo. 1v

The Book of Kells. Four-symbols page prefacing John's Gospel
Dublin, Trinity College MS A.I.6 (58), fo. 290v
Courtesy, Trinity College, Dublin

The Lichfield Gospels, carpet page and *incipit* of Luke.
Lichfield, Cathedral Library, pp. 220–21
Courtesy Lichfield Cathedral Library

The Durham Gospels. Framed text of Matt. 28: 17–20
Durham, Cathedral Library MS A.II.17, fo. 38r
Courtesy Durham Cathedral Library

The Durham Gospels. The Crucifixion.
Durham, Cathedral Library MS A.II.17, fo. 38v
Courtesy Durham Cathedral Library

Athlone Crucifixion Plaque
© National Museum of Ireland

Moore MS of Bede
Cambridge University Library MS Kk.5.6, fo. 128v
Courtesy Cambridge University Library

The Lichfield Gospels, St Luke.
Lichfield, Cathedral Library, p. 218
Courtesy Lichfield Cathedral Library

The British Isles: physical features
From Barbara Harvey ed., *The Twelfth and Thirteenth Centuries*
    (Oxford, 2001)

The distribution of amber in early modern burials
© *Medieval Archaeology*

# List of contributors

THOMAS CHARLES-EDWARDS is Jesus Professor of Celtic in the University of Oxford.

JOHN HINES is Professor of Medieval Studies in the School of History and Archaeology, Cardiff University.

ANDY ORCHARD is Professor of English and Medieval Studies at the University of Toronto and Associate Director of the Centre for Medieval Studies.

JENNIFER O'REILLY is a Statutory Lecturer in the Department of History, University College Cork.

ROBIN CHAPMAN STACEY is Associate Professor of History at the University of Washington.

### Editor's note
On behalf of all the contributors I have the pleasure of thanking all those who have helped to bring this book into being: Colin Baldwin, Sarah Barrett, Matthew Cotton, Fiona Edmonds, Nigel James, Fiona Kinnear. As editor I am deeply grateful to my fellow contributors and to Paul Langford, the General Editor of the series.

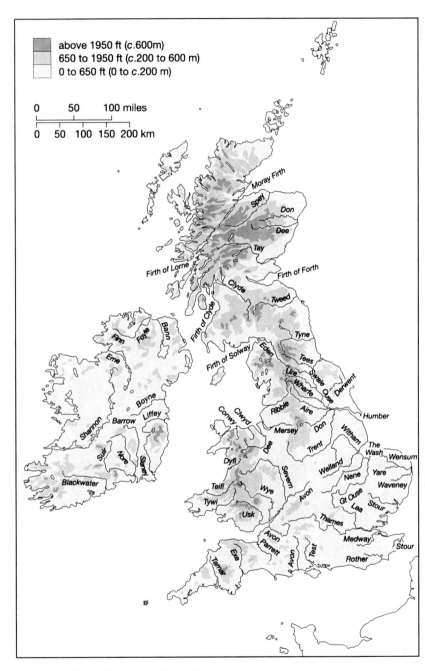

**Map 1** (a) The British Isles: main physical features.

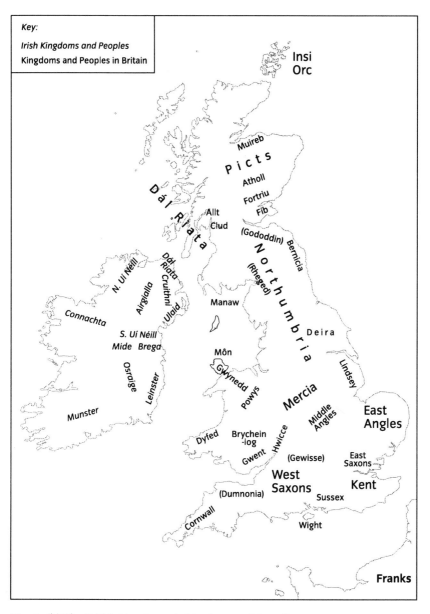

Key:

*Irish Kingdoms and Peoples*
**Kingdoms and Peoples in Britain**

Insi
Orc

Muireb

P i c t s

Atholl

Fortriu

Fíb

Allt
Clud

(Gododdin)

Bernicia

N o r t h u m b r i a

(Rheged)

D á l   R i a t a

N. Uí Néill

Airgialla

Dál
Riata
Cruithni

Ulaid

Manaw

Deira

Connachta

S. Uí Néill

Mide   Brega

Môn

Gwynedd

Lindsey

Osraige

Leinster

Powys

Mercia

Middle
Angles

East
Angles

Munster

Dyfed

Brychein
-iog

Gwent

Hwicce

(Gewisse)

East
Saxons

West
Saxons

Kent

(Dumnonia)

Sussex

Cornwall

Wight

Franks

**Map 1** (b) The British Isles: the main kingdoms and dynasties.

**Figure 1** Springmount Bog Tablet. Six tablets were found in a bog at Springmount, Co. Antrim. The illustration shows the most legible tablet. They are rectangular pieces of yew with a sunken surface containing a thin layer of wax, on which someone could write with a pointed instrument, a stylus. Wax tablets were the normal medium used for everyday writing and for drafts of texts in Antiquity and the early-medieval period. This tablet contains a scribe writing Psalm 31: 1–7. Photograph: copyright National Museum of Ireland.

# Introduction

## Thomas Charles-Edwards

One succinct characterization of the period 400–800, namely 'after Rome', is both true and false. The period opens as the Roman Empire in the West ceased to exercise power over its British provinces. The implications of that change dominate the history of fifth-century Britain. In a different way they also deeply influenced Ireland and North Britain, beyond Hadrian's Wall. The Roman frontier ceased to have the central position dividing a consciously civilized Roman Britain from the barbarians outside. At the same time it became easier for elements of late Roman civilization to be adopted by the barbarians themselves. It is as if it were easier to imitate Rome when Rome's army no longer stared one in the eye. There was also, however, a Christian, non-violent Rome, whose authority did not retreat with the legions of imperial Rome but extended its authority over the whole of the British Isles. From this point of view, the period from 400 to 800 was anything but 'after Rome'. Whereas the Irish monk Columbanus (d. 615) was proud that his people had never been conquered by imperial Rome, he was equally proud that the Irish had received the faith through a mission from papal Rome.

The end of imperial power in Britain was far more than a substitution of one set of powerful men in place of another. The entire political order and material culture were transformed. The Roman Empire had a professional army and a bureaucracy. It therefore had a division between soldiers and civilians, whereas across the frontier there was no such division. Among the barbarians any able-bodied free man was a warrior: to bear arms was an aspect of being male and free, not a profession. In order to be a civilian, a man had first to be a *civis*, a citizen, a member of the one Roman citizen body whether one lived on the Anglesey coast, looking out across the sea towards barbarian Ireland, or in the fortress town of Amida on the River Tigris.

Alongside the bureaucracy, which worked for the Emperor, there was also a landed aristocracy, most of them local gentry (*curiales*) but some with huge landed estates scattered across more than one province. One distinguishing characteristic of this aristocracy—not one shared by them all, but something which enhanced aristocratic birth and wealth—was a high literary culture. In the East the language of this culture was Greek; in the West it was Latin. In the East a schoolboy's imagination was shaped by long hours studying Homer; in the West it was Virgil. But Greek and Latin literature had been living cheek by jowl for many centuries, Latin poets imitating Greek, Latin-speaking philosophers translating Plato and Aristotle into their own language in a process that continued even as the Saxons conquered lowland Britain.

There was, however, no universal education for all citizens in the Empire. The parents of St Augustine of Hippo (in Roman Africa, where the language of government and high culture was Latin) were of the *curiales*, local gentry; yet they had to scrimp and save in order to put their son through school, and even then he had to take a year out because funds ran too low. The hope was that his education would lead to distinction as a lawyer and perhaps a post in the imperial bureaucracy. The government of the Empire required a flow of educated men; and even families of fairly modest means, such as St Augustine's parents, were prepared to spend heavily to enable a son to rise to high office. The needs of government for educated officials as well as of the elite for offices and for the display of aristocratic culture all rested on the standard education: they formed an interdependent system that linked government, high status, and culture right across the Empire. If the parents of St Patrick, the great British missionary to Ireland, also *curiales*, had not seen their son captured by raiders and taken off as a slave to Ireland, they too might well have given Patrick almost exactly the same education in the far north of the Empire as St Augustine received in the far south. Once through his education, a man shared the cultural assumptions of all those who, whether they came from Britain, Gaul, Italy, or Africa, had studied the same poets and had modelled their prose on the same great orators.

If the better-off supplied the educated recruits to man the government of the Empire, the imperial bureaucracy was paid by taxes, principally land taxes, which fell heavily on the peasants. The main consumer of these taxes was not, however, the bureaucracy but the army. The corollary of a division between a civilian population and a professional army was that the civilians were taxed in order to pay and supply the army. Across the frontier, where liability to military service was a virtually inescapable consequence of free status and male sex, rulers did not have the same problems in providing themselves with an army. On the frontier, professional Roman soldiers, paid from taxes, faced peoples for whom warfare was part of their social fabric, and for whom no taxation system was required and no bureaucracy to administer its collection and disbursement. The frontier thus divided two political orders and two civilizations.

## New nations

The frontier also separated one part of Britain from another and Ireland from Britain. For the Gallic theologian and chronicler Prosper, writing in the 430s, almost a generation after the central imperial government had last exercised control over Britain, the two islands could still be contrasted as they had been in the past. Britain was 'the Roman island', Ireland 'the barbarian island'. The frontier had existed for so long and its effects had been so profound that it left a mark upon the political and cultural landscape even when the Roman army had long left. When an Irish noble was commemorated by an inscription in fifth- or sixth-century Ireland, he was commemorated in Irish and in an alphabet, ogham, devised for Irish. The initial idea of commemorating someone by means of an inscription on stone was admittedly Roman, but the way in which this idea was given effect was carefully non-Roman. Yet, when an Irish nobleman was commemorated in Britain, he was commemorated in Latin and in Roman capitals as well as (sometimes) in Irish and in ogham.

In Northern Britain the effect of the frontier had been even more profound. For most of the period of Roman rule, the *limes* had been along Hadrian's Wall, between the Solway Firth and the mouth of the Tyne. For part of it, however, it had been further north, along the Antonine Wall between the Firth of Clyde and the Firth of Forth. Even when it lay further south, Roman control continued to be exercised over the Britons who lived between the two Walls. Beyond the Antonine Wall, however, a new grouping of peoples developed, the Picts. Initially this was a federation of smaller peoples which retained their names and identity, but by the eighth century at the very latest it had acquired the status of a distinct people. In recounting the campaigns of his father-in-law, Agricola (AD 80–83), the Roman historian Tacitus described the peoples beyond the northern frontier of Roman Britain simply as Britons. He made no distinction between them and the Britons further south, other than that one group had previously been made subject to Rome and the other had not. By AD 300 those former Britons living beyond the Forth and the Clyde were no longer perceived as Britons but as Picts. A similar process took place on the Rhine frontier: in the first and second centuries numerous small peoples lived across the Rhine, but by the fourth century they were grouped into two great federations, the Franks across the lower Rhine and the Alamans across the upper Rhine. They, too, would develop into distinct peoples—the Franks into the most important Continental neighbours of the British Isles.

The Roman frontier shaped the political geography of the British Isles, even after Roman rule had come to an end. By the eighth century the Picts had their own separate form of Celtic. Yet, if one examines the list of features by which eighth-century Pictish had come to differ from British (the language of the Britons, ancestor of Welsh, Cornish, and Breton), it soon becomes apparent that all these distinctive features date from the period after the formation of the Pictish federation. The Roman frontier thus created a new linguistic divide: between Pictish, derived from the form of British spoken beyond the Antonine Wall, and late British, spoken by those Britons under Roman rule. The whole process was a notable example of the way in which a new people could emerge: from a military federation via subsequent separate linguistic development beyond the frontier and, at the same time, an emerging distinct material culture. Whereas long-cist cemeteries are found both south and north of the Forth, the few Pictish symbol stones found outside Pictish territory were probably conscious imitations of a neighbouring culture.

If the formation of a Pictish people began when Rome still ruled most of Britain, other peoples appeared later, after the end of Roman power in Britain. In 400 there was no England and no Scotland, and likewise no English or Scottish people. That is why this book mentions Scotland, if at all, only as a modern geographical expression. Instead, 'Northern Britain' will refer initially to that part of the island that lay beyond Hadrian's Wall, later to the lands north of the Humber. The people known as Scots (*Scotti*) in the seventh and eighth centuries were the Irish; that some Irish (*Scotti*) were already settled in what is now Argyll in western Scotland is a potential source of confusion. Similarly, any confusion between a British and an English identity is wholly anachronistic for this period. The term 'British Isles'—used without any hesitation by the Irish geographer Dícuil, writing in 825 about his experiences in the Hebrides thirty years earlier—has nothing whatever to do with the English. The English, like the Irish, were newcomers to Britain. It was even believed in this period that the Picts were also newcomers. This, as we have seen, is a half-truth: any Pictish identity as a distinct people was indeed novel, but the Pictish people was created by political circumstance within Britain not by a migration from outside. Only the Britons were not believed to be recent immigrants.

Part of this book is thus about the creation of new peoples. As the example of the Picts illustrates, the process of creation was not always what later people believed it to have been. In the case of the English it very probably did involve mass migration across the North Sea and the Channel. That is not to say that the migrants brought their English identity with them: they included members of different peoples along the North Sea littoral from the Rhine to the Jutland peninsula. Englishness came later. Nor does it imply that the English were simply the biological descendants of these migrants from Germania to Britain. The creation of an English people dominant from Thanet to the modern Welsh border also proceeded by recruiting Britons; they were induced to abandon the British language and culture—and probably also the Christian religion—in favour of the language, culture, and gods of the immigrants. What they adopted, however, was not the culture of any one immigrant group but a new language created through a colonial mix of different Germanic peoples (explained more fully in Chapter 2).

The Britons were believed both by themselves and by their neighbours to be the original inhabitants of the island. After all, had they not given their name to Britain? No doubt in the long perspective of archaeological time this belief was false. Yet it was nonetheless an important element in contemporary understanding of the history and shape of Britain. No one knew of a people before the Britons. The English might bring new names for hills and rivers, but the old ones, indeed those believed to be the original ones, were British. Some effort seems to have been made by the Britons to remember their names for places in their island, even when those places had been taken from them. For one thing, the Britons could use their status as the original inhabitants to argue that the island was their inheritance, that the newcomers were intruders who should, by justice, be ejected. The English, however, were proud to have been the conquerors of the better part of Britain. Later, when the English became Christians, their historian, Bede, could appeal to Gildas, the historian of the Britons: had he not testified that it was through their sins that the Britons had lost their lands to the English? In God's plan immigrants were not necessarily intruders: had not Israel migrated from Egypt through the desert to the land of the Canaanites?

A more modest misfortune, in addition to English conquests, gradually overtook the Britons. From Gildas and from the earliest laws of those Britons who themselves migrated to north-western Gaul in this period it is apparent that the Britons regarded themselves as *cives*, 'fellow citizens', together with the Romans. The Emperor's armies might have such pressing duties close to Rome or Constantinople that rescuing the Britons was out of the question; but that did not imply that the Britons had left that immense political community, the citizens of Rome. Their haircuts (ever a reliable index of cultural loyalty) were Roman; a fierce line was taken with any Briton who wore his hair long like the barbarians. Yet the Romans themselves did not continue to be so sure that the Britons were their fellow citizens. For the sixth-century poet Venantius Fortunatus, educated in Ravenna but settled in Poitiers in Frankish Gaul, the Britons were just another barbarian people. One of his patrons was the bishop of Nantes, Felix, of a noble Aquitanian family from the south-west but with a hereditary claim to the bishopric of a city that lay close to the mouth of the Loire and on the edge of British (or, as we would say, Breton) territory. Venantius Fortunatus' praise for Felix's handling of his British neighbours was in remarkably similar terms to the traditional ways in which a successful Roman general could be praised for putting down a barbarian incursion.

British perceptions of who they were thus diverged from the ways in which they were perceived by their neighbours to the south. The earlier view of them as just another provincial people within the Empire is reflected in the history of the words 'Wales' and 'Welsh'. The Franks used these terms of their Roman neighbours in Gaul, just as the English used them of the Britons: there were Welsh in what is now France just as there were Welsh in Britain. The division was between settlers within the Empire who spoke Germanic languages and the population that had been part of the Empire for centuries. Germanic speakers called those Welsh whom Gildas, the Briton, called fellow citizens, whether they were Romans or Britons. On both sides of the Channel, moreover, Welshness was a matter of status as well as ethnicity. If someone killed a Welshman, the compensation paid for the homicide was generally half that paid for the Frank or Englishman of corresponding rank.

The main change to outsiders' perceptions of British identity came about as a result of British settlement in north-western Gaul, namely the creation of what would henceforward be another lesser Britannia, or Brittany, south of the Channel alongside the older Great Britain to the north. The British settlers (whom it is convenient to call Bretons while always remembering that contemporaries called them simply Britons) were different in language and in other ways from the Gallo-Romans, the Romans who lived in Gaul. Most Bretons spoke British (that is, a Celtic language); the Gallo-Romans, however, had largely ceased to speak the closely related Gaulish (also Celtic) and now spoke Latin, which would develop towards French and Occitan. Even though some Bretons, and indeed some Britons back home in Britain, also spoke Latin, they were a minority. |

There was also a crucial political dimension. The Franks and the Gallo-Romans reached an accommodation: military force was controlled by Frankish kings and initially largely provided by the Franks themselves. The Gallo-Romans predominated in the Church and in the bureaucracy. Gallo-Romans paid taxes; Franks fiercely resisted any attempt to tax them. Effectively this accommodation was a version of the old division between a professional army and a civilian population, the latter being taxed to pay the former; but also, and most importantly, the Frankish King Clovis (c.482–511) had converted to Catholic Christianity, the religion of the Emperor, and not to Arian Christianity, the religion of his fellow barbarian Gothic kings, Theodoric in Italy and Alaric II in Toulouse and in Spain. By the terms of this accommodation the Gallo-Romans gave their political allegiance to Frankish kings, while the Franks allowed local government to continue in the old Roman *civitates*—cities with appendant territories, such as Tours with the Touraine or Angers with Anjou. In the *civitas* the leading figures were the bishop, often of Gallo-Roman aristocratic background, and the count, sometimes Frankish, sometimes Gallo-Roman.

No such accommodation was made with the Bretons in Gaul, or by the Britons with the English back home in Britain. The Bretons ruled their territory in north-west Gaul in effective autonomy. They might acknowledge the overlordship of the Frankish kings; and the Franks, for their part, might regard Breton rulers as mere counts, not kings; yet Frankish kings did not appoint their men to local offices within Brittany. In Francia, the appointment of a bishop regularly began with the local *civitas*, or factions within it, expressing support for a particular candidate; but no one could become bishop until a standard letter was received from the king commanding a particular named person to be consecrated. Especially, but not only, when the *civitas* was divided over its preference, the king would himself take the initiative. Royal control of episcopal appointments was essential to the cohesion of the Frankish kingdoms; but no such powers were exercised by any Frankish ruler in the heart of Brittany. Moreover, whereas in the early days of Breton settlement their representatives might take part in Gallic episcopal councils, this became rare in the sixth century. Ecclesiastically, politically, and linguistically Brittany became an alien enclave on the north-western edge of Frankish Gaul.

Romans were, therefore, now one people, Britons (including Bretons) another; and since, for the Romans, peoples other than themselves were barbarians, the Britons were now barbarians too, just like the Franks or the Saxons. Yet what the Britons thought was very different, as we have already discovered from Gildas and from the early Breton laws.

# Fifth-century Britain

When the Emperor Honorius told the Britons in 410 to look to their own defences, the recipients of this unwelcome instruction were the British *civitates*. Examples are the Cantii, who gave their name to

Kent, the Iceni of East Anglia, the Dumnonii of Devon and Cornwall, and the Demetae of Dyfed in south-west Wales. Characteristic of Roman political organization was the way a man from Gwynedd was described in an inscription now preserved in the church of Penmachno on the southern edge of the Snowdonian mountains (line breaks are marked by /, a shift from one face of the stone to another by //):

CANTIORI HIC IACIT / VENEDOTIS CIVE FVIT / [C]ONSOBRINO // MA[G]LI / MAGISTRAT ⏗
Cantiori lies here; he was a citizen of Gwynedd, a cousin of Maglus the magistrate.

The date cannot be fixed more precisely than somewhere in the fifth or sixth century: probably not earlier because of the formula 'lies here', which is Christian; probably not later because the use of Roman capitals throughout indicates that it is unlikely to be of the seventh century. The Latin of the inscription is bad, but in interesting ways. For example, CIVE should, correctly, read CIVIS; but the two apparent mistakes in this one word, the loss of a final -S and -E in place of -I-, are characteristic of late spoken Latin. Although British was the dominant language, Latin was still spoken as well as written by those responsible for the text of this and similar inscriptions. If we did not know that British (on its way to Welsh) would become the universal language of Wales, we might deduce from this inscription on its own that the local language was Latin (on its way to a British counterpart to French). The language of the inscription is entirely consistent with its content: Cantiori (admittedly a good Celtic name) was a citizen of Gwynedd and his cousin was a magistrate. As well as the language, the political discourse of the Empire survived.

The Emperor's instruction to the British *civitates* that they should defend themselves implied a transformation of the relationship between the Empire and its citizens. The *civitas* had been a central institution of civilian political life; the central government had been responsible for the army. The British *civitates* thus had a choice: either to hire defenders from among the barbarians or to defend themselves. For the most part the Britons took the second course, whereas their Gallic neighbours on the whole took the first. The last independent Roman military force in Gaul was overwhelmed *c.*487, but the Britons continued to challenge English dominance in Britain until 634. In Gaul, a British army led by a British king, Riothamus, fought for the Empire against the Visigoths in 469. The settlement which created Brittany probably occurred in more than one wave, but one of them may have been associated with Riothamus and his army, and more than one of them may have been military. The implication is that British society in the fifth century had been effectively militarized: the old separation between soldier and civilian had ended.

The other tactic was to ally with one barbarian war-leader against the rest. His army would then defend Roman civilians in exchange for subsidies and supplies. To a considerable extent this put the barbarian ruler and his army into the place formerly occupied by the Roman army, since it was now the taxation system of the Empire which would supply and pay the barbarians. This was the relationship which enabled the Visigoths of Alaric to cross Europe, and it was the breakdown of their treaty with the Empire which brought about the sack of Rome in 410. From this treaty relationship it was easy for the barbarian king to assume authority over the Romans whom he protected.

Even in Britain, in spite of the militarization of the British *civitates*, something similar happened. According to Gildas, writing admittedly more than a century later, *c*.540, a 'proud tyrant' hired the Saxons to defend Britain against the Picts and the Irish. The basis of the agreement was that *annonae*, the supplies formerly provided for the Roman army, should be paid to a Saxon force which was allowed to settle in eastern Britain. For a long time, according to Gildas, the arrangement endured, with the supplies being delivered on a monthly basis. (It is striking that even in the mid-sixth century Gildas knew the technical terms for such supplies: *annonae* and *epimenia*.) Subsequently, however, the treaty was broken, and the Saxon army that had been invited into Britain to repel 'the northern peoples' now became a far greater threat than any posed by the Picts and the Irish. This Saxon army did not content itself with attacking the neighbouring *civitates* but sought to conquer all Britain. This may be the event noted by a chronicler based in Gaul and assigned by him to the nineteenth year of the Emperor Theodosius II (441–2): according to him Britain now passed under Saxon control. Gildas's account is no doubt oversimplified, especially in its implication that it was not until 'the proud tyrant' and the councillors of the Britons issued their fatal invitation that Saxons were settled in Britain. As Chapter 1 will show, that is most unlikely to be true. Nevertheless, it may be true that a Saxon army was allied with the Britons, that its settlement, at least, was sanctioned, and that it was the rupture of this treaty which led to the subjugation of a large part of Britain to the Saxons. The implication of the situation as well as of Gildas's words is that there were two military forces (quite apart from hostile Picts and Irish): one was British and the other was Saxon. A breaking of the treaty by the Saxons thus presupposed an intention to defeat the British army or armies and so achieve a military domination of Britain. Gildas is also likely to have been correct in his claim that, after this major disaster, much more effective resistance was later mounted by the Britons, and that this led, by the end of the fifth century, to a limited territorial recovery by the Britons.

Two things, in the long run, made the Saxon settlement of Britain quite different from the Frankish settlement of northern Gaul. The first was that the bulk of the settlers did not come from lands adjacent to the Rhine frontier, as did the Franks, but from the North Sea littoral right round to the Jutland peninsula. For Roman writers the invaders were Saxons: primacy, in other words, was given to a people situated around the lower Weser and the Elbe, east of the Franks. In late seventh-century England, however, primacy was given to the Angles from the southern Jutland peninsula: the West Saxon king Ine contrasted Welsh with English, even though he called the people of his own kingdom West Saxons. 'English' had already become an overarching term covering all Germanic settlers in Britain, whether they were Angles, Saxons, Frisians, or others. Different peoples evidently supplied contingents to the invasion or invasions of Britain, but almost all had much less experience of the Empire than had the Franks.

The second great difference was the success of the British *civitates* in developing their own military force. The Saxon (or English) conquest of Roman Britain was never completed (at least, not until 1282, when, long after our period, Edward I conquered Wales). Just as the Saxons were less likely than the Franks to adopt Roman habits of government and the culture which sustained those habits, so also the Britons were not in the position of the Gallo-Romans, still largely civilian and willing to welcome the Franks as their new defenders and as their kings. Britain thus suffered from prolonged warfare for a much longer period than Gaul. This partially explains why British cities did not survive as did most in Gaul.

# Ireland: territories, peoples, and dynasties

As Britain lost territory in the east, so its missionaries spread Christianity, literacy, and knowledge of the Latin language in Ireland. By the end of the sixth century the main territorial strength of Christianity and Latin culture was no longer in Britain but in Ireland. First, however, we need to have a picture of the political shape of Ireland, and then we can consider why it came to be fertile ground for a Christian Latin civilization. We may examine one specimen area, part of the province of Ulster as it existed in the eighth century.

The province of Ulster was regarded as one of the major provinces of Ireland—the so-called 'Fifths' of Ireland. It was also one of the most enduring: the people called the Ulaid, 'Ulstermen', had been known to the ancient geographer Ptolemy, whose ultimate sources are likely to have been merchants sailing to Ireland in the first century AD. The territory of the province had, however, been restricted to the lands east of the River Bann, which runs approximately from south to north through Lough Neagh to reach the sea close to Coleraine (Cúl Raithin). In 735 the kingdom of Conailli Muirthemne, in what is now Co. Louth, was also detached from Ulster. The effect was that the province was now confined to the modern counties of Antrim and Down.

In these two modern counties there were five kingdoms attested in the annals and three others which can be identified in genealogies and hagiography. The latter three are not easy to distinguish with certainty from a third category of 'population group' (an all-embracing term much loved, with good reason, by historians of early medieval Ireland). This third category embraced those minor peoples which did not have their own kings and yet are also attested in hagiography, narrative literature and genealogies.

Names for kingdoms were sometimes territorial (*mag*, 'plain'), sometimes dynastic (Uí X, 'the descendants of X'), and were sometimes derived from what Adomnán, in his Life of St Columba, called *gentes*. These latter were perceived by some as large kindreds, but status as much as descent may have determined membership. And, finally, *gentes* formed elements within a people. We may begin to find a way through these complexities by beginning with a territory, Mag

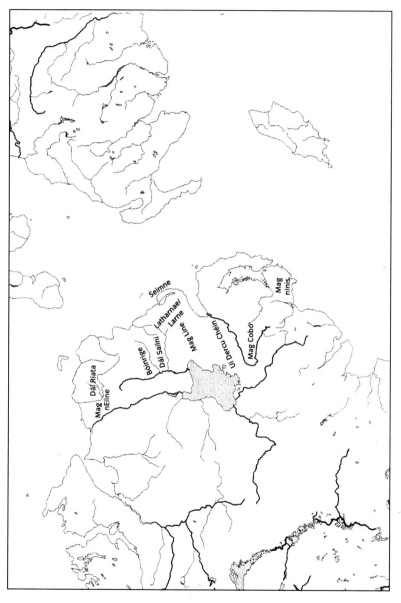

**Map 2** The Province of Ulster, c.700.

Line. Its boundaries cannot be precisely defined for this period, but for practical purposes we can make progress by using three types of evidence. First, after the reform of the Irish Church in the twelfth century Mag Line, like many other such territories, became a deanery. This enables us to know what parishes belonged to Mag Line in the later Middle Ages. Secondly, a variegated collection of earlier evidence, especially hagiographical, offers a number of places which were situated within Mag Line. Examples are the pair of ring forts on the eastern edge of Antrim Town, Ráith Mór and Ráith Becc, 'Large Fort' and 'Small Fort'. Similarly, other places are said to be in different territories. Thirdly, local topography indicates that the valley of the Six Mile Water, running from east to west and draining into Lough Neagh by Antrim Town, and including both of the two forts mentioned, must have been the heart of Mag Line. When combined together, this evidence shows that the name Mag Line always referred to something very like the area of the late medieval deanery. This could not be assumed: the next deanery to the north, Turtrye, bears the name of an early dynasty, Uí Thuirtri, but until the eleventh century they ruled land on the north-west side of Lough Neagh, outside the province of Ulster.

Mag Line was ruled by a dynasty called Uí Chóelbad, 'the descendants of Cóelub'. This can be shown by noting which kings were

Table 1 The Ulaid and the Cruithni: kingdoms and population groups (names in square brackets belonged to genealogical theory)

| Territories | Dynasties | Gentes | Peoples |
| --- | --- | --- | --- |
| Mag Line | Uí Chóelbad | Dál nAraidi | Cruithni |
| Mag nEilni/Eilne | Uí Chóelbad | Dál nAraidi | Cruithni |
| Mag Cobo/Cuib | Uí Echach Cobo | Dál nAraidi | Cruithni |
| | Latharnae | Dál nAraidi | Cruithni |
| | Uí Dercu Chéin | Dál nAraidi | Cruithni |
| | | Dál Sailni | Cruithni |
| | | Dál mBúain | Cruithni |
| Mag nInis | | Dál Fiatach | Ulaid |
| | Uí Echach Arda | Dál Fiatach | Ulaid |
| | Cenél nGabráin | Dál Riata | [Érainn] |
| | Cenél Loairn | Dál Riata | [Érainn] |
| | Cenél Comgaill | Dál Riata | [Érainn] |
| | Cenél nÓengusa | Dál Riata | [Érainn] |

associated with such sites within Mag Line as Ráith Mór and Ráith Becc. The genealogies of the Uí Chóelbad were preserved in several major medieval collections; and they enable the scholar to associate further names with Mag Line. Here, however, we meet the first serious trap. By the middle of the seventh century one branch of the dynasty had acquired the kingship of Eilne, further north between the Bann, the Bush, and the sea, and including Coleraine. One scrap of evidence in the Book of Armagh suggests that this northern branch, although kings of Eilne, retained control of a church within Mag Line, Domnach Combair, which has plausibly been identified with Muckamore, on the southern edge of Antrim Town. This bears an ancient type of name—using *domnach*, from an early Christian Latin term for a church, *dominicum*, no longer used for new churches after AD 500—and it is likely to be an older foundation than Óentrab, the church of Antrim. The latter was subordinate to the great monastery of Bangor and later became a more important church than Domnach Combair: the site is marked by a post-Viking round tower. So far, then, we have a dynasty, Uí Chóelbad, with two branches, ruling two territories some miles apart; and yet the links of the junior, northern branch with its old territory of Mag Line were preserved in the ecclesiastical sphere. The subordinate position of the northern branch may also be marked by the demotion of its principal church, Coleraine, said by Adomnán to have been the seat of a bishop in Columba's time, but by 700 only a former episcopal church.

The next step in an enquiry into the political shape of the province of Ulster is to note that the genealogies associate the Uí Chóelbad with three other dynasties, the Uí Echach Cobo, Latharnae, and Uí Dercu Chéin. Moreover, their relationship, as expressed by the genealogist, explains the name of the last of the three, Uí Dercu Chéin; it cannot therefore be the personal invention of one genealogist. The story has it that Cóelub, ancestor of the Uí Chóelbad, Echu, ancestor of the Uí Echach Cobo, and Nainnid, ancestor of the Latharnae, were sons of Crond ba Druí by Indecht, daughter of a king of the Ulaid. They also had half-brothers, sons of Crond ba Druí by a second wife, Findchóem, who came of the Ciannacht of Glenn Geimin (the valley of the Roe Water, around Dungiven, Dún nGeimin). This is a statement of the inner composition of a ruling *gens*, Dál nAraidi: Uí Chóelbad, Uí Echach Cobo, and Latharnae are given a status higher than that accorded to Uí Dercu Chéin, since the Ulaid, the people of their ancestors' mother, was a more powerful and pres- ·tigious people than the Ciannacht Glinne Geimin. The meaning of the name Uí Dercu Chéin was 'Descendants of a daughter-member- of-the-*gens* of Cian' (namely Ciannacht). With *dercu Chéin* one may contrast the name of the founder, patron saint, and first abbot of Bangor, as recorded in Adomnán's Life of St Columba, Comgall moccu Araidi, 'Comgall son-member-of-the-*gens* of Araide'. Com- gall belonged to Dál nAraidi, although he was descended from none of these ancestors of ruling kindreds within his *gens*. Royal dynasties only formed part of a *gens*.

We began with a dynasty, Uí Chóelbad, which ruled one territory, Mag Line, and subsequently acquired the kingship of another, Eilne. Now that we have moved from dynasty to the larger and more com- plex group known to Adomnán as a *gens*, things have become more complicated: Dál nAraidi was, in part, a group of dynasties supposed to be related to each other, but in complex ways which denoted dif- ferences of political status. Dál nAraidi, so far, seems to be a super- dynasty, grouping together the rulers of five territories: Uí Chóelbad, rulers of Mag Line and Eilne; Uí Echach Cobo, rulers of Mag Cobo (roughly the diocese of Dromore in west Co. Down); Latharnae (the name is preserved in the modern town of Larne, but it extended as far north as to include Glenarm); and, finally, the lesser dynasty of Uí Dercu Chéin, impossible to locate with any strong probability, but plausibly to be situated in the Laggan valley around the modern Belfast. Yet, as the descent of Comgall shows, that characterization is insufficient. There were other members of the *gens*, Dál nAraidi, who were not members of any of these royal dynasties. Sometimes the genealogists say of one branch of a lineage, 'and they are the royals (*rígrad*)'. If, then, the descendants of Crond ba Druí were seen as the royals of Dál nAraidi, there were also non-royals. Moreover, the head of a monastery such as Bangor was accorded a status in the laws equivalent to a king. In any reasonable list of the five most important churches of pre-Viking Ireland Bangor would be one, together with Armagh, Iona (in a part of Britain settled by the Irish, but also highly influential in Ireland), Clonmacnois, and Kildare. Bangor was not in the heartland of Dál nAraidi but close to the frontier between them and the Ulaid.

The final and largest 'population group' was the people. In

Adomnán's Life of St Columba, Comgall moccu Araidi, abbot of Bangor, was said to belong to 'the peoples of the Cruithni'. The Cruithni (occasionally Cruthin or Cruithin, but Cruithni is normal) are well attested in the annals during the pre-Viking period. From one entry for 563 it looks as though a single Cruithnian people could be called a Cruithne, -e being a singular ending while Cruithni, with -i, is plural. Not all the Cruithni belonged, however, to Dál nAraidi. The most important church within the modern Co. Antrim was Connor (in Old Irish a plural, Condairi, referring to the people of the church, not the buildings). This lay north of Mag Line in the territories lying between it and the other kingdom of the dynasty, Eilne. Its founder and patron saint, Mac Nisse, and also its 'second patron', Colmán Ela, belonged to another gens called Dál Sailni. In the genealogies, this is regarded as 'a base-client people', aithechthuath, and seems to be non-royal. Yet it retained a position of some consequence through its connection with Connor, and also with two other churches, one among the Southern Uí Néill, Lann Ela, and the other just over the boundary into northern Leinster (and next door to Maynooth), Láthrach Briúin.

Less prestigious was the neighbour of Dál Sailni to the north, Dál mBuain (or Bóinrige), in the valley around Broughshane and including Slemish, famous for its supposed connection with St Patrick. This was the gens to which belonged, according to a story already current by the end of the seventh century, Patrick's master when he was a slave, Míliucc maccu Buain, king and druid. What is instructive about this story is that it is almost certainly false. There is good evidence in Patrick's own Confessio that he was a slave near Killala, Co. Mayo—in Connaught, not Ulster. The story was told in order to contrast the iniquitous king of Dál mBuain with Patrick's friend from the Ulaid, Díchu, ancestor of the ecclesiastical family of Saul, Co. Down, reputed to be Patrick's burial place. A further implication of the story was that Dál mBuain, however powerful it may have been in the past, was now tributary and non-royal. Among the peoples of the Cruithni, therefore, some were known by the names of gentes and some were royal, while others were thought to have lost royal status.

'A tuath without a scholar, a church, a poet, and a king is not a tuath.' This resounding declaration by an eighth-century Irish lawyer indicates that, for him, a local people, tuath, was not defined by ethnicity or territory but by political standing; and that political standing was enhanced by possession of any person of high status, by scholar or poet as much as by king. All the evidence—of annalistic obits as much as of the laws—shows that this statement represented assumptions universal among the Irish. The standing of the Dál Sailni was enhanced by their association with the church of Connor, even though they were a lesser *gens* than Dál nAraidi, with its kings and also its connection with Bangor and other lesser churches. Both a church and its kingdom gained from possessing scholars of high status. This is the reason why Ireland was fertile ground for the new Latin civilization introduced by Christian missionaries in the fifth century.

Earlier the Irish had been willing to accept that, although one people in language and culture, they were not all of one race. They were, in other words, very like the English, who, though all English, also saw themselves as Saxons or Angles or Jutes. By the eighth century, however, the Irish were increasingly seeing themselves in more Old Testament terms, as a single descent group, one huge kindred going back to a remote common ancestor, Míl Espáine, Míl of Spain (a character invented out of Isidore of Seville's *Etymologies*, a favourite text among Irish scholars ever since the mid-seventh century). Yet, what they were coming to believe about the Irish as a whole they still tended to deny, or at least heavily qualify, when it came to small peoples, *tuatha*, such as those of Eilne or Latharnae. Some were of high political standing and were then seen as interrelated, as the Uí Chóelbad, Uí Echach Cobo, and Latharnae were descended from three full brothers. Others, however, were less closely related, such as the Uí Dercu Chéin; and yet others were alien, immigrants from another province, such as the Dál Riata of north-west Co. Antrim and Argyll. The Dál Riata never supplied a king of the province of Ulster, whereas the Cruithni, although distinct from the Ulaid, Ulstermen in the narrow sense, did provide kings of the province.

Finally, the political culture created a further use for scholars: they were needed to rewrite the past. As we have seen, the province of Ulster had come to be confined by 740 to the lands east of the River Bann. Its great days were in the remote past, the days of Conchobor, their king, and Cú Chulainn, their hero. The pre-eminent seat of kingship was then Emain Machae, Navan Fort just to the West of Armagh. But this lay outside the eighth-century province of Ulster, in the territory of 'the Easterners', *ind Airthir* (a unique case of a topographical name for an Irish people situating them in relation to another people, similar to 'East Saxons' among the English). Moreover, within the province the population as a whole were not regarded as Ulaid, Ulstermen. The Ulaid were the people of east Co. Down, to be distinguished from the Cruithni of west Co. Down and most of Co. Antrim, and also from Dál Riata in the north-east of Co. Antrim. Yet the Cruithni sometimes succeeded in elevating their kings to be kings of the entire province; indeed, the last king of Tara (the leading king of Ireland) to come from outside the Uí Néill came from the Cruithni. It is not surprising, therefore, that genealogical arguments came to be advanced that the Cruithni were 'the true Ulaid' and that they were descended from the heroes of 'the Ulster Cycle', the stories of the heroic age of Conchobor and Cú Chulainn.

It is very probable that, even before the Irish were converted to Christianity, poets and other 'people of art' had high rank and conferred prestige upon their peoples. For the first missionaries, Patrick among them, men of art were likely to be pagan and associated with pagan religion. Yet, ultimately Christianity strengthened the prestige of the people of art: the clergy were given the same high status and in turn bestowed the same standing on a local people.

There are two fundamental imaginative difficulties faced by any modern student of the period 400–800. The first is to translate oneself from the British Isles of today, in which the different nations each have a millennium or more of history behind them, into the British Isles of 400–800, when these nations either did not yet exist (the Scots) or were currently being formed (English and Picts) or were being transformed in nature (Britons). The second is to translate oneself from a period when Christianity in Western Europe is in decay to a period when it was spreading rapidly. The two are not entirely independent: the work of Gildas shows how the Jewish people, as the Chosen Nation of God even though frequently rebellious against Him, was a model and a warning to all Christian nations.

A further reason why studying the history of the British Isles between 400 and 800 is both difficult and rewarding is that three of the early Insular peoples speak to us in two languages. For the Franks, the sources of the same period are almost all in Latin, yet the Franks were not, in origin, a Latin-speaking people, though some came to be so. For them, therefore, there is a problem of translating their ideas in two directions: from the Latin of the sources into the modern

**Figure 1.1** Aberlemno Churchyard, battle scene. This stone is of critical importance for the chronology of Pictish sculpture, since there is a good chance that it commemorated the battle of Dunnichen (Nechtanesmere), which was fought only a few miles away in 685. The Northumbrians are represented as helmeted and mail-clad cavalry, the Picts without armour. The fallen figure on the bottom right, who is being pecked by a carrion-crow, emblem of battle, may represent the Northumbrian king, Ecgfrith, who was killed in the battle and is likely to have been buried on Iona. Photograph: RCAHMS.

# 1

# Nations and kingdoms: a view from above

Thomas Charles-Edwards

In the late fourth century Roman Britain was subject to major invasions mounted by sea as well as by land. One threat was from Ireland, from people called Scotti by the Romans and perhaps also from a little-known people, the Atacotti. Another was from the Picts to the north of the Firth of Forth. A third was from a people whom Roman historians called 'Saxons', but who appear to have included contingents from several peoples along the North Sea coast, from Frisia, Saxony, and the Jutland peninsula. In the very long run two of these sets of invaders would change the political shape of Britain. From the settlements of the Saxons in southern and eastern Britain would come by 700 a new nation, the English, and, in the tenth century, a kingdom of the English. From settlements by the Irish in North Britain would come, in the tenth century, a kingdom of the Scots, called Alba in the vernacular (the name for Scotland in Gaelic to this day). The Picts, however, achieved no new conquests, and by the tenth century their name would have been removed from the political map. In England, nation preceded kingdom: there was a nation of the English centuries before there was a kingdom of the English. In Scotland, kingdom preceded nation: the Scots were the Irish settled in Britain. Only half a century after an Irish (or Gaelic) dynasty had come to rule the Picts did a Scotland appear in tenth-century annals.

# The fifth and sixth centuries: Britain

The two centuries from 400 to 600 are the period for which written evidence is most exiguous on both sides of the Irish Sea. Annals deriving from the monastery of Iona in the Inner Hebrides began to be written not long after its foundation by St Columba in 563 × 565, but for a century they remained a sparse record. Among the Britons one source stands out, Gildas, described by Bede as 'their historian', namely the historian of the Britons. Gildas probably wrote *c.*540, before the plague which swept across the Middle East and Europe in the following decade. There is no contemporary written source from among the English, but this is balanced by a rich archaeological record from excavations of early Anglo-Saxon cemeteries. The English historian Bede, who completed his *Ecclesiastical History of the English People* in 731, depended heavily on Gildas and on a very limited array of Continental sources for the period before 597, the arrival of the Gregorian missionaries in Kent.

The fifth century began with Britain, south of Hadrian's Wall, still part of the Roman Empire; it ended with much of lowland Britain under Saxon control and subject to Saxon settlement. Our understanding of what happened is rendered more difficult, however, because it is hard to keep two things distinct: settlement was not the same thing as political conquest. In the fourth century the Roman army had recruited heavily from the barbarians across the frontier. Most such recruits in the West were of Germanic origin, but a detachment of Irishmen is also recorded. Moreover, large groups of barbarians were sometimes settled on land within the Empire after the Roman army had recovered control from invaders: in north-east Gaul there was a settlement of Franks of this kind. The Empire's frontiers were now under heavy pressure, even where that frontier consisted of the sea. There is no difficulty, therefore, in supposing barbarian settlement in Britain before any part of Roman Britain was taken from the Empire.

To judge by Gildas the period from 440 to 500 was marked by violent shifts in military control of territory. A swift and extensive victory for the Saxons was followed by a slower, partial, and interrupted British recovery. The Saxon victory, if Gildas is to be believed, extended across the whole island, a fire 'licking the western ocean with its fierce red tongue'. Such changes in territorial control may well have left some Saxon settlers under British rule as well as many more Britons under Saxon rule.

Barbarian settlement suggests an inability to defend Roman Britain from the sea. Yet that is not the whole story, as shown by the distribution of Irish settlements on the western seaboard. These were established from Cornwall in the south to Argyll in the north. Some, therefore, were within Roman Britain, but Argyll lay outside; and it was the settlement which had the longest future: Roman weakness was not the all-embracing explanation. What is presupposed, however, is that the defenders of the former Roman Britain largely lacked control of the sea. Although raiders had the advantage of surprise, the establishment of a territorial foothold in Britain and its strengthening from the homelands across the sea required relative security from interruption of communications. Something about the background to invasion from the sea can be inferred from the 'Saxon Shore' forts and from their more infrequent counterparts on the western coast, such as Cardiff. Something also can be inferred from the evidence of Ammianus Marcellinus, late Roman historian and former military officer. According to him, the Romans had a treaty with the Scotti in Ireland, but this was broken in 360. Raids followed leading to the great catastrophe of 367, when Scotti, Picts, and Saxons combined together to attack Roman Britain. A treaty which, once broken, led immediately to massive raids, and also to a major invasion concerted with other peoples, suggests two things: an effective political authority among the Scotti and the possession of large numbers of ships. The latter, in turn, indicates something else: that among the functions of those ships had been trade between Ireland and Britain, a trade allowed under the terms of the treaty broken in 360. If the Scotti had not had numerous ships accustomed to making the voyage across the Irish Sea before 360, it is hard to see how their attacks from the sea could have had such an impact immediately after 360; and, if this argument is correct, we have a context which can explain the continued vulnerability of Britain to attack from the Irish Sea, both before 410 and afterwards.

A possible chronology for the conquests of the barbarians can be proposed once a crucial error made by Gildas has been corrected. The correction can be justified by using two witnesses from Gaul. The first is a Life of St Germanus of Auxerre, bishop and former provincial governor, who visited Britain with a colleague, Lupus, bishop of Troyes, in 429. The Life was written about 480–90 by a priest of Lyons, Constantius—in other words half a century after the events in question. This visit has a double importance: not only does it offer a snapshot of Britain at that date, but the visit was also the background to the mission of Palladius to the Irish. Palladius was closely involved in arranging that Germanus' visit to Britain should have papal authority, and this led to Pope Celestine sending him as the first bishop for a group of existing Irish Christians. The second witness is a Gallic Chronicle ('the Chronicle of 452' after its cut-off date) which may be connected with Faustus, abbot of Lérins and subsequently bishop of Riez, who was himself a Briton.

Gildas's account depends on one crucial assumption: that, up to the time when the Britons sent a letter to the great Roman general Aetius asking for help against barbarian attacks, the barbarians in question were Irish and Picts, not Saxons. Aetius' refusal to help was followed by a treaty made with a Saxon army by 'the proud tyrant', later identified with Vortigern, together with the councillors of the Britons. The Saxon army was to be allowed to settle in eastern Britain and was promised monthly supplies. The treaty endured 'for a long time', but eventually it was broken by the Saxons. That led to major attacks by the Saxons on 'neighbouring *civitates*'; these attacks did not stop there, but spread to 'almost the whole island'.

The letter to Aetius is, therefore, central in Gildas's account: before it was sent, the enemies faced by the Britons were Irish and Picts; that threat was successfully countered by the treaty with the Saxons, made after the letter to Aetius; but this eventually led to even greater disaster for the Britons. Since Aetius was entitled 'thrice consul', an approximate date can be deduced: Aetius was consul for the third time in 446 and for the fourth time in 453, and thus the date of the letter must be 446 × 452. Hence, this date, not given by Gildas, shows that his assumption was that no Saxon settlement occurred in Britain until after 446, the earliest year in which the appeal to Aetius could have been made. This was the basis on which Bede was to establish his date for what he called 'the arrival of the English in Britain'. He had Gildas's account; he also had a list of Roman consuls, year by year; and by putting these two witnesses together he made his calculation. Indeed, Bede also had the Life of St Germanus; but unfortunately, that Life, like most others of its kind, is largely free of dates. The chronology of Germanus has to be established by using yet further sources, and these Bede did not have.

Overwhelming evidence is available, however, to show that Gildas's central assumption was wrong. To cite only three items: the Saxons were part of the great attack of 367, and when Germanus visited Britain in (as we can deduce) 429, he gave encouragement to a British army fighting Saxons who were already located in Britain. Finally, the Gallic Chronicle of 452 cited a major disaster suffered c.441 by the Britons at the hands of the Saxons—a disaster which led immediately to the Saxons achieving a military domination within the former Roman Britain. The only thing which matches this calamity in Gildas's account is the breaking of the treaty by the Saxon allies of the proud tyrant; and yet, if the entry in the Gallic Chronicle is correctly dated to 441/2, before the third consulship of Aetius in 446, it shows not merely that the Saxons were in Britain but that their power was reaching its climax before Gildas thought they were first settled in the island; and since Bede's chronology depended on Gildas's central assumption, that too is fatally undermined.

Yet Gildas evidently had some genuine information about the fifth century. For one thing, it is most unlikely that he invented the address to Aetius 'thrice consul'; for another, his account of the treaty with the Saxons uses the right late Roman terminology, such as the term for the monthly supplies they were to receive, *epimenia*, originally a Greek word. It is worthwhile trying to revise his account allowing for his central mistake. This was connected with some reasonable ideas: first, with his realization that, although the Picts had been a major threat, they no longer were, and had indeed made no territorial gains within Roman Britain; this he could explain on the basis that the Saxons in alliance with the proud tyrant succeeded in repelling 'the northern peoples'. This may well have impelled him to place the Picts first, together with their Irish allies—in other words, 'the northern peoples'—and the Saxons second.

A revised version of Gildas's account also has its central assumptions; and, if these turn out to be incorrect, the entire reconstruction of events will collapse. The principal assumption is an acceptance of Gildas's story about a treaty between the Britons and a Saxon army, which, when broken by the Saxons, led to military disaster for the Britons. On the other hand, what is not accepted is that, before this treaty, the Saxons had no settlements in Britain. It is further assumed not only that Gildas was intending to write about Britain as a whole (so much is evident) but that he knew enough about the broad trend of events in fifth-century Britain for his statements to be evidence for Britain rather than for some smaller area. A further element in the revised account is that the disaster suffered by the Britons after the treaty was broken is to be identified with the disaster recorded by the Gallic Chronicle of 452; that is made plausible by the scale of the disaster being the same, and the only difficulty was the date in relation to the letter addressed to Aetius (in Gildas some time after, in the Gallic Chronicle before the date of Aetius' third consulship). As will be obvious, the revised account is a conjectural reconstruction.

We may start with the context in which the Emperor Honorius wrote to the British *civitates* in 410 telling them that they should organize their own defence. At the end of 406 the Vandals, Suevi, and Alans had crossed the frozen Rhine and had broken into Gaul. In these circumstances the ability of the central government, based in northern Italy, to control events beyond the Alps was slight. In 407 a general called Constantine led a British army to Gaul, initially as a tyrant (a general who took power by force), but subsequently recognized as co-emperor by Honorius. Constantine III's power was, however, soon undermined by his principal lieutenant, Gerontius, and by 409 his regime was crumbling. The British *civitates* could expect no defence from him and they proceeded to expel his officials. Their subsequent appeal to Honorius was, however, singularly unfortunately timed: relations between the Emperor and Alaric led in that very year to the sack of Rome by the Goths. Imperilled in its Mediterranean heartland, it was hardly to be expected that the Empire should send its forces to defend the Britons.

By 429, the date of Germanus' visit, Saxon forces were established within Britain. In that year, at least, the army created by the British *civitates* succeeded in defeating the Saxons. At about this time we may place the treaty made with the Saxon army by the proud tyrant and by the councillors of the Britons. The 'considerable period' during which the treaty endured may have included most, if not all, of the 430s. The treaty, however, may have obliged the Saxon army to fight against other Saxons and not just against Picts and Irish, as in Gildas's account.

The breaking of the treaty may be placed towards the beginning of the 440s. The catastrophic defeats endured by the Britons were the subject of the entry in the Chronicle of 452 and were also the reason for the appeal to Aetius, 446 × 452, then in command of Roman forces in Gaul. This was the point at which considerable swathes of lowland Britain passed under Saxon rule. Indeed, to judge both by Gildas and by the Chronicle of 452, there was a serious possibility at this time that all of Roman Britain would now be ruled by whatever Saxon general led the army that broke the treaty. If that had happened, the fate of Britain would have been much more similar to that of Gaul, especially if the Saxon ruler had called upon the services of British administrators to govern Britain (all this assumes that this Saxon general still retained overall command on the Saxon side and that he called himself a king, as did most of his Continental contemporaries). Instead, the Britons in the West, those more remote from the original settlement of the Saxons in the east, mounted a counter-attack under the leadership of a man called Ambrosius Aurelianus. He was described by Gildas, who was a contemporary of his degenerate grandchildren, as 'a gentleman who, perhaps alone of the Romans, had survived the shock of this notable storm: certainly his parents, who had worn the purple, were slain in it.'

The victory of Ambrosius Aurelianus initiated a period in which the war went one way and then the other, until a major victory at a place called Mons Badonicus, won in the very month in which Gildas was born, forty-three years and one month before he was writing. If Gildas was writing c.540, this battle should have been in the closing years of the fifth century. Since then, so he says, 'external wars', namely wars against barbarians, had ceased. The period covering roughly 497–540 is sometimes called 'the Gildasian peace', since it coincided with the period of his life up to the time when he was writing. It also appears to be the period in which trading connections between south-western Britain and the Mediterranean were at their height.

The breaking of the treaty by the Saxons, their subsequent shattering victories, and the British revival under Aurelius Ambrosianus foreshadowed the fundamental shape of Britain. Roman Britain was not to become a Saxonia as much of Roman Gaul became a Francia, and eventually all of it France. There would remain a Britain beyond England. Britons and English would come to define themselves in opposition to each other. Gradually the terms of the opposition would shift: in place of Gildas's Roman-style conflict between *cives*, 'fellow citizens', and the barbarians, among whom the Saxons were only the worst, the division would increasingly be between two nationalities. Moreover, these nationalities would come to define themselves in terms of language. In 500 that part of Britain which would become Wales contained speakers of three languages: British, Irish, and Latin. By 700 the descendants of the Irish and Latin speakers of 500 probably all spoke British, now well on its way towards Welsh. On the other side, as John Hines argues in the next chapter, English was forged as a new colonial variety of Germanic, retaining no differences derived from the dialects spoken by Angles, Saxons, Frisians, and others. On the other side of the Channel the development was very different: by 700 some Franks spoke 'the Roman language' while others still spoke Frankish; both counted as Franks. The defining characteristics of nationality thus became non-linguistic south of the Channel but linguistic in Britain.

The 540s, the decade immediately after the writing of Gildas's *The Ruin of Britain*, saw a major pandemic. Plague, certainly bubonic and presumably also the related pneumonic variety, spread across the Roman world from Egypt. In 540 a well-informed observer might well have thought that a major Roman revival was under way. The armies of the Emperor Justinian had retaken Africa and were then engaged in a struggle to recover Italy from the Ostrogoths. The Franks, Catholic allies of a Catholic Emperor (although prone to look to their own interests first and the Empire's second, if at all) dominated the lands across the Channel all the way from the Pyrenees to the Elbe: the Saxons of Old Saxony now paid tribute to a Christian Frankish king. The plague was the first major dent in this revival, seriously reducing the largely peasant population of the Empire and thus the capacity of the land taxes to pay for the Emperor Justinian's wars. The arrival of the Avars, a new steppe people, in southern Russia at the very end of Justinian's reign in 665 was the second, exerting a fatal pressure on the Danube frontier. In Britain the Gildasian peace appears to have ended in the middle of the sixth century with new and widescale English advances, in particular the foundation of a new kingdom in North Britain, known by a British name, Bernicia, and centred around Bamburgh and Lindisfarne.

# The fifth and sixth centuries: Ireland

In Ireland the fifth and sixth centuries had also seen major political change. Admittedly this was not nearly so momentous as those in Britain, but nevertheless it led to the creation of a new political order which would endure until the end of the tenth century. Far more important than these political developments, however, was the conversion of Ireland to Christianity (discussed in Chapter 3). Yet the triumph of the new political order came at much the same time as the triumph of Christianity; and together they shaped the Ireland of the seventh and eighth centuries, in which art and literature, both Latin and vernacular, flourished.

The Roman historian Ammianus Marcellinus, writing about the 360s, noted that two sets of barbarians were involved in the attacks across the Irish Sea, Scotti and Atacotti. Scotti became a normal term in Latin for the Irish, alongside Hiberni, but the Atacotti vanished entirely. What is puzzling is that, although Scotti had acquired the sense of 'Irish' by the time of Patrick in the second half of the fifth century, it was not used before the late Roman period. This raises the possibility that the Scotti and Atacotti were two federations of Irish peoples involved in attacks on Roman Britain, very much as the Picts were a federation of British peoples beyond the Empire to the north. As we have seen, the Scotti and the Atacotti should have been led by people involved in the trade with Roman Britain under the terms of the treaty broken in 360. Two areas, however, have most archaeological evidence for trade with the Empire: the coastal areas of northeast Ireland (the later province of Ulster) and the fertile region between the Boyne and the Wicklow Mountains.

This possibility may be linked with another change, lying on the very edge of what can be surmised from later Irish evidence. The prehistoric site of Tara lies in the centre of what Muirchú, in the late seventh century, called 'the great plain of Brega'. Tara is a complex of structures of very different periods, from the Neolithic to (perhaps) around the second century AD. It is a site bearing a distinct resemblance to an early Irish kindred: just as in the kindred the dead still played an essential role, so also at complex sites such as Tara, what was important included both currently used structures and those which had become monuments, given meaning by an evolving narrative and by the way they defined the local landscape. By the early Christian period, it seems, Tara was all monument: no permanent structures were still in use. Yet meetings could still be held there, since it was entirely normal for great men to camp out for special occasions in the summer. Half the elite of Ireland camped at Tailtiu in the north of Brega for the 'Fair' at the beginning of August: a mixture of horse-racing, other entertainments, and serious political business. A readiness to camp out was not peculiar to the Irish: when the Frankish king Chilperic was assassinated in 584, his body was prepared for burial by a bishop who was encamped by the royal hall at Chelles in order to have a meeting with the king.

In the early Christian period Tara was the pre-eminent seat of kingship in Ireland, just as Cashel was the pre-eminent seat of kingship in Munster. The king of Tara was the leading king in Ireland and might even sometimes be termed king of Ireland. Normally, from c.500 to 637, the king of Tara was a descendant of Niall mac Echdach, Niall 'of the Nine Hostages' as medieval Irish historians termed him; and the Uí Néill, 'Descendants of Niall', were thus the principal royal dynasty. After 637 and until the end of the tenth century the Uí Néill had a monopoly of the kingship of Tara. Before 500, however, it looks as though Tara may have been largely controlled by the Laigin (who gave their name to Leinster, and probably also to the Llŷn peninsula in north-western Wales). The province of Leinster may, in the fifth century, have included Brega, to the north of Dublin, and Mide, 'the Middle Land', between the Shannon and the upper River Boyne; it may thus have resembled the modern province of Leinster, whereas the early medieval province lay south of Dublin. The implication of all this would then be that the coastlands from which the great raids on Roman and post-Roman Britain were launched were mainly within this early Greater Leinster. Perhaps the Scotti of Ammianus Marcellinus were a confederation led by the Laigin, while the Atacotti may have been another confederation, further north, perhaps led by the Ulaid, the Ulstermen.

The events which lie on the edge of reliable Irish annalistic memory constituted the destruction of Leinster power in the Irish midlands—that broad swathe of fertile land including Brega (and therefore Tara) in the east and Mide further west. These midland kingdoms would later often be known as 'the land of the Uí Néill' between the Shannon and the Irish Sea. The conquest of this area by the sons and grandsons of Niall may be placed in the period 490–540, sufficiently late to be remembered when annals began to be written in the second half of the sixth century on Iona, and when Iona acquired a dependent house, Durrow, within Mide.

Munster may have seen a related change of dynastic leadership. From the sixth century until the late tenth a group of related dynasties called Éoganachta shared the kingship of Cashel. The very name Éoganacht was used as a virtual title: those who rejected the claim of the Éoganacht Locha Léin in West Munster to take a turn in the kingship of Cashel called them the Uí Choirpri Luachra; similarly, the enemies of the Éoganacht Áine (east Limerick) called them Uí Éndai, of the Éoganacht Raithlind Uí Echach Muman. This political order, in which Éoganachta were scattered across the province, replaced one in which the Corcu Loígde and Osraige had constituted branches of a single people ruling Munster, even though by 600 the Corcu Loígde were confined to west Cork and the Osraige were on the eastern frontier with Leinster, from the Slieve Bloom area in the centre of Ireland down the Nore valley almost to Waterford. An ogham inscription, probably of the first half of the sixth century, situated close to the Nore, and thus in Osraige territory, commemorates a man who belonged to Corcu Loígde. This bears out later testimony of a link between these two peoples, of east and south-west Munster respectively.

The triumph of the Éoganachta and of the Uí Néill in the northern half of Ireland may have been linked. There is some reason to think that northern kings were active in Munster in the sixth century, and also that in the seventh and eighth centuries a treaty of alliance, called a *cairde*, was normally in force between the Uí Néill and the Éoganachta. According to origin-legends dating from the eighth and ninth centuries, and from both Munster and the lands of the Uí Néill, the ancestors of the Uí Néill and the Éoganachta jointly triumphed over an early warrior-king of the Corcu Loígde. These legends purport to tell their story about the remote pre-Christian past; but if one may allow for this chronological displacement, they may well contain a historical truth.

The new dynastic order in both the southern and the northern halves of the island more or less coincided, as we have seen, with the triumph of Christianity, and thus marked the dividing point between the largely prehistoric and historical periods, between Late Iron Age Ireland and Early Christian Ireland. On current archaeological evidence, this dividing point followed the start of a revival in agriculture, shown especially in the extension of settlement.

The change to a new dynastic order may also have had a direct impact on Irish culture. Old Irish is a standard written language with remarkably little evidence of dialect. It prevailed between the late sixth century and c.900. Although we know it in a written form, it was probably also a spoken form of the language since it changed over time and the changes were phonological and grammatical, not just matters of spelling conventions. Old Irish was thus very different from Old English before the second half of the tenth century. Even though no dialect distinctions were inherited from the pre-migration period, political distinctions within Britain were effective in creating separate English dialects by the eighth century. Yet for Ireland, a country conspicuous for its many small kingdoms, we have no such evidence. The easiest way to account for such a unified language, in an island marked by local divisions of the kind prone to encourage dialect, is to suppose, first, that the standard language was, in origin, the dialect spoken by a politically dominant group, and, secondly, that their dialect was adopted by the poets and the lawyers as the language of 'the people of art', *áes dána*. The situation of Old Irish would then resemble that of Late Old English after the Benedictine Reform of the tenth century, a standard language derived, very probably, from the dialect of Winchester. The prevalence of Old Irish as the standard literary language of Ireland may thus be associated with the triumph of the Uí Néill and their allies, the Éoganachta. The language of Old Irish vernacular literature—the richest written vernacular literature of early medieval Europe—was the language of a new political order.

# The seventh century

In an addition made about AD 700 to Tírechán's account of Patrick's journeys round Ireland, Patrick is recorded as having made three solemn petitions to God. One was that God should never permit 'foreign peoples to acquire power over us'. An Irish legal tract on status, written between 697 and c.750, illustrates one of the powers enjoyed by a king: 'For there are three edicts which it is right that a king should pledge upon his peoples: an edict to expel a foreign race, that is, against the Saxons . . .' At the end of the seventh century there were reasonable fears in Ireland that an English invasion might be launched. The fears were caused by experience: in 684 the Northumbrian king, Ecgfrith son of Oswiu, sent his right-hand man Berht with an army to attack Brega. At that date the ruler of Brega was Fínsnechtae Fledach, who was also king of Tara. He belonged to Síl nÁeda Sláne, 'the Seed of Áed Sláne', namely that branch of the Uí Néill that ruled Brega; and in 684 Síl nÁeda Sláne had held the kingship of Tara for a generation, for four reigns in succession. Fínsnechtae Fledach intended that this grip on power should last indefinitely. Ecgfrith's army, however, 'laid waste the plain of Brega, including many churches, in the month of June' (Chronicle of Ireland). It took many captives, perhaps in the hope of using them as hostages, to induce Fínsnechtae Fledach to submit. Less than a year later, however, on 20 May 685, Ecgfrith was defeated and killed by the Pictish king Bruide son of Bile at Dunnichen near Forfar (north-north-east of Dundee). This put an end for the foreseeable future to the huge ambitions of the Northumbrians, and especially of one branch of the ruling family of Bernicia, Æthelfrith, his sons, Oswald and Oswiu, and Oswiu's son, Ecgfrith.

The developing scale of Northumbrian ambition is the principal theme of political and military developments across the British Isles for most of the seventh century. Yet what is remarkable about Northumbrian history at this period is how slight was the territorial basis on which it all began.

Northumbria is a term used by Bede for the Anglian territory north of the River Humber. It is sometimes matched by a corresponding term, 'Southern English', for those south of the Humber, as in the Life of Gregory the Great written early in the eighth century by someone from Whitby. Bede himself was a Northumbrian, and in the year before he died in 735 he revealed his hopes and fears for his native kingdom in a letter he sent to Ecgberht, bishop of York—hopes that Ecgberht would receive the papal pallium and be recognized as metropolitan archbishop of an ecclesiastical province embracing Northern Britain; hopes that Ecgberht would use his authority to create new dioceses; but fears that pursuit of aristocratic family ambitions at the expense of the kingdom and its Church would draw down upon Northumbria the anger of God, as once the sins of the Britons had led to their defeat and loss of most of Britain.

Yet Bede's loyalty to Northumbria could not entirely conceal the deep division between its southern and northern sections—two old kingdoms, Deira (roughly Yorkshire) and Bernicia (from Co. Durham northwards to the Forth). Until 651 Bernicia and Deira had two distinct royal dynasties, and from the reign of Æthelfrith until 651 those dynasties were in a bitter feud. It ended with the killing of Oswine, king of Deira and especial friend of Aidan, monk of Iona and bishop of the Northumbrians. Even in the early eighth century Æthelfrith was remembered at Whitby, the greatest monastery of Deira, as a tyrant who had expelled their rightful king, Edwin. Yet Deira, the kingdom conquered by its northern rival Bernicia, was the only part of Northumbria for which there is good evidence of extensive English settlement in the sixth century. Before the reign of Æthelfrith (592–616) Bernicia was confined to a small territory around Lindisfarne and Bamburgh in the north of the modern Northumberland. The foundation of Bernicia's power was laid, therefore, by Æthelfrith. In Bede's words,

At this time [namely around 597] King Æthelfrith ruled the kingdom of the Northumbrians, an exceptionally powerful ruler and most desirous of fame. More than all the leaders of the English he laid waste the people of the Britons . . . For no one among the leaders, no one among the kings made more of their lands either tributary to, or available for settlement by, the English, having slain or subdued the inhabitants. (*HE* i. 34)

The target of Æthelfrith's attacks were the Britons of what is now southern Scotland and northern England, of the Gododdin out of whose territory Bernicia was carved, of the kingdom of Dumbarton, the royal fortress and capital on the north side of the Clyde, of Rheged, probably around Carlisle, and perhaps others. Further south there was a British kingdom called Elmet in west Yorkshire, a name which endured after English conquest and remains in such modern names as Sherburn-in-Elmet. Lancashire and Westmorland would all have been British at this date.

Up to 592 the Northern Britons had largely escaped the calamities that had overtaken their southern fellows. The Picts, who had been their most dangerous and immediate enemies, had ultimately made no territorial gains. Their partially successful struggles against Deira and against the infant Bernicia became the stuff of heroic verse: Urien, king of Rheged, and his son Owain, together with their English enemy, nicknamed Fflamddwyn, 'Flame-bringer', were models of heroic warfare in Wales until the end of the Middle Ages. Yet Æthelfrith's conquests changed the political map of the north. The central belt of modern Scotland may be defined, for present purposes, as lying between a northern line from the head of Loch Lomond east to Dundee and a southern line from Ayr in the West to Berwick in the east. Here most Scotsmen live—across the most dangerous fault-line in early medieval Britain. Across the middle ran the Antonine Wall between the Firths of Clyde and Forth. Because the Picts to the north had made no permanent conquests to the south, it remained a zone of contact between Picts and Britons. In addition, the Irish of Dál Riata had extended their territory in the West, probably as far as Clach nam Breatann, 'the Stone of the Britons', on the west side of Glenn Falloch close to the head of Loch Lomond—Llyn Llumonwy to the Britons, one of the marvels of the island according to the *Historia Brittonum*. Around Loch Lomond and southwards across the Clyde was the kingdom of Dumbarton (Welsh Allt Clud). Initially, most of the central belt was British—both Glasgow and Edinburgh have British origins—but Fife and Strathearn, at least, were Pictish. For this reason, when Æthelfrith compelled many of the Britons to pay tribute, he transformed Bernicia from a small kingdom at the south-east corner of the central belt into a power that threatened all his neighbours; and, in this area, that meant the three other nations of Britain apart from the English, not just the Britons but also the Picts and the Irish of Dál Riata. According to Bede's account it was Áedán mac Gabráin, king of Dál Riata, who was so disturbed by Æthelfrith's triumphs over the Britons that he mounted a counter-attack. This led in 603 to the battle of Degsastan, in which Áedán was defeated but the contingent of Æthelfrith's brother, Theodbald, was destroyed and Theodbald himself killed. The battle was, therefore, an expensive victory for Æthelfrith and also a foreshadowing of Bernician dominance in Northern Britain.

About 604, just after the battle of Degsastan, Æthelfrith took control of Deira. As we have seen, a hundred years later this seizure of power was still regarded in Deira as the act of a tyrant. It entailed the expulsion of Edwin, son of the previous king, Ælle; and later, when

Edwin had found himself a powerful patron in Rædwald, king of the East Angles, Æthelfrith would attempt to secure his killing through bribery. When he became king, after Rædwald had defeated and killed Æthelfrith, Edwin followed his enemy's example, took control of Bernicia as well as of his native Deira, and expelled Æthelfrith's sons. The ambitions of members of two English dynasties to dominate Northern Britain lay behind the emergence of Northumbria. Edwin was defeated and killed in 633 at the hands of an alliance of those whose power he had threatened: Cadwallon, king of Gwynedd, and Penda, royal hopeful and future king of Mercia. After an ensuing year of military disaster, one of Æthelfrith's sons, Oswald, took power; he, like his father, seized power in Deira as well as in Bernicia. The surviving descendants of Edwin then had to go into exile, some as far as Francia. The last native king of Deira, Oswine, ruled for seven years, 644–51, after Oswald's death in 642, and in a period of relative weakness for the latter's brother and successor, Oswiu; when Oswine was killed, that was the end of the Deiran dynasty in the male line.

A third way in which Æthelfrith set the agenda for his Northumbrian successors was in his intervention in the Welsh marches. In 615 or 616, very shortly before his own death in battle against Rædwald, Æthelfrith won a final great victory at Chester, in which a British king, Selyf ap Cynan, was killed and also numerous monks of the great monastery of Bangor-on-Dee. Chester, although still remembered in its name, Cair Legion, as a former legionary fortress, may well have been joined with the former Roman *civitas* of the Cornovii to the south, with its capital at Wroxeter. In the eighth century these districts would be western appendages of Mercia, facing a British kingdom named in ninth-century sources as Powys; Selyf ap Cynan, Æthelfrith's opponent, was linked by later Welsh genealogists with the dynasty of Powys.

The significance of this victory is, as with many Northumbrian events of this period, that it reveals the scale of ambition rather than that, of itself, it changed the political map. The classic situation in the eighth century was that the three most powerful English kingdoms each had their British hinterland: that of Northumbria was the land of the Britons ruled from Dumbarton; that of Mercia was Wales; and of Wessex Cornwall. Partly because these British neighbours could be compelled to pay tribute, as Æthelfrith compelled the Northern

Britons, partly because, if they rejected English overlordship, they could be subjected to raids designed to take British booty and to lay waste British lands, these British borderlands seem to have enhanced the power of their English neighbours. In the early years of the seventh century, south-eastern English kingdoms, Kent and East Anglia, were the most powerful south of the Humber; yet after 625 they would never again exercise any hegemony over their neighbours. The Sutton Hoo ship-burial, close to the North Sea over which the Angles, Saxons, Frisians, and Jutes had come, and containing a rich collection of artefacts, some looking north-eastwards, back over the North Sea towards Scandinavia, probably celebrated the achievement of Rædwald, king of the East Angles, and the last leading king of the English to come from eastern England, from the original settlements of the English. Future leading English kings ruled peoples of the British frontier.

In the eighth century the leading English kingdom would be that of the Mercians, Mierce, the Marcher people *par excellence*. Hence the significance of the battle of Chester was that the Northumbrian king now sought to exploit not just the adjacent Britons but those across the *mearc*, the frontier, from the Mierce, the frontier people. It was a bid for dominance by means of military exploitation of the Britons of Wales as well as the north. It is a fair guess that Æthelfrith's defeat and death at the hands of Rædwald shortly afterwards was partly a consequence of the alarm felt by the leading English king south of the Humber at this bold intervention into his zone of influence. Yet, after Rædwald's death *c.*625, his protégé, the Deiran Edwin, now himself king of all Northumbria, would pursue the very same grand plan inaugurated by Æthelfrith.

Quite why there should be a close relationship between power over neighbouring Britons and power among English kingdoms is not wholly clear, but some further suggestions can be made. Kings and those members of their dynasties who had any prospect of kingship were accompanied by noble retinues. One element in a royal retinue was composed of young men who had not yet married or settled on a landed estate. These young men—what in Old English was called the *geoguð*, the 'Youth'—were different from their elders in more than age. First, they were mobile: when Edwin drove the sons of Æthelfrith into exile, the latter left Northumbria accompanied by 'a Youth of nobles'. Secondly, because they were mobile, kings could compete for their loyalty. In a slightly surprising passage of the Ecclesiastical History Bede says that Oswine, king of Deira, was

attractive in appearance, imposing in stature, pleasant in conversation, cultivated in his mode of behaviour, and generous in giving to all, both nobles and commoners. For that reason, because he was a king worthy in mind and appearance and deserts, he was loved by all, and from everywhere even the noblest from almost all provinces came together to serve in his retinue.

This is remarkable because Oswine's reign only lasted seven years before he was killed on the orders of his Bernician rival, Oswiu, in 651.

Tribute and booty taken from neighbouring British kingdoms enabled some English kings to be more generous than others, allowing them to recruit a larger retinue and so deploy more military force. In Northumbria, Mercia, and Wessex, which not only profited from British tribute but were also expanding by taking over British territory, the king will more often have been able to offer meritorious young retainers the opportunity to settle, whichever province it was from which they derived. Finally, the wealth derived from the Britons gave the neighbouring English kings the ability to arm their retainers well and thus to invest in future victory. The ordinary warrior at this period was equipped with spear and shield; the one who had a sword was already exceptional; mailshirts and helmets were even rarer. Part of the reason for Northumbrian, Mercian, and West Saxon power may have been this relationship between an English king, his subjugated and exploited British neighbours, and an aristocracy eager for fame, for wealth, for weapons, and for land. A stone monument, probably put up to celebrate the Pictish victory over the Northumbrians in 685 at Dunnichen, shows helmeted Northumbrian horsemen clashing with bare-headed Picts: these would be the small army of horsemen mentioned by Stephen in the Life of Wilfrid. Ecgfrith was perhaps relying on mobility and superior equipment, very much as the Normans would in a later period. One reason for the credibility of Northumbrian military ambitions was thus the scale of their investment in war. In 655 Penda, king of Mercia, mounted a great campaign against Oswiu of Northumbria. According to the *Historia Brittonum* he brought in his army British contingents together with those supplied by Southern English kingdoms; and when he had driven Oswiu into the far north and besieged him in Stirling, he compelled him to 'deliver all the riches that he had in the fortress into the hand of Penda and Penda distributed them to the kings of the Britons; and that is called "the Restitution of Stirling" '. To force Oswiu to disgorge the treasure he had taken from the Britons was a dramatic display of the rewards of victory on the part of Penda; but it was also shrewdly calculated, for it struck at the heart of Oswiu's power.

Both Edwin and Oswiu added further elements to the grand strategy inaugurated by Æthelfrith. Edwin struck much further into Wales, as far as Anglesey. Indeed, according to Bede, Edwin subjugated both Anglesey and the Isle of Man; and both were, in his day, British islands. The significance is evident from any map of the British Isles. Those two islands straddled the broader, northern section of the Irish Sea. On the one hand, they would allow the Northumbrians to gain access to the trade from the Mediterranean and from Spain and Frankish Gaul, along the Atlantic seaboard and northwards into the Irish Sea, a trade that had continued in the post-Roman period. On the other, Anglesey and Man also offered the Northumbrians the prospect of using sea power along the coasts of both western Britain and eastern Ireland. This development foreshadowed the invasion of Brega in 684 and recalled earlier uses of sea power, by the Irish against Roman Britain and by Áedán mac Gabráin, king of Dál Riata, who had sent a fleet as far as the Orkneys.

In the first half of the seventh century the main victims of Northumbrian overlordship were the Britons; but in the reigns of Oswiu and his son Ecgfrith (642–70 and 670–85) the Picts and the Irish of Dál Riata were also affected, especially the Picts. At the same time it becomes clear from the evidence that there were degrees of overlordship. The minimum required seems to have been military and political collaboration. When Penda and his son Wulfhere, kings of the Mercians, organized major expeditions against Northumbria, they 'roused all the southern nations against our kingdom' (Stephen's Life of Wilfrid). Political collaboration revealed itself principally in dealings with dynastic rivals in exile. Royal kindreds were agnatic lineages descended from a named ancestor, as the Iclingas of Mercia were the descendants in the male line of Icel, someone who apparently flourished in the mid-sixth century and was accepted as the founder of the dynasty. Anyone descended in the male line from Icel was a potential contender for the kingship of Mercia. When a reigning king was faced by a kinsman from another branch of the dynasty who made an active bid for the kingship, he often drove him into exile; and he would then expect client, and allied, kingdoms to refuse to offer a safe haven to the exile. This degree of overlordship, involving no more than military and political collaboration, we may term 'light domination'. It could be made heavier (and less similar to an alliance of equals) in a number of ways: most obviously, tribute might be exacted, as Æthelfrith took tribute from the Northern Britons and Ecgfrith took tribute from the Mercians between 675 and 679. Other possibilities included treating the local ruler as a retainer, a thegn, of the overlord, to the point at which land grants by the client ruler required the consent of the overlord; imposition of territorial settlements, as when Wulfhere, king of the Mercians, transferred the border province of the Meonware from Wessex to Sussex; and control of church appointments, as the Mercian kings decided who should become archbishop of Canterbury for much of the eighth century.

It was probably in the reign of Oswald that Lothian, the last remaining portion of the territory belonging to the Gododdin, fell to the Bernicians, as a result of a siege of Edinburgh recorded in the Chronicle of Ireland for the year before Oswald's death in 642. This brought direct English rule into the heart of the central lowland belt of modern Scotland. Oswald is also said to have exercised overlordship over the Picts and Dál Riata. Yet this is likely to have been a light domination, since Bede also says that Oswiu—unlike, apparently, his elder brother—imposed tribute on the Picts and on Dál Riata. This policy was continued by Ecgfrith in spite of Pictish attempts to free themselves from the Northumbrian yoke.

The increased harshness of Northumbrian domination in Northern Britain may be linked to the adoption by Oswiu of the role of defender of the orthodox Roman faith in Britain. At the Synod of Whitby in 664, Oswiu himself took the decision in favour of the Roman Easter. He subsequently wrote to Pope Vitalian; and Bede quoted part of the pope's reply. This makes it evident that Oswiu had declared his readiness to use his power in Britain to bring the entire island into accord with Rome on the Easter question. Yet, as a result of Whitby, the division in this dispute in Britain now ran along largely national lines, whereas this was not true in Ireland. What Oswiu was proposing was to use Northumbrian overlordship to compel the Northern Britons, the Picts, and the Irish of Dál Riata to abandon the Celtic Easter. In his reign and that of his son, Northumbrian ambition was linked with a general adherence to Rome. Anyone who examines the dedication inscription of Jarrow (cut in 685 at the end of Ecgfrith's reign and still preserved in the church) can see from the Roman capitals what line a royal foundation was expected to follow. The Northumbrian domination in Northern Britain was now anxious to emulate Roman ways and prone to regard the Picts as 'bestial tribes' and the Irish as 'barbarians'.

The peculiar position of Dál Riata, a kingdom straddling the North Channel between Antrim and the Mull of Kintyre, and of the island monastery of Iona, 'which', Bede says, 'belongs by right to Britain . . . but was granted to Irish monks', meant that the ambition to dominate Northern Britain could not but affect Ireland. That this was fully appreciated is shown by a declaration of faith made in Rome in 679 by Wilfrid, bishop of York, 'for all the northern part of Britain and of Ireland and for the islands which were inhabited by the peoples of the English and of the Britons and also the Irish and the Picts'. The justification of this claim to speak for, and by implication have authority over, the northern parts of both islands was twofold. For Britain there was Pope Gregory the Great's plan by which the northern half of Britain was to be subject to a metropolitan bishop of York; for Ireland there were two plain facts—that the southern half of Ireland, unlike the north, had already adopted the Roman Easter, and that the authority of Iona, belonging to Britain, extended to subordinate churches in the northern half of Ireland; and there was one crucial but controversial claim: that those who kept to the Celtic Easter were heretics and schismatics.

There is no direct evidence to show why Ecgfrith sent an army to attack Brega in 684. Any such venture presupposed a Northumbrian presence in the Irish Sea. By this period what is now Galloway was probably under Northumbrian rule; the same may temporarily have been true for the Isle of Man, as in the days of Edwin, even though a British dynasty survived there until the ninth century. We do not know the reasons for Ecgfrith's attack because Bede was strongly opposed to it (even though Ecgfrith granted land for Wearmouth and Jarrow) and so reported only the arguments against the attack. Yet it is a fair guess that the arguments would have been straightforward: that the cause of Northumbrian imperialism in the northern half of the British Isles was also the cause of Roman orthodoxy.

In May 685, after the dedication of St Paul's at Jarrow, Bede's monastery, and the consecration of St Cuthbert as bishop of Lindisfarne, Ecgfrith led an army north to repress another Pictish uprising against Northumbrian overlordship. It was six years since the battle of the Trent against the Mercians, which had ended Northumbrian overlordship south of the Humber, and in which Ecgfrith's younger brother and co-ruler, Ælfwine, had been killed. It was less than a year since the attack on Brega. Now the opposition was one that Ecgfrith had defeated before, using, as we have seen, a highly mobile cavalry force (itself perhaps the successor to the cavalry of the Gododdin remembered in the heroic elegies of Aneirin). On this occasion, however, 'the bestial tribes of the Picts' triumphed and Ecgfrith was killed. Bede, quoting Virgil, remembered the battle as the end of Northumbrian domination in Northern Britain:

From that time, 'the hope and strength' of the kingdom of the English began 'to ebb and slide backwards away'. For the Picts recovered their own land which the English had held; and the Irish who were in Britain, and also one section of the Britons, recovered their liberty, which they have now enjoyed for about forty-six years.

It has been plausibly suggested that a cross-slab in the churchyard of Aberlemno in Angus, about three miles north of the battlefield, which has a cross on one side and a battle scene on the other, commemorates this battle. It is also likely that Simeon of Durham, a twelfth-century historian with access to earlier sources now lost, was correct in saying that, after the battle, to which he gives its English name, Nechtanesmere, 'Nechtan's Lake', Ecgfrith's body was taken away and buried on Iona. Two considerations support his statement: it was on Iona that Aldfrith, Ecgfrith's half-brother and successor, was then living, and Ecgfrith was commemorated in *The Martyrology of Tallaght*, much of which derived from Iona (no likely explanation for this warrior-king's appearance in the Martyrology, in the company of Irish saints, has been suggested other than that he was buried on Iona and Aldfrith ensured that the monks prayed for his soul).

These two battles in which Ecgfrith was defeated, the Trent in 679 and Dún Nechtain (Dunnichen) or Nechtanesmere in 685, marked a major turning point in the history of Britain and Ireland. Britain was now divided between southern and northern halves, and because of the battle of the Trent the boundary was the Humber. For almost all of the next 150 years the Mercians would be the dominant people in the southern half of Britain. But Dún Nechtain had ensured that the Northumbrians would not enjoy a similar hegemony in the northern half. The next great war leader who would aspire to, and in some measure, achieve a domination in the north was a Pict, held to be of part-Irish descent, known to the Picts as Unust son of Wurgust, to the Irish as Óengus mac Forgguso.

# The long eighth century, 685–825

In 697 Adomnán, abbot of Iona, author of the Life of St Columba, organized the holding of a great assembly at Birr, close to the frontier between Munster and Mide in the centre of Ireland. The purpose of this assembly, composed of great churchmen and scholars, of kings great and small, was to promulgate a special kind of law, a *cáin*. It was enforced by a special apparatus of guarantors and included special penalties for violation. As a legal mechanism, it was, unless renewed, valid for a limited period. This law, called variously 'the Law of Adomnán' or 'the Law of the Innocents', offered special protection for non-combatants, for women, children, and clerics. Although the intention was that the protection should be permanent, and thus the law was termed, in the text itself, 'a perpetual enactment', the mode of enforcement was renewed in 727. The text itself makes it very clear that the initiator of the entire project was Adomnán, but at the beginning it contains a long list of names, clerical and lay, who are said to have ordered that the law be imposed 'upon the men of Ireland and Britain'.

In one way, this law was the counterpart of the remarkable scale of the ambitions expressed in the actions of Northumbrian kings up to 685: the law was for Ireland and Britain. Moreover, Adomnán, already abbot in 685, was the friend of Aldfrith, king of Northumbria, and had made two visits to Northumbria, probably in 686 and 688, to negotiate the freeing of the captives taken in Brega in 684. 'Britain' in the text of the Law of Adomnán was not, however, the whole of Britain or even the whole of the northern half of Britain. Iona itself, as we have seen, belonged to Britain, and Coeddi, bishop of Iona and present at Birr, was, to judge by his name, English. Bishop Wihtberht, recorded in Bede's *Ecclesiastical History* as an early and unsuccessful missionary in Frisia, and now living in ascetic exile in Ireland, also attended, as did Bishop Curetán, probably of Rosemarkie in Cromarty among the northern Picts. On the secular side, the names of Fiannamail ua Dúnchatha, king of Dál Riata, and of Bruide son of Derilei, king of the Picts, were included among those who 'have sworn, both lay persons and clerics, to fulfil the entirety of the Law of Adomnán'. Yet the list did not include Aldfrith nor any representative of the Northern Britons. 'Britain', therefore, embraced the two 'northern peoples' of Britain, those whose origins lay beyond the Antonine Wall, who had both been freed from the heavy domination of Northumbria.

The provincial kings of Ireland were all included, headed by Loingsech mac Óenguso, Adomnán's own cousin, member of his branch of the Uí Néill, Cenél Conaill from the far north-west. Since Loingsech was king of Tara, there was a separate king of Cenél Conaill, Congal mac Ferguso. Among the provincial kings were Niall mac Cernaig, king of Brega, and Cellach Cualann, king of Leinster. In the following half century several of these dynasties would have lost their pre-eminence: after the death of Cellach Cualann in 715, the Uí Máil dynasty never again held the kingship of Leinster; Cináed mac Írgalaig, killed in battle in 727, was the last king of Tara from Síl nÁeda Sláne, apart from one exceptional tenth-century ruler. When Flaithbertach mac Loingsig—son of the king of Tara of 697—abdicated in 734, there was no further king of Tara from Cenél Conaill.

Partially similar changes occurred in England, also in the early eighth century: the descendants of Æthelfrith lost their monopoly of the kingship of Northumbria in 716; and in the same year the descendants of Penda lost their hold over the kingship of Mercia. From 724 until 729 a whole series of battles and other acts of violence involving four different Pictish kings ended with the triumph of Óengus mac Forgguso.

In part, it was merely an accident that so many dynastic changes occurred in the period 715–34. For one thing, the changes themselves were not all of the one type. In England, both Æthelfrith and Penda had been highly successful in war and in extending the territory of their kingdoms. It is hardly surprising that their successes benefited their descendants, since those successes had enriched the nobilities of their kingdoms. Yet this effect did not endure: the political power of the descendants of Æthelfrith and of Penda did not entail the extinction or wholesale dispossession of other branches of their dynasties. Penda's brother Eowa was probably killed in the battle of Maserfelth (Oswestry) in 642; none of his descendants held the kingship of Mercia until his grandson Æthelbald gained the throne in 716; and he had been in exile for some years before that date. Although it was no doubt acceptable for kings to act against individual rivals, it seems not to have been acceptable for them to destroy the rival branch as a whole or to deprive it of its lands. It is notable, first, how Alcuin explained the killing of Offa's son Ecgfrith, already consecrated in 787 as co-ruler of the Mercians with his father: he wrote a letter to a Mercian magnate declaring that, according to the morality of the feud, the violence of the father had been avenged upon the son:

That most noble young man has not died for his own sins; but the vengeance for the blood shed by the father has reached the son. For you know very well how much blood his father shed to secure the kingdom for his son.

Secondly, it may also be noted that, when Æthelbald was still an exile, he received a welcome from St Guthlac, by this time a hermit at Crowland in the Fens, but earlier himself a contender for the kingship and probably for that reason an exile among the Britons: Guthlac, like Æthelbald, was an Icling, a descendant of Icel, the founder of the Mercian dynasty. A temporary monopoly of the kingship by one branch of the royal kindred may have encouraged all the other branches to act together to break that monopoly.

As in Offa's case, much intra-kindred feuding was liable to bring disaster. A different kind of feud caused the decline of Síl nÁeda Sláne in the early eighth century. This branch of the Uí Néill had, as we have seen, been exceptionally successful in the seventh century. In the first half of the eighth, however, two developments occurred which may help to explain its decline. First, it divided into several branches and these branches split ('segmented') according to their local territorial interests; secondly, it acquired some of these local territories at the expense of leading client peoples. An example of segmentation is Síl Conaill Graint, 'the Seed of Conall Grant'. Conall himself was killed in 718, in the course of the feuding within Síl nÁeda Sláne, but his lineage became kings in south-west Brega with their seat at Calatruim. The descendants of Conall's brother, Niall mac Cernaig, established themselves a few miles further east: their seat was a *crannóg*, an artificial island in a lake, Loch nGabor (Lagore). Together, these two lineages formed Uí Chernaig, 'the Descendants of Cernach', namely of the father of Niall and Conall Grant. The Uí Chernaig were the ruling kindred of Southern Brega, so that, when one of them was recognized as overlord of them all, he was 'king of Southern Brega', *rí Deisceirt Breg*, but there were also rulers who were only kings of Calatruim or Loch nGabor as the case might be. The Uí Chernaig of Southern Brega were one branch of Síl nÁeda Sláne, the Uí Néill of Brega. Another two branches had their seats in Northern Brega: Síl nDlúthaig in the Blackwater valley, between Navan and Kells, and Uí Chonaing on the lower Boyne.

Both the northern and the southern branches acquired territory at the expense of client peoples. The kings of the Uí Chonaing displaced the ruling kindred of the Ciannacht of Brega from the lands around Duleek, between the lower Boyne and the Delvin; they themselves became kings of Ciannacht, while the native dynasty was confined to the region north of the Boyne, where the modern barony of Ferrard bears the name of their kingdom, Fir Arda Ciannachtae, 'The Men of the Upper (= Outer) Part of Ciannacht'. In South Brega the displacement was into the Church, where the principal local dynasty was transformed into the clerical dynasty of the church of Lusk.

The feud within Síl nÁeda Sláne continued until 737. It was not responsible for the internal segmentation in the dynasty, but it hardened the divisions. Moreover, it gave an opportunity to Cland Cholmáin (remote cousins but also rivals of Síl nÁeda Sláne), rulers of Mide to the west. Cland Cholmáin had not allowed the same segmentation between different branches that divided Síl nÁeda Sláne. To a remarkable extent son followed father in the kingship of Mide; and the ruling kindred never became tied to a single local territory. The main client peoples of the Southern Uí Néill, Ciannacht Breg, Gailenga, Luigne, and Delbnae Assail, some of who had suffered territorially from Síl nÁeda Sláne, loyally supported their rivals, Cland Cholmáin.

In Northern Britain and Ireland there may have been more connection between the major political changes of the early eighth century. In north-western Ireland, Cenél Conaill lost power to Cenél nÉogain largely because the latter had an unusually aggressive ruler who succeeded, in repeated annual campaigns, in humiliating the

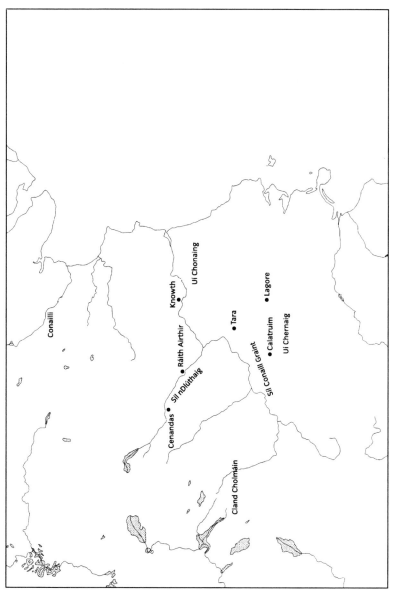

Map 3  Brega, Eastern Mide, and the Conailli.

Cenél Conaill king of Tara, Flaithbertach mac Loingsig, and, more importantly, in conquering a strategically vital area of the Foyle basin, Mag nÍtha. In 733 Flaithbertach mac Loingsig 'brought the fleet of Dál Riata to Ireland', but this attempt to use the sea power of these allies of Cenél Conaill failed. Moreover, Dál Riata was now itself threatened by a new king of the Picts, Óengus mac Forgguso (Unust son of Wurgust). No longer were Cenél Conaill, Dál Riata, and the Picts all within one constellation of power embracing the far north of Britain and much of the northern half of Ireland, as in the days of Adomnán.

Because of the information given by the Chronicle of Ireland, still being written on Iona, and now a richer source, the 720s and 730s are the one period of Pictish history for which we have some detailed information on the sequence of events. But first some background knowledge is required. Britain north of the Antonine Wall was divided between two peoples, the Irish of Dál Riata to the West of Druim Alban, 'the Back (or Ridge) of Britain', and the Picts to the east. The Picts had the better lands, both the southern Picts and northern Picts, divided by the eastern extension of the main Highland massif, which almost reaches the sea by Stonehaven, south of Aberdeen. This part of Britain was divided as by a cross, of which the vertical post ran northwards up Druim Alban and the horizontal bar ran from the point of Ardnamurchan in the West to Stonehaven in the east. The south-east and north-east sections contained the southern and northern Picts, the south-west Dál Riata, while the north-western was probably Pictish in the sixth century—its subsequent history is deeply obscure. Communications across Druim Alban were mostly through high and difficult passes, but the great geological fault that lies along the Great Glen and Loch Ness provided a relatively easy route from Dál Riata in the south-west to the northern Picts—the modern route from Fort William to Inverness.

Pictland was, often at least, a unified kingdom; but it was divided among several provinces, and, sometimes it seems, they were ruled by provincial kings. Good examples of Pictish provinces are Fife (which included St Andrews), Fortriu (in the valleys of the Earn and the Almond, and later, at least, extending southwards through Strathallan between the Ochils and the main Highlands to include Dunblane, and northwards to the Highland line), and Atholl, to the north of Fortriu and including Dunkeld. Fortriu was usually the leading province, with the result that in the ninth century it was synonymous with southern Pictland, perhaps excluding Fife and the neighbouring Fothriff. In origin, however, Fortriu was the land of the Verturiones, one of the constituent peoples that made up the Pictish federation. If that federation was defined, as has been argued, by the Roman frontier on the Antonine Wall, it may well have coalesced around a particular people located immediately to the north of the frontier, namely the Verturiones; and this might explain the leading role of Fortriu in the Pictish kingdom.

Evidence for Pictish client kings all comes from Iona, but it should not be dismissed on that account. In Adomnán's Life of St Columba there is a story about a meeting near Inverness between the saint and Bridei son of Máelchú, king of the Picts. To judge by the contemporary lament for Columba's death in 597, *Amra Choluim Chille*, the king's native province seems to have been near the River Tay in Perthshire. When near Inverness, therefore, he was on progress in a subordinate province (presumably the one later called Muireb, Moray, as in the Moray Firth). On this occasion an under-king, ruler of the Orkneys, was present; and Columba asked Bridei to command his under-king to protect Cormac ua Liatháin, Columba's friend and an inveterate voyager out into the Atlantic hoping 'to find a place of retreat in the ocean'. In the Chronicle of Ireland (here derived from Iona annals) there are obits for a king of Fortriu, Bridei son of Bili, the victor of the battle of Dunnichen, Dún Nechtain, in 685, and thus presumably dominant at least among the southern Picts, and a Talorgan son of Drostan, king of Atholl (693 and 734 respectively). The Pictish kingdom seems to have been not unlike an Irish province or late seventh-century Mercia: a relatively stable over-kingdom including client kingdoms.

In Ireland and England, the early medieval historian has two crucial categories of evidence for royal kindreds and succession: regnal lists giving the succession of kings, typically with the number of years of their reigns, and genealogies. For Wales, however, there are only genealogies, and for the Picts only regnal lists. This is especially unfortunate for the historian of the Picts, since the whole question of Pictish royal succession is highly controversial, partly because of an origin-legend reported by Bede. According to this legend, the forefathers of the Picts arrived at the British Isles by sailing around the top of Britain and landing first in Ireland. There they asked for land from the Irish but were encouraged to go to Britain, where they were promised Irish help in making a settlement. The Picts had left their women behind; and the Irish offered to make good their oversight with Irish women on condition that 'when there was a dispute, they should choose a king for themselves from the female lineage of kings rather than from the masculine'. The legend, then, had a dual purpose: to explain the close connection between the Picts and the Irish and to explain the Pictish royal succession, unique in the British Isles.

Elsewhere in Britain, men of the royal kindred usually married women of other royal kindreds, and the women came to live with the men. Thus Northumbrian royal men married Mercian royal women, who then lived in Northumbria, and Mercian royal men married Northumbrian royal women, who then lived in Mercia. Between the children of Oswiu and Penda, inveterate enemies, there were three such marriages; they put the women into the difficult, even dangerous, position of 'peace-weavers' between hostile kindreds and kingdoms, born into one kingdom but resident in another. The last of the three, Osthryth daughter of Oswiu, wife of Æthelred son of Penda, king of the Mercians, was killed by the Mercian magnates in 697, the very year in which Adomnán engineered his 'Law of the Innocents' to protect women, as well as children and clerics, from violence. Among the Picts, however, the position was reversed. The sons of Æthelfrith of Bernicia were driven into exile in 616 by Edwin of Deira; Oswald and Oswiu took refuge in the kingdom of Dál Riata, Eanfrith among the Picts. Between then and the autumn of 633, when he returned to Bernicia, Eanfrith fathered a future Pictish king, Talorgan son of Eanfrith (who died in 657). According to the *Historia Brittonum*, the two kings who fought at Dún Nechtain, Ecgfrith of Northumbria and Bridei son of Bili, were cousins in the male line, presumably because of Eanfrith's marriage. Bridei's own father appears to have been a king of Dumbarton.

The Pictish regnal lists are constructed on the basis of a single monarchy; there are no separate lists of kings of Atholl or of Fortriu. This does not refute the proposition that there were Pictish provincial kings; it only shows that they were all expected to be subordinate to the king of the Picts as a whole. Confirmation comes from the period 724–9, when there was a struggle for the single kingship of the Picts between four contenders, each of whom may have ruled over smaller, provincial kingdoms. In 706 Nechtan son of Derilei succeeded his brother, the Bridei son of Derilei who appears among the guarantors of *Cáin Adomnáin*; Nechtan had expelled the community of Iona westwards across Druim Alban in 717, the year after Iona had adopted the Roman Easter but before, in 718, it adopted the Roman tonsure. In 724, Nechtan was 'made a cleric', and thus removed from the kingship. Drust succeeded, but it appears that Nechtan did not accept his removal from power: he had to be imprisoned by Drust in 726. Later the same year, Drust was removed from the kingship in favour of Eilpín; but he too only lasted for two years. In 728 Óengus son of Forggus defeated King Eilpín at Moncrieffe Hill, close to Perth, and again at an unidentified fortress the same year. This second defeat was decisive, but initially it was not the victor, Óengus, who succeeded but the old king, Nechtan son of Derilei. The next year, 729, saw further battles: first, Óengus was victorious against Nechtan at 'the battle of Monad Carno near Loch Loogdae', where 'the tax-gatherers of Nechtan fell'; subsequently, Óengus went on to defeat Drust, now again entitled king of the Picts. Nechtan would not die until 732, but by that time Óengus was unquestionably king of all the Picts.

His path to the kingship was uniquely violent in the known history of the Pictish kingdom. It accords entirely with a contemporary Northumbrian annalist's assessment of the reign as a whole:

In the year 761 Óengus, king of the Picts, died. He continued his reign to the end as he had started it, like a tyrant and a butcher, with blood-stained violence.

Óengus's rise to power makes it look as though he was something of an outsider who took advantage of strife among better-established rivals: first Nechtan was removed by Drust, then Drust by Eilpín; then Óengus emerged, defeating Eilpín, who was replaced by Nechtan; then Nechtan, too, was was defeated by Óengus, but Drust succeeded. Only when he had finally defeated and killed Drust did Óengus become king. Perhaps the Northumbrian annalist's description of him as a tyrant referred not just to the manner of his rule but to a rise to power deemed illegitimate as well as violent—tyranny in the Roman sense.

The annalist used the Irish form of the Pictish king's name: Óengus rather than the Pictish Unust or Unuist. At Lindisfarne, however, or perhaps Wearmouth–Jarrow (depending on the original home of the Durham 'Book of Life'), he was remembered as a benefactor for whom the monks ought to pray and was given his Pictish name, Unust. The two Northumbrian impressions of Óengus are, however, compatible and explicable. Two annalistic entries, both for 750, one from the Chronicle of Ireland, the other from the Northumbrian Continuation of Bede, show what position Óengus had gained. The Chronicle of Ireland records, first, a defeat for Óengus's brother Talorgan at the hands of the Britons of Dumbarton, and secondly, later the same year, 'the ebbing of the power of Óengus'. The Northumbrian annalist states that 'Cuthred, king of the West Saxons, rose against King Æthelbald and Óengus'. Óengus would not die, as we have seen, until 761, and Æthelbald not until 757, yet this year, 750, marks the 'ebbing' of both their overlordships.

What is startling is that a Northumbrian annalist should say that Cuthred, ruler of a kingdom to the south of the Thames, rebelled against Óengus, king of the Picts, as well as against Æthelbald, king of the Mercians. In what sense could a king whose territory comprised Hampshire, Berkshire, Wiltshire, Dorset, Somerset, and Devon rebel against another king whose territory came no further south than the Forth? The answer to this conundrum can only be that Æthelbald and Óengus were in some sense joint overlords of Britain. Their alliance can be seen earlier: in 740 Æthelbald attacked Northumbria when the Northumbrian king, Eadberht, was himself campaigning against the Picts. In the next year, 741, the Chronicle of Ireland records, 'the hammering of Dál Riata by Óengus son of Forggus'. In the eighth century, as later, it was a principle that 'my neighbour's neighbour is my friend': Æthelbald was hostile to Northumbria but allied with Óengus; similarly, Óengus's enemies were his immediate neighbours, Northumbria, the Britons of Dumbarton, and Dál Riata, but with Æthelbald of Mercia he could dominate Britain.

An Irish genealogist claimed that Óengus was 'king of Alba'; and Alba, in the eighth century, meant Britain. A Worcester charter of 737 described Æthelbald as 'king of Britain' and also as 'king of the Southern English'. Loingsech mac Óenguso, Adomnán's cousin, who led the kings assembled at Birr in 697, was described both as 'king of Tara' and as 'king of Ireland'. In all three cases the grander title of the two rested upon alliance rather than mere subjection: Óengus and Æthelbald were allies and by their alliance dominated Britain; the claim of an Uí Néill king of Tara to be king of Ireland relied upon a double alliance—between the Uí Néill and the Connachta, and between the Uí Néill and the Éoganachta of Munster. In the seventh and eighth centuries an Uí Néill king of Tara might, with luck, impose his dominion upon the Leinstermen and the Ulstermen at the point of the spear, but with Munster and Connaught, alliance was the tried and tested method.

There were differences between the great political hegemonies of the British Isles, and some of these will be examined, but there were also broad similarities. A distinction has already been drawn between light and heavy domination: between a domination which entailed only military and political support and a domination which also exacted tribute. It will now be apparent that light domination was close to a straight alliance. What made the difference was which king led the combined army, if there was one. Æthelbald and Óengus may have concerted military activity against Northumbria, but neither is likely to have marched in a combined army summoned by the other. Penda, however, and his son Wulfhere both attacked Northumbria leading combined armies of the Southern English (sometimes also including British kings). Similarly, when it came to political support, if one kingdom was the centre around which the alliances of other peoples revolved, that would suggest that the situation was tending towards light domination.

To understand how these hegemonies worked, a further distinction is required, which can best be made by means of two early Irish terms: the *bóraime*, 'cattle-tribute' and the *cuairt ríg*, 'king's circuit'. Edwin, king of Northumbria, was a Deiran, yet he visited 'royal vills' in Bernicia and used his visits to influence the local population. The vill he is known to have visited, Yeavering, has been excavated and shown to consist of a complex of structures adapted to grand political hospitality and local assemblies as well as to the reception of the food-renders of the neighbourhood. On the occasion described by Bede, Edwin stayed for thirty-six days, during which the local district must have provided the kind of render said to be due from ten hides according to Ine's laws: 10 vats of honey, 300 loaves, 12 'ambers' of Welsh ale, 30 of clear ale, 2 full-grown cows or 10 wethers, 10 geese, 20 hens, 10 cheeses, an 'amber' full of butter, 5 salmon, 20 pounds of fodder, and 100 eels. No doubt there was local variation, but the essential point is that it contained both bread (the 300 loaves) as well as other grain products (the ale), meat, fish, and dairy products: it was a balanced diet for a royal household. Contrast with that the tribute demanded of the Leinstermen by kings of Tara: simply cattle, and hence *bóraime*, 'cattle-reckoning' and so 'cattle-tribute'. Where the king went on his circuit, the local population had access to the king, could seek his justice, and could even share his feasts. Although it might be onerous, it was honourable. But the king did not go on circuit in a territory from which his steward exacted his cattle-tribute. The inhabitants of that territory gained no access to the king. This was widely regarded as deeply injurious: Bede and Stephen of Ripon both described it as political slavery. Edwin of Deira was probably regarded as a foreigner by the men around the Bernician royal vill of Yeavering, as his enemy Æthelfrith was certainly regarded in Deira; yet Bernicia was within Edwin's circuit. On the other hand, the tribute Edwin sought to exact from Anglesey consisted of cattle: a Welsh poem in praise of his enemy, Cadwallon of Gwynedd, declares proudly that Cadwallon's cattle 'did not bellow'—that is, Gwynedd did not pay cattle-tribute to be driven off by the tribute-gatherers of Edwin.

Two scales are thus necessary to gauge the inner workings of an early medieval hegemony. On the one hand, there was the degree of subjection: a client people which owed only military and political support was less subject than one which owed tribute. On the other hand, there was the form of subjection: Edwin may have demanded tribute of a sort from both the Bernicians and Gwynedd; yet the food-renders of the Bernicians gained them access to the king and thus associated them with a ruling elite, whereas if the men of Gwynedd were to pay cattle-tribute they would merely see their wealth departing on its own hooves before the goads of Edwin's drovers— and they would see nothing in return unless it were, perhaps, defence from third parties.

What has been said so far would apply as readily to the overlordship of Edwin in the seventh as to that of Offa in the eighth; it would apply, with minor variations, to Óengus son of Forggus, king of the Picts, and to Donnchad mac Domnaill, king of Tara. There were, however, new developments in the eighth century, especially the increasing importance of trade across the Channel and the North Sea from the last quarter of the seventh century. This was associated with the creation of *emporia*, specialized trading towns under royal protection and a distinct legal regime; it was also associated with the creation of a coinage issued in very considerable volume (coins of this type are generally called *sceattas*). The distribution of single finds of sceattas—because single finds probably derived from accidental losses—offers a good indication of where these coins were in most use, whereas the sites of deliberately hidden hoards have no close relationship to where coins were used. The conclusion is that, in the eighth century, the use of coins in exchange had a south-eastern distribution within Britain and are associated with *emporia* such as London, Hamwich, and Ipswich. Quite apart from the profit to be made from royal control of a coinage, such as charging moneyers for the right to coin, there was also revenue to be gained from control of an *emporium*, as well as political advantage to be obtained by forgoing revenue in special cases. To take one example, a charter of 734 shows Æthelbald granting remission of toll on one ship in the port of London to the bishop of Rochester. Rochester was one of the two Kentish bishoprics, in a kingdom unwillingly subject to Æthelbald; but, because the bishop wished his ship to use the port of London, subject to Æthelbald, he faced the prospect of paying tolls, and the king could thus display his benevolence by remitting the obligation.

Cultivation of relations with major churches was a marked feature of Uí Néill policy. A major component of Cenél nÉogain power after 734 was its close association with Armagh. In the midlands numerous major monasteries had been founded in the period 550–620 within the kingdom of Cenél Fiachach, a branch of the Uí Néill but excluded from the kingship of Tara. By the eighth century these monasteries were often very powerful institutions, with numerous so-called *manaig*, literally 'monks', but in fact lay or semi-lay clients of a church. Some might be subject to a rule and to an ascetic regime, but they were married and also often carried arms. A royal patron of a powerful church thus provided himself with an army on the cheap. So many were the major churches in the kingdom of Cenél Fiachach that it came to be known as Tír Cell, 'Church Land', and its people as Fir Chell, 'Men of Churches'. Among the Picts an association between king and great church is exemplified by one of the finest surviving works of art in the period, the St Andrews Sarcophagus, which arguably depicts King David as emperor and as a model of Pictish kingship. The most likely person to have commissioned the sarcophagus is Óengus son of Forggus.

One theme running through much of the period 400–800 is the creation and reshaping of nations. These are not to be imagined as

**Figure 2.1** Lagore motif piece. This bone was found at Lagore, one of the principal royal sites of the Uí Néill of Brega (Map 3). The surface was polished and then used for designs also found in contemporary metalwork. Some of the designs are lightly sketched, some are finished. This example is exceptional for the chip-carving technique used for the finished designs, which was also employed in metalwork. It illustrates the role of royal centres as places where craftsmen were employed (also demonstrated at Dunadd in Argyll) and the way motif pieces were vehicles by which designs could be transported from place to place and from one medium to another.

# 2

# Society, community, and identity

## John Hines

Anyone wishing to understand the life and relationships of the population of Britain and Ireland in the first four centuries of the post-Roman Middle Ages truly has to peer into a melting pot. In Britain, as elsewhere, the breakdown of the Roman imperial order in western Europe saw the emergence of entirely new nations and identities. The most conspicuous change was the introduction of Germanic culture and language from the Continent to create a new English identity and culture (which we usually call 'Anglo-Saxon') over much of southern Britain. Politically, as we have seen in the previous chapter, this area became organized into a series of kingdoms. In the remainder of Britain and Ireland, meanwhile, archaeology as well as history reveals marked differences in the organization and practicalities of life. It is understandably tempting to look at these all together as embodying a 'Celtic' culture, and not entirely unrealistic to do so, athough it is crucial to appreciate the many differences within this zone. Immediately adjacent to Anglo-Saxon England to the west and north was an extensive band of land in which another series of kingdoms appeared (and frequently disappeared), where the British language from which modern Welsh survives became the norm. North of these in Britain were the lands of the Scots in western and Picts in eastern and northern Scotland. The period of the fifth to eighth centuries is the period in which Ireland moves absolutely from prehistory into documented history. What we know about life in Ireland in this period has many features quite different from conditions in contemporary Britain, although

Ireland was by no means a uniform or unified society, least of all politically.

The political history of kingship and kingdoms in this time of extraordinary change has been discussed in the previous chapter. As that makes clear, our direct historical evidence tends to reflect the interests of especially powerful and successful groups within the total population. Equally, it tends to report or reflect the results of processes of development rather than to give substantial accounts of how those changes came about. It is the business of this chapter to introduce other means of studying this period: in particular to interpret the evidence of the superficially silent remains of the culture of the populations of these islands. Primarily this means turning to what we can observe of the material culture of the period—the domain of archaeology—together with the evidence of language history, which is unusual amongst historical phenomena in that the precise rules of grammar and linguistics allow unrecorded prehistoric linguistic situations to be reconstructed with a high degree of confidence from later records.

This should set the historical sources in their context. To do so is inevitably a corrective exercise in some sense, but not to the extent that it is assumed that those historical sources are massively or even deliberately misleading. Their limitation is that they are selective, and our understanding of this period can be much enhanced by the writing of a demotic history to complement the history of the political and ecclesiastical elites who inevitably dictated the production and survival of the documentary sources. One can understand all sides of the range of life and experience in the period much better as parts of an interrelated whole.

This foray into cultural history must itself select a theme and structure, however. The most appropriate target in the broader context of this book seems to be a deeper characterization of the complexities of social life in Britain and Ireland from AD 400–800—in particular to illustrate the imperatives and constraints acting upon the human population, and to explore its range of responses to those controlling factors. The scheme of discussion is therefore thematic rather than regional or chronological: it follows a series of central economic and social issues, each of which can be examined comparatively from area to area and period to period, subject, inevitably, to the quantity and quality of known evidence. Only at the end do we need to make the major ethnic and territorial divisions that we can assign to this period—between Britons, Anglo-Saxons, Irish/Scots, and Picts—the principal focus in themselves. This is not to achieve a pre-set objective of diminishing the significance of those large categories of identity. It is, however, intended to suggest that these divisions within the Isles were sustained and modified for practical reasons through social relationships that were deeply rooted in the real needs of the living communities, every bit as much as such identities were predetermined by deep roots in the past and lived on through inheritance and inertia.

# The natural environment

Both archaeologists and historians have found that they can write coherent and satisfactory explanations of the practices and events of this period in terms of human motivation and agency. But we must not think of this historical world as one that was entirely made and governed by man. The impact on the course of history of natural and environmental phenomena has been rather sidelined in recent historical writing. It is true that long before the beginning of the fifth century AD the areas in the agricultural landscapes of Britain and Ireland that had not been modified by human cultural agency— especially in terms of changing the plant cover—were marginal and few. But while nature can be driven out by the fork, it is endlessly creeping back in, and in lowland England, which had seen the most intensive economic exploitation both for agriculture and for other resources in the Roman period, there are areas where local study has revealed a reversion of open and worked landscapes to scrub and woodland at the beginning of the Middle Ages: for instance, in an area that had seen concentrated iron extraction in the Rockingham Forest area of Northamptonshire. More widespread than un-controlled woodland regeneration, however, seems to have been an erosion of features of the agricultural landscape, such as the filling up of ditches, combined with a redeployment of formerly cultivated land as pasture, and limited reforestation. This is well attested, for example, in the area of southern Oxfordshire and Berkshire.

But even without a major collapse or widespread abandonment of land, there was a linked economic and demographic contraction in some areas of Britain following the end of Roman rule. (This may very well, indeed, have begun in the late Roman period.) In what was to become England it is likely that settlement became more concentrated in viable cells and niches within the overall landscape. This could be relevant to the political history of the early Anglo-Saxon period, as it is widely suggested that the national and political entities recorded for us in those sources are the products of the union of originally much smaller, independent, local building blocks of land and communities. It is, however, only in England that we can illustrate contraction of this kind around the fifth century relatively clearly. Altogether too little is known about general patterns and levels of settlement in Scotland and Wales for any such comparisons to be made between the Roman and post-Roman periods. In Ireland, by contrast, datable settlements, usually enclosed by banks or walls (known as raths and cashels), become particularly numerous in this period. Without good reason to doubt the essential continuity of land use and occupation in the more upland areas of Britain, we can tentatively take the view that there was greater retrenchment in lowland Britain (southern and eastern England) at the end of the Roman period than elsewhere.

The climate in Britain and Ireland in the period AD 400–800 was temperate but changeable, as it has been in modern times. A population that was highly dependent on agriculture for basic subsistence would have been equally sensitive to climatic vicissitudes, and there is evidence of a significant deterioration in conditions from a particularly warm period during the Roman occupation to colder and wetter weather in the fifth and sixth centuries. A serious crisis must have been the extreme climatic downturn apparently implying a dust-cloud in the sky and exceptionally low sunlight beginning in AD 536 and lasting for about a decade, identified first from tree-ring sequences in Irish bog oaks, which has occasioned much discussion recently, both popular and academic. We do not need to reach a view as to whether the cause was an extraterrestrial collision or near-miss with a comet or meteoroid (cf. Tunguska, Siberia, 1908) or a massive volcanic eruption on the scale of Santorini in the Bronze Age or Krakatoa in 1883. And whether or not this climatic disaster was also the cause of the devastating pestilence that struck Constantinople in 542 and was gruesomely described by Procopius there, and which seems to be represented by either or both of the *mortalitas prima* and *mortalitas magna* in Ireland, recorded in the Annals of Ulster under the years 544 and 548, such plagues were recurrent calamities for early medieval populations. Altogether more thought-provoking for the archaeologist is the fact that so far it has not been possible to demonstrate convincingly that the dark-sky disaster or subsequent plague of the mid-sixth century had any detectable, let alone radical, impact on the course of cultural history for the population of these islands. The implication is that cultural systems of the time were economically and socially resilient in the face of sudden famines and mortality. They did not collapse under these blows, and the populations that survived could pursue essentially the same practices and goals as before. This could be a sign of either simplicity or sophistication.

# Economic life

Agriculture was absolutely the core and the most important single facet of economic life in early medieval Britain and Ireland. It was vital for human subsistence. Hunting and gathering in the form of fowling and fishing, fruit, egg, and shell collection, were certainly important as forms of food supply, but the production of cereal crops and vegetables, and the farming of livestock for milk, wool, and leather as well as for meat, were manifestly the rationale of most settlements and their communities. In different geographical circumstances we find different types of small settlement group ranging from what we tend to call, a little vaguely, single or isolated farmsteads—meaning single sets of functional buildings, including the dwelling space, for whoever lived there—to small 'villages', where there may be between two and perhaps a dozen broadly equivalent but separate and duplicated working homesteads of this kind (Figs. 2.2 and 2.3).

The farming practices of this period can be inferred from residual deposits of the products of agriculture and from chance finds of tools. Cereal grains can be found, usually in a charred state incorporated in the fills of features such as pits, post-holes, ditches, and wells from the settlements, or as in imprints in pottery in areas where pottery was produced. Cereal and other plant pollens retrieved from samples of contemporary soil deposits can identify and even quantify

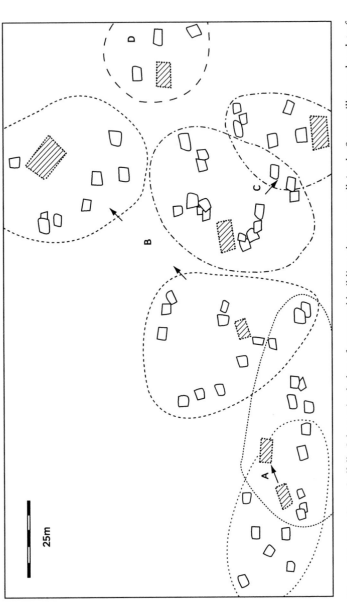

**Figure 2.2** West Stow, Suffolk. Schematized plan of excavated building plots at a small Anglo-Saxon village or hamlet of the fifth to seventh centuries, showing inferred shifts between earlier and later phases of three or four contemporary farmsteads consisting of one post-built rectangular house and several smaller sunken huts.

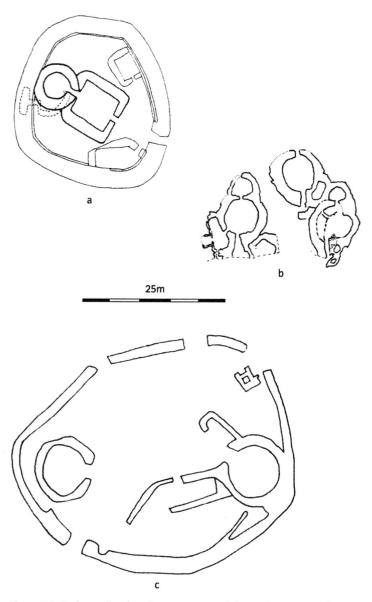

25m

**Figure 2.3** Early-medieval settlement-types and domestic structures from Ireland, Scotland, and Wales. (a) Cashel (stone-walled 'ring-fort' with souterrain chamber), Leacanabuaile, Co. Cork. (b) Figure-of-eight or cellular houses, Bernerar, Western Isles. (c) Enclosed hut-group, Pant-y-saer, Môn (Anglesey). Scale bar, 25m.

the ranges of both cultivated plants and weeds characteristic of particular agricultural regimes. The results show a rather limited range of crops, with few surprises. Barley was widely grown, together with various types of wheat in the milder climes. Hardier crops such as rye, and later oats, were prevalent in the west and north. Evidence for vegetables is more selectively reported, but points to the deliberate cultivation of pulse-bearing peas and beans, cabbages, and onions at least. Flax proves to have been a widespread crop, for the production of linen and linseed.

Animal husbandry is represented primarily by the bones of domesticated species: cattle, sheep, and goat (these caproids are difficult to distinguish from one another) for their meat, leather, and wool, and milk; pigs for meat and hides; domestic fowl for meat, feathers, and eggs; horses, oxen, and dogs principally to work. The proportion of species inevitably varied from area to area, as different animals were better suited to the local environment. A particularly important item of information that can be gleaned from settlement-site bone assemblages is the kill-pattern of the various species: specifically, the proportion of animals of particular species slaughtered at different ages. A relatively high average age amongst caproids, for instance, at Wicken Bonhunt, Essex, reflects the importance of wool production. Higher numbers of young cattle bones reflect the use of breeding to maintain lactation and the milk supply, as well as the careful targeting needed in face of the fodder cost of keeping a stock of cattle over winter when they are unable to graze all the time. Distinct profiles of meat supply may characterize sites where meat was brought for consumption rather than produced. At the ostensibly high-status hall site at Dinas Powys, south Wales, for instance, slaughtering of most of the relatively high proportion of pigs in the bone assemblage under the age of 2 may imply privileged access to particularly tender meat. The situation with pig is similar at the Moynagh Lough crannog, Co. Meath, where also 75 per cent of cattle were slaughtered under the age of 3. In the eighth-century urban context of Hamwic (Southampton), meanwhile, beef was always predominant in the meat supply, and the average age of the cattle gradually rose. This can be interpreted in terms of increasing demand for food supplies, both dairy products and meat, which could thus gradually decline in quality.

What is altogether most important to appreciate, however, is the level of organization the agrarian economy demanded. From the hunting bands of the earliest Stone Age onwards, human subsistence strategies have required cooperation and social organization. Up to a point, a system of practical and social interdependencies should have served to strengthen these early medieval agricultural communities. Mixed farming (arable and pastoral) has many advantages. A diversity of resources rather than dependency on a single product provides greater security in adverse circumstances. In practical terms, cultivation and livestock farming are mutually supportive where 'waste' plant products such as hay can be used as animal fodder and animal dung is valuable for manuring crop plots. Specialized farming, of which we have some evidence from Roman Britain, implies an elaborate economic superstructure in which redistribution and sharing of products is organized at a high level.

A special, non-domestic agricultural facility that first makes its appearance in Ireland is the watermill, of which examples are known from several early medieval sites, including dendrochronologically dated ones at Little Island, Co. Cork, of AD 630 and Drumard, Co. Derry, of *c*.782. Contemporary Irish laws and tracts testify extensively to the importance of the mill, and assign a relatively high status to both the millwright and the mill owner. The occupation of miller also appears as a distinct one. What is also implicit, however, is that mills could be communally owned, and that every grade of free man could have a share in one. The laws seem to be assiduous in controlling access and the right to use the mill. It may therefore be no coincidence that one early mill in England, dated to the ninth century, has been found at a Mercian royal residence at Tamworth. An example dated to about a century earlier has recently been discovered by excavation close to another Mercian royal residence at Wellington, Herefordshire.

From the seventh century onwards, Anglo-Saxon charters nicely illustrate the range of resources usually required to maintain a full working agrarian landscape at that time. Even if their listing of resources is formulaic rather than a careful inventory of everything that was actually available in each case, we find that the very large estates being defined in these sources characteristically include fields, ponds, rivers, marshlands, meadows, woodlands, pastures, and even sea shores, for cultivation, herding, fishing, fowling, the management and supply of timber, and pannage, as well as for any other natural resources that were available. A special charter of 689, however, granted a piece of cleared land (*assart*) on which there was an iron mine in Kent to St Peter's, Canterbury. Although of uncertain date in themselves, equivalent formulas, and with that at the very least a trustworthy recognition of the same economic desiderata, occur frequently in the Llandaff charters from south Wales, the earliest of which seem to derive from our period.

The very large estates with this multiplicity of resources described in the earliest Anglo-Saxon charters were explicitly designed to produce a surplus in order to support the activities of an elite, whose own occupations were different—be they the ecclesiastical duties of a religious house or the administrative and military duties of an aristocracy. This would affect the size of estates within which such a range of resources was collected, but was not the only circumstance in which a balance and diversity of resources was of fundamental importance. There is, of course, much of Britain and Ireland where the environment is not so diverse. Away from the south-east of Britain, extensive pastoral farming had to dominate the landscape, with cultivation focused on scattered pockets of land. Here, inevitably, domesticated animals were a more staple commodity of both diet and economy, and the population densities are never as high as they can become in areas more favourable to arable farming. As the historical records show, however, these areas were no less organized into territorial units, such as the polities (*túatha*) in Ireland, and the kingdoms, principalities, and estates in Wales and Scotland, which supported special establishments in the form of either aristocracies and their households or clerical establishments, if not both. To some degree these demonstrably embody further forms of economic domination.

Everyday life in Britain and Ireland at this date involved the use of products deriving from various crafts, all of which in turn required certain basic materials to be supplied. Craftwork provided productive tools, and basic utensils such as cooking pots and storage containers, as well as the clothing essential in these climes. Materials for footwear and garments were, of course, secondary agricultural products; and textile production, both spinning and weaving, was manifestly a domestically based craft throughout the islands, represented by ubiquitous finds such as spindle whorls, loomweights, and thread pickers. This does not, however, imply that textile production was exclusively for domestic use, and by the end of our period a letter of

Charlemagne to Offa of Mercia in 796 documents the exportation of English woollen cloaks, albeit as a suspended practice. An example of what could be one of the earliest specialized production sites for textiles in medieval England has recently been identified on the basis of remains of a very large loom excavated at Pakenham, Suffolk, from as early as the sixth century, paralleling the interpretation of a slightly later site at Bejsebakken, Ålborg, in northern Jutland (Denmark). As yet we have no clear evidence of precisely where and how tanning was usually done in this period, but the occasional finds of pointed iron and bone tools or awls from both burials and settlement sites may also represent leatherworking as a domestic craft.

Vessels for cooking could be of iron, pottery, or even stone, while storage containers could equally be of wood. The majority of basic tools and utensils at this time would undoubtedly have been wooden, but inevitably little of this perishable material has survived. Ceramics were not produced in every part of Britain and Ireland: indeed, there is a marked contrast between the Anglo-Saxon cultural zone, where pottery production was high and the tradition of using pottery strong, and the areas to the west and north, where only a relatively restricted tradition can be found before the end of our period involving similar but simple pottery, first in Cornwall and later in the north-east of Ireland, spreading up into the Western Isles of Scotland. Much of the pottery that has been found in the west and north was in fact imported from as far away as the eastern Mediterranean (in the fifth and sixth centuries) and western France (seventh century), and arrived as a container for some other commodity, although the imports do also include tableware. In England, close study of the forms and fabrics of the huge numbers of sherds and vessels known from both burials, where they were used as cinerary urns in the fifth and sixth centuries, and settlements again presents us with the image of a domestic craft advancing eventually into bulk and centralized production. At the early stage, there is no direct evidence of production in the form of securely identified kilns, although possible clay dumps and a handful of antler stamps for decorating the clay before firing have been found. Study of stamp links between vessels has, however, allowed the distributional ranges of a number of 'potters' to be identified in the sixth century: most of them within radii of just a few kilometres although a few longer distance connections have been identified, as one between Sancton, east Yorkshire, and Baston in south Lincolnshire. None of these, however, matches the puzzling evidence of a clay with distinctive granite inclusions in the fabric which is apparently uniquely localizable to the Charnwood Forest area, close to Leicester. This fabric has been found not only copiously but also over a remarkably wide area of the East Midlands, from the Thames to the Humber, at just as early a period. So far nothing consistent, let alone distinguished, has been noted in respect of the form of these pots. It is genuinely difficult to believe that they were made and distributed from the centre implied by the identified source of the clay, but the peculiarities of this fabric have yet to be explained in any other way.

Definite production in bulk and distribution from an 'industrial' centre comes in the form of Ipswich ware (Fig. 2.4). Ipswich ware consists of a rather utilitarian range of vessels, finished, for the first time in Anglo-Saxon England, on a slow turntable, and hard-fired at a reducing temperature. Kilns in which this pottery was produced have been excavated at Carr Street, Ipswich, and the products themselves are found widely distributed over settlement sites, again primarily in eastern England between the Thames and the Humber. While it was thought for some time that Ipswich ware came into production before the middle of the seventh century, a recent but as yet unpublished reassessment of this pottery by Paul Blinkhorn has concluded that we should date this development no earlier than the eighth century.

A major class of materials in widespread demand and use which required even more specialized skills for both provision and working was metals. Copper, invariably alloyed with a considerable amount of tin and/or zinc to form a range of bronze- or brass-like amalgams, and silver and gold constitute a semi-precious to precious range of metals used for more prestigious items. Iron, meanwhile, was a staple commodity, used for basic tools and items of practical equipment, although it too could be used in highly prestigious and specially crafted items, such as the massive cauldrons and elaborate suspension chains found as seventh-century grave goods in the extremely rich Sutton Hoo and Broomfield barrows, as well as for weaponry ranging from spearheads and shield bosses to sword blades and (very rarely) helmets and chainmail. Apart from a small range of items of personal equipment—buckles, knives, and keys—basic iron tools are rarely

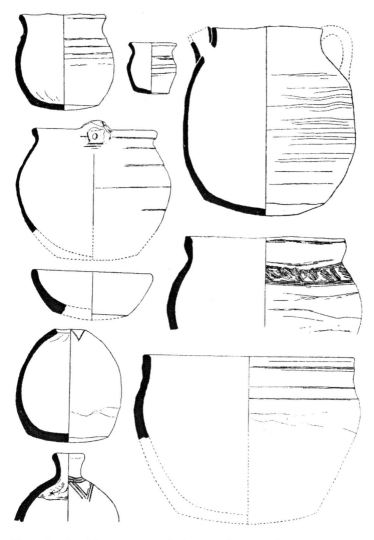

**Figure 2.4** Ipswich-ware pottery. Scale 1:5. © *The Society for Medieval Archaeology* (1959)

found, presumably because such material was habitually recycled when an object became damaged.

Fresh iron can be obtained from either stone ore or bog ore, which are available in different parts of the islands. Evidence of ironworking itself can take the form of remains of furnaces and forges, but is most frequently encountered in the form of the by-products of ironworking, namely smelting and forging slag or smithing scale. When looking at Anglo-Saxon settlements, our expectations cannot but be influenced by the clear evidence from excavations at a Continental Saxon settlement of the third and fourth centuries at Feddersen Wierde on the north German coast, where there was evidently a primary workshop site within what was chiefly a farmstead, dominating production in a village of considerable size—perhaps as many as twenty contemporary farmsteads. But we do not yet have the evidence to show how centralized or widely dispersed either the extraction or the working of iron was anywhere in Britain at this time. On Irish settlements, evidence for ironworking is almost ubiquitous, although without a definite distinction between smelting and forging in the available analyses from most sites. In England, we again eventually find evidence of sites specializing in iron production, as at Ramsbury in Wiltshire, where there are the remains of smelting furnaces datable to the late eighth century.

From a strictly utilitarian viewpoint, items made in other materials requiring special skills both to produce and to work, such as the non-ferrous metals and glass, were not essential to practical, daily life, although it would be a serious mistake to regard them therefore as functionally ephemeral. A wide range of personal jewellery and dress accessories was produced, very rarely in iron except for simple pins or the pins of brooches, or the buckles mentioned above. Dress fasteners such as brooches or clasps originally had a practical function on the costume, but by this period this had become largely redundant, and in respect of their form served primarily for display. This allowed for striking changes and variations in fashion, both within the period and between different communities. In Anglo-Saxon England, for instance, jewellery was worn almost exclusively by women so that, apart from exceptional figures such as the probable king whose treasures were buried in the mound 1 ship-burial at Sutton Hoo, or a religious leader such as Cuthbert of Lindisfarne with his jewelled pectoral cross, men must have had to use other forms of display. In

Scotland, Wales, and Ireland, by contrast, it is not clear that dress accessories were gender-specific, but most evidence associates the ostentatious penannular brooches with men, while it appears that women were more likely to have gathered and fastened their garments with various forms of pin. Besides dress accessories, it is in the form of bowls and other vessels that we see the largest amounts of non-ferrous metals being used in this period. At the simplest level, this takes the form of copper alloy mounts from turned wooden cups or bowls, or bands from stave-built wooden buckets (both of which, of course, required woodworking skills too). At the other end of the spectrum, from the seventh century in particular, we find a large number of hanging-bowls, made of beaten sheet copper alloy with richly decorated suspension and decorative mounts, often inlaid with enamel. This is an artefact type whose origins may be traced from late Roman Britain into British, Irish, and Pictish contexts of the early Middle Ages, but which became widely used in England.

As the diversity of this range of more markedly artistic objects is higher, so is the available information about their manufacture more complex. This is partly because we can infer more about techniques and organization of production from the objects themselves: in the case of separate items, for instance, which reveal some definite connection at the point of manufacture, just as the stamp-linked pots. Our best evidence in the form of the detritus of actual production comes from sites in the west and north: crucibles and moulds from various sites such as Garryduff and Garranes in Co. Cork, southern Ireland, and consistently from reoccupied Iron Age hill-fort sites in Britain such as Cadbury by Congresbury, Somerset; Dinas Powys, south Wales; the Mote of Mark in south-western Scotland; and Dunadd in Argyll. This presumably reflects a particular social and economic structure, with the manufacture of prestigious goods being concentrated at specific foci, obviously centres of regional power and control in the British-, Gaelic-, and Pictish-speaking areas. In Anglo-Saxon England, meanwhile, we have not been able to discover any substantial production site of the fifth to seventh centuries, and an increasing quantity of scattered metal-detected finds of failed or unfinished products supports the view that such production was largely peripatetic. Again, though, in the town sites of London, Ipswich, and Hamwic that had emerged by the end of the seventh century, we eventually see some concentration of production of metalwork, and especially of bone, antler, and leather artefacts.

# Social units

The brief survey of economic production in Britain and Ireland from the fifth to eighth centuries above offers an outline of the practical parameters of life. It is evident that extensive social interdependency and collaboration were required to live, materially, in the ways described. Every individual homestead had to organize its human resources, not only to have all the requisite farming jobs done adequately and at the right time but also to nurture and train children, and to produce whatever other practical or status-laden artefacts they could. We clearly cannot entertain ideas of a population made up essentially of self-sufficient farmsteads, subsisting on their own efforts and the land and resources immediately available to them. Levels of self-reliance and independence, and reciprocally the extent and objects of trade of exchange, must naturally have varied from area to area, site to site, and even household to household. Within the whole range of economic activities discussed above, however, we find that site-specific specialization is always present, and in the case of England is clearly an advancing trend. We can therefore understand how economic needs are fundamental to an investigation of how the populations were organized, from above or from within.

The term 'household' is a deceptively easy one to use to denote a basic social unit, without any substantial implications of how that would be constituted except, incongruously, in terms of the extrinsic detail that presupposes the unit to have a common home. Our basic concept is also likely to embody the archetype of the nuclear family that we are familiar with: a monogamous adult couple, children, and probably further household members in the form of dependent adult relatives, most likely elderly or widowed, and possibly a number of bond or dependent adults providing labour services to the household. Nothing in our early documentary sources would suggest that this is seriously anachronistic, although inevitably the specific life histories we are able to look at are usually reflections of far from ordinary practices in royal circles, where it is clear, for instance, that considerable latitude was possible in marriage alliances.

But can we trace any sort of 'average' families on (or in) the ground? We could start by trying to evaluate domestic arrangements as implied by dwellings excavated at settlement sites. These in fact provide anything but a uniform or easily interpretable set of data, even within particular areas or at individual sites. Building types themselves vary, especially from region to region (see Figs. 2.2 and 2.3). In Cornwall, Wales, and Ireland, round structures are typical for basic domestic structures in this period, although a rectangular form appears as the norm for larger buildings interpreted as halls, and square to rectangular domestic buildings appear in both Ireland and Cornwall before the end of the period. Rectangular structures constructed with timber posts were the normal dwelling type in England, but not—on the evidence of the post-Roman settlement excavated at Poundbury near Dorchester, Dorset—only for communities that were Anglo-Saxon in culture. Tradition and innovation in Scotland produce a more diverse range of building types, with evidence for the continued use of round wheelhouses and enclosed duns from the early centuries AD, and the introduction of rectangular hall-like buildings especially in the south and east. Examples of a distinctive cellular type of structure are best known in the northern and western Isles. They have been labelled as characteristically Pictish, which may indeed be the correct label for their inhabitants in most cases; but their absence from most of mainland Scotland renders the ethnic term somewhat misleading.

The sizes of known buildings also vary considerably; even amongst buildings we can reasonably regard as basic houses, the largest examples have up to three times the internal ground area of the smallest. There does, however, appear to be a consistent middle range of recorded sizes, with buildings between about 30 and 50 square metres in area, that comprises a substantial majority of buildings irrespective of shape and locality. In most cases we do not have good evidence for the specific function of these buildings, particularly in relation to neighbouring structures that were probably in contemporary use. Furthermore, the amount of domestic space we should allot on average per person in a household is a contentious issue, so that it is speculative in the extreme to try to translate these figures into a calculated normal household size. We can at least note that if we apply the commonly used yardstick of 10 square metres per person to this evidence, we must conclude either that few buildings were constructed to house a group of more than five persons, or that larger households either occupied more than one such building or made do with less space per head than this model would allow them. Altogether, this points us in the direction of relatively small and compact household units rather than diverse and extended ones.

Demographic studies based on the skeletons found in Anglo-Saxon cemeteries of this period give us the best information from which to try to picture such household units. What we must appreciate from the outset is that nothing could be less realistic than a freeze-frame picture of a supposedly average family. Both for individuals and even more for relationships and roles within such a group, these units were naturally and essentially in a state of constant change, with ageing, illness, and external influences such as times of plenty and want affecting their capacity and activities between the extremes of birth and death. We can nevertheless describe the fixed parameters within which each individual found his or her own particular place. We can state, for instance, that mean life expectancy was about 25 years, although on its own this figure is potentially misleading. It effectively means that half of those born would die by their twenty-fifth birthday. Juvenile mortality was quite high, and if one reached one's 20s one could reasonably hope to live to 40 or more. Overall, life expectancy for adult males was a little higher than that for women, but not by much. If we sought to picture a notional family unit around a healthy adult couple, we might risk an assumption that men were more likely to pair with women a number of years younger than themselves than to have spouses of equal age. By her mid-20s a healthy woman should be expected to have had the absolute minimum of two children a couple would need to rear for the population level to be maintained. To compensate for juvenile mortality and other adults who failed to reproduce to the necessary level, there may well have been several children in a household. Adult dependants that might be added to the household could include elderly parents, especially widowed women, and adult brothers and sisters who may not yet have formed a household of their own. It is manifest just how widely and randomly the population of a household could vary.

There are two kinds of relationship in a nuclear kin group, blood relationship and created kinship, especially marriage. We should appreciate that other forms of kinship can be created, through the fosterage of children, for example, or adoptive fraternity. But while there is wide scope for variation in size and structure between household units within the range of kinship, the greatest uncertainty we face relates to the actual place of unrelated dependants—household servants/labourers, bondmen/women and slaves—within the household. Our historical sources leave us in no doubt that servitude was an accepted fact of life, presumably right across the British Isles at this time. And there would have been degrees of servitude, depending partly on the context, partly on the characters involved, from the slave regarded as a complete chattel and beast of labour to the bondman or client with limited freedom and a series of obligations. Some households presumably housed individuals who through the quirks of fortune had become rootless, and who freely traded service to the household for a home there. But the relative numbers of individuals in a servile condition, and where they might be represented in the archaeological record, remain unanswered questions.

There is no archaeology of slavery from this period: no slave chains, no obvious slave accommodation. It has been suggested that some Anglo-Saxon burial evidence could be interpreted in terms of servitude, for instance as an explanation of the poorest end of the wealth scale of furnished burials in individual cemeteries, or, more plausibly, of abnormal burials including a few cases where it is conceivable that one individual was sacrificed to accompany another in the grave. An example is the prone burial (face down—an unusual position) of an older woman above that of a younger one in a single deep grave at Sewerby, East Yorkshire, of the sixth century. The lower burial is very richly furnished. However the upper body, lying prone, was itself far from poorly clad when buried, undermining the case for low social status as the explanation for the deviancy of this burial from the norm. Even possible cases like this are extremely few, and do not provide us with any sort of generalizable pattern. Pathological analysis of skeletons from Anglo-Saxon cemeteries, meanwhile, has revealed communities in which all individuals, whatever their apparent status as implied by the level of grave furnishing they were buried with, led lives of sustained strenuous physical exertion.

Age and sex were natural conditions of decisive importance for an individual's role and status within the community. The condition of childhood is generally obscure, although we can assume that it involved such work as could be managed by the immature, and gradual training for adult duties. Historical sources and law codes indicate at least two major thresholds in the case of boys: one around the age of 7 to 8, at which serious education and training of those accepted into the Church ('oblates') could begin, and another between 10 and 12, when legal adult responsibility was attained. Anglo-Saxon cemetery evidence paints a rather different picture. Here girls can be seen to qualify for burial in the standard adult female costume from the usual age of adolescence (generally 12–14), and predictably they would have been regarded as marriageable from this stage onwards. In the case of teenage boys it seems to be a little later, around the ages of 15–18, that they are more likely to be accompanied by the definitive adult male accoutrements of weaponry in the grave. An exact counterpart is the age at which the period of fosterage of children ends according to the Irish law book *Senchas Már*: 14 for girls and 17 for boys.

Gender roles amongst adults were sharply distinguished. The persistent association of women with domestic occupations and men with military activities is strongly represented in the grave goods of early Anglo-Saxon burials. The indoor craft of textile production is overwhelmingly linked to the female. Shears, spindle whorls, and occasionally thread pickers and weaving battens (the latter apparently a prestigious, status-bearing object, and intriguingly sometimes made out of an item of weaponry such as a spearhead or sword) are the only pieces of productive equipment persistently found in these burials, and occur exclusively with women. This gender link is also explicitly recognized in Irish laws, albeit with an additional social distinction between employment in textile work for women of a higher social status and kneading and grinding for those of lower class. Another domestic role in which some women appear to have been attributed special status over others was that of housekeeper: specifically, the keeper of the household's stores and valuables. This is reflected in the symbolic association between the adult woman, well established in her society, and the key. Functional iron keys hanging from the belts or chatelaines of women buried in Anglo-Saxon cemeteries are common finds, and in some areas in the sixth century what appears to have been a purely symbolic pair of model keys in copper alloy occurs in relatively well-furnished adult women's graves (see fig. 2.5, a and b).

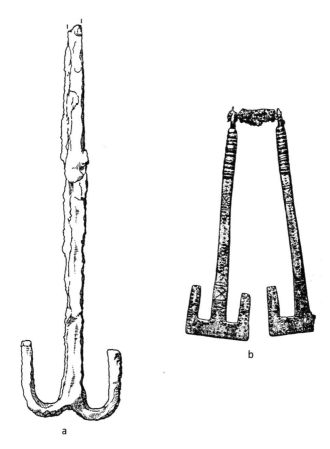

a

b

**Figure 2.5** Anglo-Saxon key and girdle-hangers. (a) Iron key. Edix Hill, Cambridgeshire. (b) Pair of copper-alloy girdle-hangers. Little Eriswell, Suffolk. Scale 1:2.

None of this means, of course, that we can expect many women to have enjoyed remission from laborious farming tasks such as harvesting and threshing corn, milking and dairywork, grinding and food preparation. The pathological evidence for women from Anglo-Saxon cemeteries shows no difference in the effects of manual labour between the sexes, while the Old Irish tract on social relations and marriage, *Cáin Lánamna*, makes it clear that burdens were effectively balanced between the sexes, although not identical. Adomnán's Life of Columba refers incidentally to a woman herding a flock. With the exception of potting, however, such evidence as we have attributes the other crafts discussed above to the male sphere. The Irish law code *Uraicecht Becc* has an elaborate set of provisions on craftsmen with an unquestioned assumption that the individuals concerned should be male, as is also the case with references to individual skilled artisans in Irish hagiography. Unlike weaponry, however, and the women's textile-working equipment, it is—with one exception, unusual in other ways as well—unknown in Anglo-Saxon England for craft tools to appear as grave goods.

There could be no more obvious illustration of the fact that grave goods offer us a selective and deliberately focused image of gender roles and the communities that buried them. This is not, however, to suggest that the frequency of weapon burials in the period of furnished burial gives a fictitious view of male roles in this society. It is true that none of the weapons buried in England has yet been shown to bear the scars of battle, and indeed in some cases the quality of iron used for, say, spearheads is considerably poorer than that of the general-purpose knife. On the other hand, the skeletal pathology at Edix Hill, Cambridgeshire, revealed a number of men carrying what seemed to be weapon-blade injuries. The social organization of warfare below the level of the aristocratic warrior band is something that we unfortunately catch only scattered glimpses of, like this. But we may still conclude that in these early post-Roman centuries, any distinction between civilian and military society effectively collapsed. The majority of men had to be prepared to bear weapons, at least to fight for themselves and their immediate household and property. Socially, however, what one would greatly wish to know is how far and in what directions their obligations for military service would have extended.

Such obligations could not be distinguished from the social rank a man held or aspired to. Like slavery (which is of course an extreme aspect of it), social hierarchy is something which has no doubt existed in one form or other, always and everywhere, within our field of discussion, but we often have only limited and unclear information about it, with the lower strata in particular being poorly recorded. A ruling elite of kings sprang up in post-Roman Britain, presumably principally on the basis of the Roman-period aristocracy although there is also evidence for successful invasions and conquests by ruling groups, both British and Irish, establishing dynasties in Britain. The constituent elements of Irish political organization, involving tiers of kingship and ruled groups called *túatha*, are clear in the Irish historical sources, even if the social realities underlying them are likely to have been even more complicated and inconsistent than the surviving written records show. In England we gain our first real views of social hierarchy towards the end of the sixth century, a period from which King Æthelberht of Kent's lawcode refers to a social scale involving grades of king, nobleman, freeman, churl, and slave, at the same time as the range of furnished burials in England shifts to show both wider distinctions and special concentrations of wealth. There has consequently been considerable discussion of how 'egalitarian' fifth- and sixth-century Anglo-Saxon society may have been. The term can only imply a fluidity and instability of positions of eminence and control, not the absence of power relations in a notionally democratic or republican society: a state of affairs which in a strict sense is more *an*archic than *hier*archical, in which individuals' ambitions and abilities could create and relocate positions of power. In such circumstances it is obviously not practicable to construct models positing general or typical ranges and structures of group affiliation involving military commitments.

# Social networks

In the society of early medieval Britain and Ireland as we understand it, there would also have been a direct equation between an individual's status in society and the range of that individual's contacts. Such a range could be measured in terms of the quantity and diversity of goods and services the individual could obtain: the wealth and variety of sources to which he (or she) had access. It is consequently no surprise that the probably royal funeral treasure from Sutton Hoo mound 1 comprises not only local works of consummate skill and value but also items showing contacts with both Scandinavia and the Continent, including items from as far off as the eastern Mediterranean. Alliances between individuals and families could be created and cemented by both material and personal forms of exchange within these networks: the giving of gifts to create reciprocal obligations; marriages to create ties of kinship; agreements to trade available commodities to mutual advantage.

While it would be anachronistic to think of the movement of goods in this context in terms of a commercial market, the need for specialist skills in production, for raw materials to be acquired, and for the products to be distributed would have created opportunities for entrepreneurship. One of the most likely categories to emerge would be the skilled craftsman able to claim a special category of status—as in the Irish laws—or even to trade and profit freely on the basis of the demand for his skills and products. If the finer pieces of metalwork known from sixth-century Anglo-Saxon England were, as suggested, the work of peripatetic craftsmen, it is difficult to see how such craftsmen could not have been largely free agents, subject to the limits and opportunities their market afforded them. Similarly, the variety and diversity of production on small, fixed plots in the early towns may reflect the use of such plots on individual producers' initiatives—taking advantage of the guaranteed market in an agreed meeting and trading place, and the protection that would be afforded (at a price) by the controlling authority there. Soon enough, too, such a situation would give rise to a group of professional merchants as well, transporting and trading goods rather than producing them. Nevertheless the laws of both Æthelberht of Kent and Ine of Wessex, from either end of the seventh century, refer to unspecified 'smiths' who were tied to the king and a nobleman respectively.

The importation and distribution of commodities over considerable distances is visible at every stage in Anglo-Saxon England. A popular item of sixth-century women's jewellery, for instance, was a necklace including amber beads, some of which could have been supplied from raw amber found on the east coast of England, although it is difficult to believe that that source was sufficient for the huge quantities of beads found right across England (Map 4). The importation of supplies from the southern Baltic is highly likely. At the same time, a considerable number of women had purses fitted with elephant ivory rings, a commodity that obviously had travelled a very long way indeed to sixth-century England. In the seventh century cowrie shells from the Indian Ocean were arriving, as well as a considerable amount of wheel-thrown Frankish pottery, especially in the south-east. The provenance of stone used for querns or whetstones can be determined; and it can thus be shown that it came

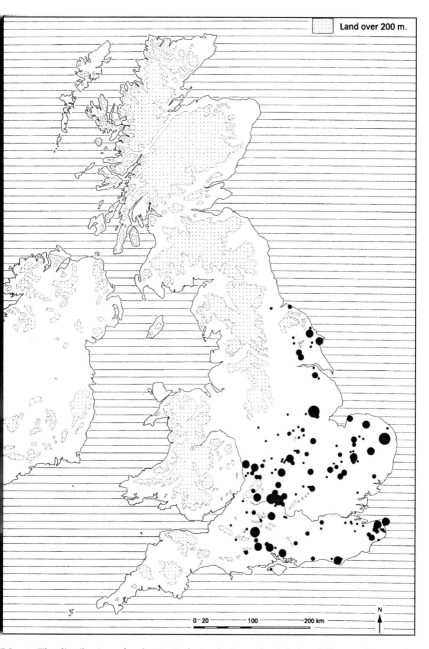

Map 4 The distribution of amber in Early Anglo-Saxon burials, late fifth to early seventh century.

eventually to be transported around England, including a distinctive basalt lava from the Rhineland.

We have not yet identified any of the earliest coastal landing places of England that we can assume to have been the predecessors of a series of port towns that appears in the seventh century. However, the cemetery of a rich and particularly martial community at Sarre opposite the mouth of the Stour on the south coast of what was then genuinely the Isle of Thanet may well point to where one of these lay, just as distinctly well-equipped groups burying inland at Mitcham and Croydon in Surrey, at collection points in the old Roman communications system south of Londinium, were presumably located there to continue to control the produce of the surrounding territory as early as the fifth century. The re-emergence of urban ports in the seventh and eighth centuries was part of a wider northern European network, embracing both sides of the Channel and the North Sea from Southampton to York in England, as far as Ribe in Jutland, and extending even into the southern Baltic. While the same story does not account for the primary origins of the sites in every case, there is no doubt that they became established and flourished under royal protection: Hamwic in the kingdom of Wessex, London originally in Essex and Ipswich in East Anglia although soon under Mercian supremacy, and York in Northumbria. The king would profit from these towns via tolls and taxes.

A special feature of the development of trading systems is the increasing use of coinage in eastern and southern England from the sixth to eighth centuries. For about a century after the demise of Roman government in 410 the occurrence of coins from the Continent in England was exceptional in the extreme, but for most of the sixth century and increasingly into the early seventh a steady if still thin stream of gold coin, Byzantine and Merovingian, appears, the great majority of it in Kent. Regular English minting of a gold coinage began in the second quarter of the seventh century, gradually being taken up in more than one area within the south-east. Around the 670s the now massively debased gold coinage was superseded by a silver coinage of proto-pennies, most commonly known as *sceattas* (sg. *sceatt*), a coinage which became a common currency of the North Sea port network and which survived into the later eighth century, when a reform of King Offa replaced it in most of England with a broader and thinner silver penny, a coin type already standard in Carolingian Francia.

Profuse finds of sceattas from a large area of England imply that this coinage was in very widespread use there—indeed, at a level of circulation not to be reached again until the thirteenth century. While intrinsically valuable and tradable, there is reasonable doubt over whether the small amounts of high-value gold coin present in the sixth and early seventh centuries could have played any great role in economic transactions. In the eighth century, by contrast, especially in the first half, it seems that we have to regard eastern and south-eastern England as thoroughly monetized in its economic life. There is, however, a marked and continuing decline in coin loss (and, by implication, circulation) from the last three or four decades of the eighth century onwards. The cause of this is quite obscure. There is no reason to associate it with any severe decline in economic activity, at least at this date. The Continental coin reform of Pepin the Short in 755 was intended to impose royal control over this medium of exchange, and much the same goals are evident in Offa's policies. This may, then, have extended to restrictions on access to and the circulation of coinage as well as control over its production, although it seems that the coinage remained essentially a practical, economic utility, not a special form of aristocratic wealth.

There is a thorough systemic contrast in the west and north of Britain and in Ireland. Here a number of coastal landing and trading sites, several of them represented by activity layers within sand dunes, are known from the fifth century onwards: for instance at Bantham, south Devon, Longbury Bank in south Wales, Meols on the tip of the Wirral peninsula, Luce Sands in Galloway, Dalkey Island and Dundrum on the east coast of Ireland. Our best plot of the pattern of importation and distribution in this whole zone comes in the form of the imported ceramics, especially amphorae and types of red-coated bowls of the fifth and sixth centuries and what is known as E-ware of the seventh to early eighth. There is a distinct shift in distribution between these two phases of importation, with E-ware proving very scarce in south-western England apart from the Scilly Isles, in sharp contrast to the earlier amphorae. E-ware distribution patterns have been studied in detail by Dr Ewan Campbell, revealing clear concentrations at particular centres, such as Dunadd in Argyll, from where some limited redistribution to satellite sites appears to have taken place. The near-absence of E-ware in south-western England coincides with the incorporation of this area down to the Cornish border within the kingdom of Wessex. The clear implication is that political control was always a key and apparently direct factor in obtaining and supplying such valuable commodities in this zone. We may suspect that this was also largely the case with high-quality metalwork and other crafts. As noted, it is at the special settlement sites of this zone that we find production evidence in the form of moulds and crucibles, and also, indeed, fragments of reusable scrap metal and glass, often originating in the Anglo-Saxon east or from across the Channel in Frankish lands.

The former Roman town of Viriconium at Wroxeter in Shropshire, however, is an exceptional site that demonstrates how a common pattern will not necessarily be a uniform one. Sub-Roman activity here is dated by a coin of Valentinian III from around 430, and archaeomagnetic and radiocarbon dates continuing to the early seventh century. The character of activity in the late- and sub-Roman 'town' is represented by the occurrence of a series of unsophisticated adaptations of the area of the old baths basilica—a large public building—followed by the laying out of what looks like a street bounded by a series of rubble platforms, capable of supporting a considerable number of timber-framed buildings, at least one of them impressively large, although these can now be reconstructed by imagination alone. Yet whatever administrative and trading functions were going on here, in what must have been British territory down to the seventh century, at most one sherd of imported pottery, actually of uncertain date, has been found, and no fine metalwork or other prestigious portable artefacts at all.

Throughout our period, in summary, there is evidence for direct contacts over great distances, and in every feasible direction: from early England to the Continent and Scandinavia; between the various territories of an Atlantic zone that stretched southwards to western France and Iberia; and between Anglo-Saxon England and its neighbours in Britain. In most cases, it appears to have been the intrinsic value of the commodities traded to the communities that obtained them that provides the basic reason for the existence of the networks. However the provision and distribution of the goods was controlled, we can regard these forms of contact as essentially impersonal, object-oriented trade. Within England, meanwhile, archaeology may provide us with an insight into other networks, of a medium extent between long-distance and local, that we can suggest were more socially oriented.

These appear within the rich supply of dress accessories in early Anglo-Saxon women's graves. As has been noted, women's fashion was variable, and many distinctive forms of brooch and pendant ornaments are known from these burials. Combinations of different brooch types and other dress accessories are far from haphazard, and a wide variety of different sets or costume groups have been identified. Amongst some of the more richly and skilfully crafted objects, such as the ostentatious 'square-headed' brooch, cast in relief and usually gilded (see Fig. 2.6(a)), and similarly showy 'florid cruciform' brooches, we can observe the distribution of closely related types over certain consistent ranges. One such range links East Anglia with Humberside, north and south; another covers a central Midland zone from Cambridgeshire westwards; a third an area around London from south Bedfordshire to Sussex and the upper Thames basin. Such brooch types sometimes reveal more local areas of inter-association even within these larger networks, as is particularly clear in the Warwickshire Avon area, and in an intriguing case between clusters in southern Northamptonshire and Berkshire apparently linked by a Roman road running straight through the upper Thames area. As we are dealing with women's personal costume accessories here, it seems inappropriate to try to account for these coherent and persistent distributional patterns purely in impersonal terms of production and trade. It is inherently likely that the articles were also moving with women themselves, passing from one family to another to strengthen alliances through exogamous marriage exchange.

We cannot find the same level of material evidence outside the Anglo-Saxon area, of course, but the Irish historical material gives clear enough testimony of the use of female exogamy in constructing social relationships. The dynamic of exogamy provides a telling insight into the essential mutability of the household unit. This, as we have seen, was a culture in which the domestic was the female domain, particularly the wife's. Yet under a system of exogamy the household is the fixed locus of a male line, and women move from one household into another—in the case of sixth-century England, it would seem, still likely to display their origins in a material way. If identity and cultural traditions were passed on in the family unit, a

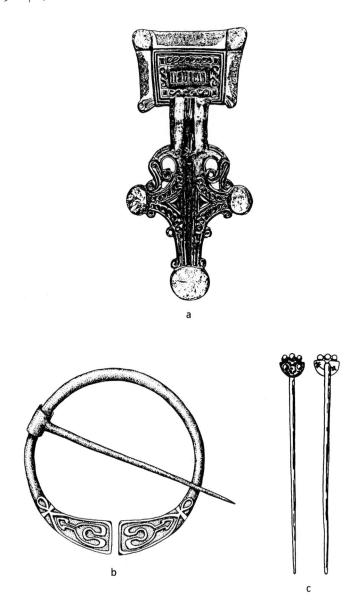

**Figure 2.6** Ornate dress jewellery. (a) Great square-headed brooch. Bergh Apton, Norfolk. (b) Penannular brooch. Dinas Powys, Vale of Glamorgan. (c) Hand-pin. Norrie's Law, Fifeshire. Scale 1:2.

constant process of cultural adoption and personal adaptation must therefore have been at the heart of their transmission.

# Macro-groups

We have suggested that the creation of long-distance, sometimes overseas, connections in early medieval Britain and Ireland was motivated by the demand for valuable material supplies rather than the social dimension of those contacts. There are nonetheless instances of long-distance political and social interference or influence accompanying these networks. King Æthelberht brought a Merovingian princess and a Frankish bishop, Liudhard (who had struck the earliest coin known to have been minted in England), to Kent in the later sixth century, and there were Merovingian claims of sovereignty over Kent and England around this time that have been thoroughly examined by Professor Ian Wood. The Iona community in Dál Riata involved itself in Northumbria by sheltering the royal pretender Oswald from the 610s to c.633, and by sending missionaries to re-establish a Christian church there when Oswald then assumed rule in Northumbria; Penda of Mercia was allied with Cadwallon of Gwynedd when Oswald's predecessor, Edwin, was slain in 633. When the first Viking raid on Lindisfarne took place in 793, Alcuin upbraided the nobles of Northumbria for copying the dress and hairstyles of the very pagans who were now threatening their land. Amongst the Britons, meanwhile, despite deep uncertainty over the precise form, contents, and date of different recensions of the ancient Welsh heroic poem *Y Gododdin*, this poem appears to have originated as early as the sixth century, and its reworkings reveal a growing determination to create a pan-British military alliance, opposed to an English enemy, in the legendary history of the poem.

At this point, then, we have finally come to those large entities British, English, Irish, Scots, Pictish: the groups that seem to be at the highest level of contrastive identity found in Britain and Ireland in our period. Useful contemporary testimony to a conception of these groups is provided around the year 730 by Bede, describing Britain and her peoples, with additional reference to Ireland. These macro-groups he saw as the *gentes* and *nationes* of Britain and Ireland. They were distinct from one another primarily in language, in their territories, and in their origins: shared identity was thus a form of genetic inheritance, as implied etymologically by the word 'nation'. Bede himself was fully aware of many levels of subdivision within such groups, particularly another relatively high-level division of the English into three further *gentes, populi,* or *nationes*: the Angles, Saxons, and Kentishmen.

For us, the reality of these groupings is corroborated by other forms of evidence—implying thereby that the distinctions subsisted in a wider range of characteristics than Bede indicated. A considerably greater challenge than to recognize these group divisions (which we can refer to as a set of *ethnic* identities) is to reach a confident understanding of the reasons for their existence, both historical (diachronic) and functional (synchronic). Bede's historical explanation is simple, and in demonstrable ways is a *simplified* version of historical fact. This does not make it intrinsically wrong. Nor does it make it easier for us to explain things in a more accurate and thorough way now. What we have to do, however, is to treat Bede as part of the history we are studying, not as an objective, unnaturally timeless bridge between his own time and ours.

Materially, the Anglian, Saxon, and Kentish groupings are amply distinctive in late fifth- and sixth-century female costume sets. Within these, and justifying Bede, there are even elements with definite origins in the Anglian, Saxon, and Jutish homelands on the Continent respectively, although these consistently make up only a small part of what became the characteristic material representation of these groups in England. They take their place amongst a range of constituent elements which were adapted and hybridized in the redefinition of these groups as they transformed themselves from Continental into English ethnic groups in the fifth and sixth century, a period widely known as the 'Migration Period' in Germanic Europe. In Anglian England, for instance, Scandinavian and even Saxon elements proved no less significant constituents than the Anglian 'small long' brooches and pottery types, while Kentish material culture owed very much more to Continental Frankish models than to Jutish ones. In a tantalizingly imprecisely dated transition around the late sixth to early seventh century, these regionally and ethnically distinctive female costume sets gave way to a more uniform dress style in England: actually a sort of continuum, with still quite contrastive northern and southern poles, but no divisions we can interpret in ethnic or national terms. Those identities certainly did not disappear at this juncture, but they had to find expression in other ways.

So active and substantial was the material investment in the redefinition of these ethnic groups in very early England that we must infer them to have had a serious regional function—at a level above those of the large social networks previously described, at least in Anglian England. They certainly represent something more than an inherited identity that simply could not be sloughed off. The historical names and associations of the groups were themselves elements available for selection from a range of cultural traditions, just like brooch or pottery types. In Kent, in fact, the group did not adopt the Jutish name even though it claimed that ancestry, and rather took the ancient, Roman and even pre-Roman name of the area, *Cantium*, calling themselves *Cant-ware*, 'people of Kent'. This process is that which is known as 'ethnogenesis': the generation of groups, rather than their smooth, continuous history. Amongst the factors that drove such a process, we should recognize the importance of the security of feeling part of a large community, represented by conformity in shared material practices. In an area that had seen such demographic and political turmoil as southern and eastern Britain in the aftermath of the collapse of the Roman Empire, such an impulse would understandably have been strong.

These processes are also particularly conspicuous in England because they happened (not coincidentally) to include furnished funerary rites, in particular widespread inhumation (burial of the body) rather than cremation. We know that such was not uniformly the case within the Anglo-Saxon area, however: in the area around London at this time, for instance, we have a curious contrast in the distribution maps of known Anglo-Saxon furnished burial sites and known settlements using Anglo-Saxon artefact types and structural types, the former appearing up on the dip slope of the South Downs, the latter on the riverine gravels closer to the Thames. The general distribution map of Anglo-Saxon Migration Period cemeteries (Map 5) nonetheless gives us a reliable picture of the extent of Englishness by the second half of the sixth century, even if not in every last detail.

A crucial question is whether the remaining areas of Britain and Ireland differed from Anglo-Saxon England primarily in the medium

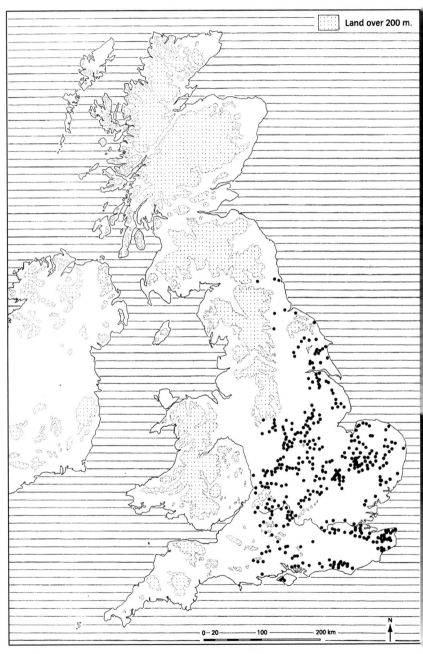

**Map 5** Distribution of Anglo-Saxon burial sites of the Migration Period (approx. mid-fifth to later sixth century).

of expression of cultural cohesion and group identity (particularly their depositional practices) or—passing through a quite different historical trajectory—simply did not experience an equivalent surge of group formation and (re)definition. Careful and deliberate study of the sources that the cultures of these areas have produced for us does in fact reveal similar processes at work. Amongst the parallels in the British area is indeed a focus on dress accessories as a sign of identity. This is represented specifically by the penannular brooch type and some distinctive, relatively large pin types (see Fig. 2.6 (b and c)). These underwent a variety of design elaborations in the period, and appear to have become popular not only widely but also rapidly right across Celtic- (and Pictish-) speaking Britain and Ireland. Work by Dr Raghnall Ó Floinn suggests that these developments stem from a productive hotspot in the Bristol Channel area as early as the late Roman period (fourth century AD). It is premature to try to explain why this happened there, but when the details and dating of the evidence are fully available this will be a crucial matter of investigation. Significant confirmation of the symbolic role of dress accessories comes, admittedly in the later A-text of *Y Gododdin*, where the group affiliation and nobility of the British warriors advancing into battle is encapsulated in their being described as *torchawg* or *kayawg*, adorned with or wearing a torque and clasp respectively.

While material culture and consequently archaeology are so revealing in the Anglo-Saxon context, language and discourse such as this poetry were crucial media in the British area. The modern Welsh term for Wales and Welsh people—*Cymru/cymry*—was earlier geographically a wider ethnic term (hence, for instance, *Cumberland*), and has been explained by Professor Thomas Charles-Edwards as originating as an ethnic denominator comprising people with a shared, vernacular, local language: like *Deutsch/Dutch*, from *þeod-isc*, 'the people's language', as opposed to the international language of ideological and political control, Latin. Although the term for the Brythonic (pre-Welsh) language, first recorded in Irish as *combrec*, a linguistic form likely to originate no later than the seventh century, is in a sense secondary—an adjective derived from a noun *\*com-brog-*, 'one of the same area', which survives for us in Welsh *cymro/cymry*, 'Welshman/-men', and in an Old English personal name *Cumbra*—this is a standard way of labelling languages, and does not undermine the proposition. The language did emerge as a major unifying factor, even if for a time it seems to have been restricted to an oral domain, and a distinctive written culture using Latin, and occasionally Irish in inscriptions, appears from Cornwall to south-western Scotland. The earliest vernacular Brythonic inscription we have is from Tywyn, Gwynedd, datable to the seventh–ninth centuries. Whether the Brythonic (British) language superseded a spoken Latin to any significant extent in this area we cannot tell, but it certainly rose steadily to normative status as the language of all facets of secular life.

The distinction between Irish Gaelic and the Brythonic language within the Celtic language family can be traced back to at least the third century BC, to when a sound change from an initial $k^w$- cluster to $p$- created the well-known $q$-/$p$-Celtic split. This is particularly interesting as the oldest division *within* one of the major Indo-European language groups in Europe (Celtic, Germanic, Baltic, Slavonic, Romance, Greek, and Albanian) surviving in separate but related languages, the only one that can be traced back to before the Roman period. The $p$-innovation was otherwise shared by most Celtic language varieties across Britain and the Continent. The insularity of Ireland is clearly a significant precondition for this split, although it is not immediately satisfactory as a complete explanation. Instead of seeing this as an early assertion of Irish unity and difference, however, we ought first to look to the apparent absolute decline in activity in Ireland between the Middle and Late Iron Age, setting in during the second century BC. While there is evidence of external La Tène-style overseas influences reaching Ireland in the third and fourth centuries BC, and there were certainly exchange links between Britain and Ireland in the Roman period, this may have been enough to marginalize Ireland at a crucial juncture of Celtic linguistic development.

The q-Celtic Gaelic language, then, appears in western Scotland in our period. This has widely been regarded as a linguistic shift for this area, with Gaelic being introduced as a result of conquest and settlement that created the Scottish Gaelic kingdom of Dál Riata out of which Scotland herself was eventually to develop. This explanation has recently been challenged on the grounds that independent archaeological and historical evidence for such settlement is negligible, leaving the putative language shift itself as the main supporting plank of what is meant to be its own explanation. In view of the proximity by sea of northern Ireland and the western coast and islands of

Scotland, it is certainly difficult to insist that the q-/p-Celtic boundary can only have followed one particular line, isolating Ireland—a point implicitly conceded in doubts over whether the pre-Viking-period language of the Isle of Man was Gaelic or Brythonic. The identification of p-Celtic elements in a handful of names recorded by classical authors in western Scotland may not be enough to provide a complete language map of this area. Where we do have evidence of the resettlement of influential individuals from Ireland in western Scotland is in the establishment of the monastic community of Iona by Columba (Colum Cille) in the 560s—by which time, though, Gaelic Dál Riata reportedly already existed. When Adomnán, another Irishman and a later abbot of Iona, wrote Columba's Life at the end of the seventh century, he was apologetic over the need to introduce 'strange' and 'crude' Irish names into his Latin text. But this was essential to represent the historical situation of Columba's life and miracles: western Scotland was thoroughly Gaelicized. In Ireland itself, Old Irish was well in advance of Brythonic/Old Welsh as a formalized and literary vernacular, used in written laws and moral tracts as well as ethical poetry, and even with its own special alphabet, the ogham script, for inscriptions from at least the beginning of the fifth century.

The Pictish language referred to by Bede, and apparently represented for us in a small number of incomprehensible inscriptions from early medieval eastern Scotland, is mysterious in many ways. Place names in Pictland include a pair of recurrent and prominent p-Celtic elements, the *aber-*, 'river mouth', of for instance Aberdeen, and *pit-*, 'piece of land', of Pitlochry etc. (cf. Welsh *aber-*, *peth*). However, the date of the latter is disputed, and there is nothing like sufficient evidence of the vocabulary and grammar of language in Pictland for us to attempt to define the affiliations of the language as a whole. Its use in inscriptions is evidence of some formal cultural status, but it eventually expired in favour of Scots Gaelic in the mainland, and the Vikings' Norse in the northern isles. This in fact means that the fate of the Pictish language was apparently one with the fate of the Pictish polity and a distinct Pictish people. Although not completely dissimilar to cases of language shift and ethnic replacement elsewhere in Britain in the Middle Ages, this is to all appearances the starkest and most absolute case of such an equation. It is possible, therefore, that 'Pictish', however it was constituted, was the language

Pictish culture thus have an inflexibly esoteric and resistant character, which might explain the eventual annihilation of Pictishness?

The language that eventually became dominant in Scotland—long after our period—even though it was not the original language of the ruling class, was English. English in the fifth to eighth centuries was the newly forming language of a population that in the fifth century had extended the geographical range of the Germanic language family across the North Sea for the first time. The language varieties it introduced to Britain would have been those of a wide arc of coastal lands on the Continent, from what is now northern France right around to the west coast of Norway. We can read something of the Germanic language in the area before and at this time in early runic inscriptions, but can particularly use reconstruction from later attested language forms to produce an extensive and detailed picture of variation within its range. It appears that substantial divergency had already set in within a North Sea Germanic linguistic continuum, a process of differentiation that was dramatically reversed in Britain, where the Germanic language varieties converged upon a set of norms that themselves represented substantial shifts—particularly in pronunciation—from the Continental norms. Dialects formed within English from the very beginning too, but we cannot map these precisely against their contemporary ethnic and cultural borders; what they do *not* represent, however, is the survival to any significant degree of pre-settlement linguistic differences within Continental Germanic.

The unification of English must reflect the pragmatic pressure for a common language within the area: this must too have accommodated a significant number of language-shift speakers, especially during the Anglicization of western England from the late sixth to eighth centuries. There is virtually no convincing evidence of Brythonic or spoken Latin substrates in the language that emerged. Interference in most areas of the vocabulary and sound system is minimal, the former either being very specialized (e.g. the term *ceaster* from Latin *castrum* for a former Roman town) or appearing as virtual one-offs, in rarely used words. Syntactically, the influence of these languages on colloquial English seems to have been nil, although language historians are still puzzled by the extraordinary parallel between English and Welsh in the now common construction of the verb 'to be' (Welsh *bod*) with a verbal noun (e.g. to be going/*bod yn mynd*), which only really emerges in English at the end of the Middle English period in the fourteenth century: had this been attested in Old English we should have little hesitation in attributing it to Brythonic influence. What we should also attach some importance to is the number of pre-English topographical, place, and personal names that remain in use in Anglo-Saxon England. Studies of language shift have found that these can be the last elements of a dying language that its speakers give up. As examples we could note the various rivers Avon in England (*afon* is Welsh for 'River'), or the springs denoted by Latin *funta* at, for instance, Bedfont and Chalfont, west of London. Meanwhile the celebrated father of Old English religious poetry, Cædmon, had a name of Brythonic origin.

Language is a medium for social exchanges, and for creating and maintaining social relationships. While it cannot be an object of exchange in itself, it is in these functions very like a currency: an element whose only function is to facilitate exchange itself. Just as we can observe political control of the currency being imposed in the area where coinage was in use, so also we eventually see political interference with forms of language and discourse, in an attempt to exercise a similar kind of control. Short of using an exclusive elite language—such as aristocratic French in nineteenth-century Russia—no dominant power can withhold or restrict language from a population. We do in fact have a story told by Bede of a Northumbrian nobleman, Imma, who betrayed his high social and therefore warrior status by speaking the elevated social dialect of his class, not the language of the peasantry. Formal uses of the language can, however, be controlled, as we see in Kentish documents of the late eighth century onwards, where dialectal norms we can rightly regard as Mercian are imposed in line with the fact of Mercian hegemony.

The histories of the languages of early medieval Britain and Ireland were thus fundamentally shaped by the active domains of these languages—the contexts in which they were used. Of course linguistic history must include linguistic origins and transmission. Here too migration and settlement are an essential part of the story of why certain languages were spoken in particular places. This is indisputably so in the case of England, although it is salutary to acknowledge that at present our best evidence for a relatively high level of Germanic migration and colonization in the fifth to early sixth centuries lies in the volume of evidence for the abandonment of agricultural land in northern Germany produced by pollen diagrams there rather than anything we can securely infer from the introduction and development of Germanic language and culture in England. Irish raiding, political conquest, and settlement in western Britain can likewise be taken as a fact, although again its quantitative level is simply not directly deducible from its qualitative impact. Contrary to Bede's view, then, we cannot see these ethnic and linguistic origins as determinative facts which imposed contrastive identities and cultural profiles on the populations of eighth-century Britain. Those historical backgrounds, rather, provided the materials out of which the peoples of these islands in successive generations constructed and reconstructed their cultures (including their language) and identities. The building blocks they used thus ranged from small and particular details to large and abstract entities.

# An overview

Of all the only partially adequate terms that could be chosen as the subheading for a final paragraph, 'overview' at least focuses nicely on the question of whether this has been a demotic worm's-eye view—looking as archaeologists tend to do, from ground level or below upwards—or an eagle's-eye view—trying to take in a huge area at once, albeit with no hope of the unfailing acuity of vision with which eagles are proverbially attributed. While detail is vital to accuracy and validity of perception, however, a conscious attempt has been made here to convey a general view of the period that is not just a mass of details, but rather one which focuses crucially on a vital and general dynamic of constant, essential change and adaptation. The people of Britain and Ireland from the fifth to eighth centuries could never just passively exist. They had to live, and to work for their economic and social security, which for some meant an ambitious struggle for power. As the whole population became involved in this, we can detect an interesting pattern by which the majority of significant cultural developments arose spontaneously and popularly, to be appropriated, if possible, by political elites rather than being imposed by them. If 'elite emulation' was a feature of this period, it could as well mean emulation by an elite as the emulation of an elite.

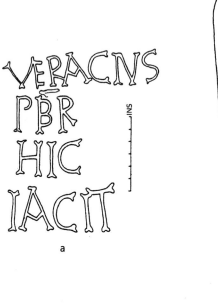

**Figure 3.1** (a) Aberdaron inscription (VERACIVS PB̄R HIC IACIT: 'Veracius the priest lies here').
(b) Inscription at Whithorn (LOC STI PETRI APVSTOLI: 'The place (church) of St Peter the Apostle').
These two inscriptions, the one on the Llŷn peninsula in the north-west corner of Wales, the other in Galloway in the south-west corner of Scotland, both attest post-Roman Christianity of the fifth or sixth century. They are linked by their unusual 'fish-tail' serifs and may thus reveal north–south connections across the Irish Sea.

mother, Matrona, gave her name to the River Marne, east of Paris. The stone in Wilfrid's crypt thus juxtaposes three religions: that of the Britons, shared in large part with other Celtic peoples; that of the Romans, the imperial religion; and Christianity, recently brought to Northumbria by the Irish from the north and by an offshoot of a papal mission from the south.

The inscription denotes the beginning and the end of a circular movement of conversion to Christianity in the British Isles. It began with the advance of Christianity in Roman Britain during the fourth century, by the end of which the religion now favoured by the emperor was dominant in political authority if not in numbers. At the same time as Christianity prevailed in Roman Britain a new Christian community was formed in Ireland, which, by 431, was strong enough to request and receive a bishop, Palladius, sent by Pope Celestine. This newly constituted Irish Church was then supported for the rest of the century from Britain; at first it was probably confined to the province of Leinster (then including Brega and much of Mide in the east midlands); in the second half of the century it reached the furthest parts of the West and north in a renewed expansion led by the man who became the apostle and patron saint of the Irish, the Briton Patrick. About the beginning of the sixth century it recrossed the sea to the British section of the kingdom of Dál Riata, now Argyll in western Scotland. There, after the foundation of the island monastery of Iona c.563, the abbot of Iona, Columba, led a mission to the Picts of eastern Scotland north of the Forth. By c.580 Christianity had a secure place among the Picts and had probably converted the leading Pictish king, Bridei. From Iona, also, was to come a mission to the English between 635 and 664, by the end of which only two kingdoms, Sussex and the Isle of Wight, continued to be ruled by non-Christian kings. In the mean time, however, in 597, the very year of Columba's death, a new mission arrived in Kent, sent by Pope Gregory the Great. After this Roman mission came others from the Continent, probably associated with the heirs of another Irish monk, Columbanus, who had settled in Burgundy in 591, had founded Luxeuil, and had subsequently travelled to northern Italy where he also founded Bobbio. As a whole it was a process which passed from one country to another within the British Isles, while it also received major initiating and supporting impulses from Rome and Francia. We will consider this circular movement in more detail later; but first what was involved in conversion needs to be examined.

## Space and time: the landscape and the calendar

Wilfrid did not mind enough about Apollo or Maponus to direct his builders not to use such relics of pre-Christian worship in his new Christian church. He may well have heard of Apollo; most probably the name Maponus would have meant nothing to him. Yet if he did know of Apollo, it would have been as part of an ancient Latin literature in whose religious underpinning he had no interest. What would have concerned him would have been the gods brought by the English from their homelands across the North Sea, Woden, Thunor, Tiw, and the rest, now known to us, if at all, only through the English names for the days of the week and the odd place name, such as Wednesbury, 'Woden's fort.' Yet, although the sacrality of names for long-lost gods has vanished, the very existence of the names for days of the week is important. For Wilfrid and for all Christians, the week was an organization of time inherited from the Old Testament, inscribed by the God of the Jews into the very constitution of the world. It may have been from the Jews that the Romans themselves adopted the week; but they gave to the different days the names of their gods: a polytheistic time confronted a Jewish time, the week of the one God of Abraham, Isaac, and Jacob. In Welsh the names of the days of the week continue to this day to bear the old Roman names, just as they do in France and the other countries of the former Western Empire; in Irish they were, at an early date, partly Christianized: Wednesday is 'the first fast', because a good early Irish Christian fasted twice a week, on Wednesday as well as Friday; Thursday was therefore 'between the two fasts'; Sunday was 'the Lord's day'. Yet even in Ireland there are traces of the Roman week. In English the Roman week appears in a Germanic guise: the Roman Mars, god of war, might be equated with Tiw, and so the day of Mars became Tiw's day.

This habit of equating the gods of one religion with another had been a glue holding the Roman Empire together. Mars is found in inscriptions in Roman Britain equated with the British god Toutatis and with a probable by-name for the Germanic god Tiw, Thingsus. There are no inscriptions, however, equating the British god with his Germanic counterpart: provincials might wish their gods to find a place in the Roman sun; Roman soldiers, on the other hand, might wish their gods to possess a residence permit even on Hadrian's Wall, in the cold north, far from their native Italy, Gaul, or Spain; nobody wanted their gods to be subsumed into the gods of mere fellow provincials, let alone the barbarians across the frontier. By 400, when Roman polytheism had weakened under the impact of Christianity, Mithraism, and other cults from the east, the Roman gods could no longer be effective divine intermediaries between the local gods of western Europe.

The divine week has further implications: it flatly contradicts the modern notion of a secular time with the occasional, and optional, day of religious observance. This was as true for the non-Christian as for the Christian, for the Englishman who thought it was Woden's day as for the Irishman who thought it was the day of the first fast, *Cétaín*. On the other hand, it also shows how elements of an old religion could be disembodied rather than replaced: the English still, in a fashion, organize their time by Tiw, Woden, Thunor, and Frig, but the ghosts of the old gods are so faint that it takes the philologist to give them any visible shape. These names of the week must, very rapidly, have become as untroubling to English Christian consciences as were the corresponding Roman names to their British neighbours. The same point holds for space as it does for time: Wednesbury and Wednesfield demonstrate that a Germanic god could be transplanted across the North Sea and acquire local territory in lowland Britain: gods, not just their worshippers, could settle in a new land; the English could make particular places sacred to their gods, and so give conquered space their own religious form. Yet, when the Mercians became Christians in the third quarter of the seventh century, they did not feel the need to rename all these places: again, the sacrality of place, like the sacrality of time, was disembodied rather than replaced.

# The implications of conversion

The upheavals of the centuries between Roman Britain and the eighth century had brought about as fundamental a change in the religious as in the political landscape. Yet, in large part, the direction of change had been opposite. By 800 the surviving Roman Empire, now ruled from Constantinople, only had toeholds even in Italy; but the descendants of those barbarians who had invaded and conquered Roman provinces ruled from either side of Hadrian's Wall in the north to Benevento in the south of Italy. By 800, however, the religion which had in the late fourth century come to be identified with Rome, Christianity, had long prevailed in Ireland as well as in Britain, and had even sent out tentative feelers as far as south-eastern Iceland. Political Rome had retreated south and east; Christian Rome had extended its influence beyond the furthest limits of the Empire at its prime. Moreover, the contrast was already apparent from the mid-fifth century. In 441 Pope Leo the Great preached one of his greatest sermons to the Roman people on the occasion of the feast of Saints Peter and Paul. Earlier in the century the city of Rome had been sacked by one barbarian army, and it was soon to be sacked again by another; but Leo could rally the citizens with the thought that, while the city of Romulus and Remus, legendary founders of Rome, was on the wane, the city of the martyr apostles, Peter and Paul, was triumphant. By 700 Western Christendom was threatened by Arab conquest in the south, and by 800 it would be threatened by Vikings in the north. Already, when Bede was finishing his Ecclesiastical History in 731, the forces of Islam had swept across Latin-speaking North Africa and Spain, and had even penetrated into Aquitaine; a new religion from the Middle East had arisen to challenge its predecessor, Christianity. Yet it was not known in the eighth century how lasting the conquests of Islam would be. Men such as Bede knew only that the triumph of Christianity had not come about because of the victories of its political patrons, but because it had converted its triumphant enemies.

Conversion, however, might mean many things according to context. We may take two examples, both of them real persons, but endowed with some characteristics which are only probable. The first is a highly educated and thus probably aristocratic Briton whose life stretched either side of our initial date, 400: Pelagius. For the sake of argument I shall endow Pelagius with some attitudes which we know through the *Confessions* of his contemporary, and later his theological opponent, Augustine of Hippo. He would almost certainly have been familiar with such attitudes, even if he did not himself share them. The second was an Englishman, Peada son of Penda, in 653 the newly converted elder son of a great Mercian warrior-king.

When he was a young adult, and thus already intellectually formed, Pelagius went to Rome and won patronage from influential figures in Roman society. We are, however, concerned with him and his contemporaries in their youth, back in Britain. Pelagius was educated in Britain in a tradition of learning which stretched back centuries to Hellenistic times and which was dominant right across the Empire. It was intended to make the sons of well-off parents into full participants in a literary culture, both because they had read those school classics, above all the poet Virgil, whom every educated person in the Latin West had read, and also because they could write a grammatically correct and logically persuasive Latin. The Latin they wrote was not the Latin they spoke: four centuries had passed since this educational pattern had taken hold of the Roman elite. Rome had encouraged the nobility in its western provinces, including Britain, to participate in a Latin culture: to read the standard Latin authors and to write correct Latin. It is not just as if we were required to read Shakespeare—many of us still are—but as if we were expected to write a prose as close as possible to the sermons of John Donne. This education may well have been at its most widespread in Roman Britain in the fourth century, when Pelagius was at school.

Peada never went to school at all. His father, Penda, a firm pagan until his death, would have insisted on the proper rearing for his son: a training which would make him a fine warrior. The traditions of Peada's people, the Mercians, the people of the frontier, had not been preserved in writing. To learn about them it was sufficient to listen to the poet, the *scop*, the shaper of words, as he declaimed his verse to the harp in Penda's hall in the evening. The language used by the *scop* was elevated: it used some archaic words not by then in common use; but with a little attention it could be followed by a child. This was not a culture of such polite language that it took years to master—if, indeed, one were sufficiently clever with words ever to succeed. For

Peada, words were not so difficult; his challenge was to master the use of horse, of spear, sword, and shield in battle; to persuade his elders by his courage in facing the wild boar in the hunt and the Welshman on the frontier that he might, in time, make a worthy king of a warrior people, the Mierce, the people of the march. Pelagius' education had fitted him to be a civilian of high status, to be a lawyer or to work in government. Peada grew up in a country where there were no civilians, apart from women and slaves. To be a poor fighter was to fail as a man and as a free Mercian.

Christianity was a religion in which written texts were central: the canonical books of the Jewish Bible, to which was added the New Testament of the Christians. In the West these books (they almost always formed a collection of books, separately bound) were known through translations into Latin. Similarly, when the central rite of this religion was celebrated, the Eucharist, that was also in Latin. Yet the Latin of the Bible and of the Eucharist was a language which had been appropriate for early Christians in the western provinces—not the highly polished Latin of the grammarian and the rhetor, educators of aristocratic youth, but the language of artisans, merchants, and shopkeepers. Worse, the Latin of the Bible was a language through which seeped word patterns and sequences of thought which came from outside the Graeco-Latin cultural stranglehold. Nobody could translate the particular rhetoric of, say, the opening of St John's first epistle into Ciceronian Latin. As some educated Christians, probably including Pelagius, came to realize, it had its own eloquence, but it was not an eloquence recognized in the schools. Initially, at least, the language of the Bible and the Eucharist sounded vulgar to men such as Pelagius, a language unworthy of profound religious truth. Christianity, therefore, was an alien competitor within a literary culture; and yet the triumph of Christianity and the greatest influence of Roman education in Britain were contemporaneous. No known Latin writer of British origin died before 400. Pelagius was the first.

We have already met one paradox: that the influence of Christian Rome became more widespread in the West as the power of the Empire declined. To this we can now add a second: that, at the same period, the range of Latin culture within Britain reached its height. In the fifth and sixth century Latin, alongside British and Irish, was a spoken language even in the far west, looking out across the Irish Sea and the Atlantic Ocean. True, some extensions of the range of Latin culture in the British Isles were simply a consequence of the spread of Christianity, but there is no reason to think that all those who spoke Latin in the far west of Britain were Christians. Western Britain, which for three centuries had been a dangerous highland zone, watched by great legionary fortresses at Chester and Caerleon, no longer had the legions, but in terms of culture and language was more Roman than in the palmy days of the Empire in the second century. Some Romans saw—and some modern scholars still see—a connection between the rise of Christianity to power within the Empire and the decline of the Roman state; but nobody made or makes or should make the corresponding point about the extension of Latin culture, as if the power of an Empire's culture could be an agent in its decline.

Conversion entailed different things to Pelagius and to Peada. To Pelagius it implied giving his first loyalty to a Bible whose origins lay outside the Graeco-Roman tradition and whose literary modes were correspondingly remote. It meant putting one's faith in the God not just of the Christians, of the New Testament, but of the Jews, of the Old Testament; it meant giving a higher authority to the product of a Semitic tradition than to Virgil, the Latin poet treasured, memorized, and annotated in the schools. An educated convert to Christianity in the late fourth century could have recited thousands of lines of Virgil ever since his youth; he learnt to memorize parts of the Bible only in middle age, and thus with difficulty.

There were, of course, other things which were difficult for Pelagius when he became a Christian. A quick reading of the surviving stone inscriptions of Roman Britain, mostly put up by those in, or associated with, the Roman army in places under military occupation, will soon persuade anyone of the power of the pre-Christian religions to encompass loyalties to place, to family, and to community. There are numerous inscriptions to the *genius loci*, the divine presence in a place; a standard form of inscription commemorating a person will begin with *D.M.*, short for *Dis Manibus*, 'To the Divine Shades', including the spirits of dead ancestors. Larger entities than a single house or sacred place in a rural landscape also had their divine companions: York, a major city and legionary fortress, had its *genius*; the goddess associated with the Brigantes of northern Britain, Brigantia, was worthy of cult on Hadrian's Wall as well as in west Yorkshire, not far from the capital of the Brigantes at Aldborough. Britain itself was a divine entity, *Britannia sancta*, 'Holy Britain'.

If places, peoples, and whole provinces had their divine aspects or companions, so also did the times and seasons of the year. In Ireland, the harvest season opened with the feast of one Celtic god, Lug, while the season of spring, with its heavy ploughing work, probably began with the feast of Brigit, the Irish counterpart to Brigantia. Time and space—and especially the most precious times and places—were part of pre-Christian religion. For the adherent of Celtic or Romano-Celtic religion, the landscape and the calendar were expressive of his loyalties to a multitude of gods; for the Christian in 400 it was a foreign land and a foreign time. By 600, however, in those areas of Britain still British, there was a new Christian landscape and a new Christian calendar; and for the years around 700 we have the Calendar of Willibrord—a Northumbrian who had gone to Ireland and from there to be a missionary to the Frisians—a calendar of Christian saints, including the Briton, St Patrick, who had become the patron saint of the Irish; but for Pelagius such developments lay in the future. Indeed, they were never completed: as we have seen, only in Ireland were the days of the week Christianized at all, whereas, also in Ireland, the beginning of August remains Lúnasa, earlier Lugnasad, the feast of the god Lug.

For Peada son of Penda, the emotional and mental upheavals entailed by becoming a Christian were in part more serious and in part easier than those experienced by Pelagius. Peada was not literate: he could neither read nor write. The authoritative books of his new religion were doubly foreign to him. The clergy and even some lay-men, such as Peada's brother-in-law, Aldfrith, later to be king of the Northumbrians from 685 to 705, learnt to read and to write Latin. For others, their knowledge of the sacred text depended upon it being read out in translation; and there was, as yet, little of that. What it might have meant to Peada is illustrated by a letter sent by Boniface, the eighth-century West Saxon missionary in Germany. He wrote to the abbess of Minster-in-Thanet asking that she should command a copy of St Peter's Epistles to be written in large-size gold letters on purpled parchment, so that, as for himself, suffering from poor sight, 'I may always have before my gaze the words of him [St Peter] who guided me along this path'; but another purpose of obtaining this precious book was so that even the heathens might see, be astonished at, and revere a canonical book of the Christians.

When Peada gave his allegiance to Christianity, he had to accept, at least by implication, the cultural associations of his new faith: the supremacy of a highly developed intellectual tradition embodied in written texts he could not read and in a language he did not know. In the last analysis, the final arbiter was not the warrior-king, such as his father, Penda, and his former god, Woden, but the man who had mastered the language and the learning which came with the Christian God. In his new religion, violence even though it might be necessary, was inherently stained with sin. No more could he march to battle against the Christian Britons calling upon the patronage of his gods, Woden, Tiw, and Thunor, who were even more powerful in their violence than he was. The Christian God was a civilian, although there were parts of the Old Testament which had another message. On the one hand, it had been asked whether a man could be in the Roman army and be a good Christian; on the other hand, it was said of Ulfila, a missionary to the Danube Goths in the fourth century, that he refused to translate the Books of Samuel and Kings into Gothic, since his people were quite violent enough already without any encouragement from Holy Writ.

There were, of course, ways of making the ultimately pacific message of Christianity cohere more easily with a warrior ethic. In the 670s, a generation after the conversion of Northumbria had begun in earnest, King Ecgfrith set about extending the subjection of his neighbours to the north, the Picts, a subjection which had been begun by his father, Oswiu. At the time when Ecgfrith was pursuing his northern wars Wilfrid was bishop of York; his authority—his 'kingdom of churches'—extended as far as the power of Ecgfrith. From 674 until his expulsion from the bishopric in 678, it stretched from the Wash northwards, through Lindsey and the whole of Northumbria, across the Forth and at least over Fife. From Stamford to Perth Wilfrid was bishop; and his biographer attributed King Ecgfrith's early victories over 'the bestial peoples of the Picts' to the guidance of Wilfrid. Ecgfrith was compared with Joash, king of Judah, and Wilfrid to Jehoiada, the high priest: 'And Joash did that which was right in the sight of the Lord all the days of Jehoiada the priest' (2 Chron. 24: 2). While Wilfrid, this new Jehoiada of Northumbria, remained bishop of York and chief counsellor of the king, Ecgfrith triumphed over his enemies, 'the bestial peoples of the Picts' among them. Once king and bishop had quarrelled, royal power began to wane.

There are two elements in this description of the great days of Northumbrian power: the first is an equation between the people of Judah, God's chosen people, and the Northumbrians—and therefore between the enemies of Northumbria and the enemies of God's chosen people; secondly, there is a more commonplace claim that the Picts are less than fully human, and that the military power of the Northumbrians over the Picts was an empire of true men over bestial inferiors. Although, therefore, Christ as understood by the great fourth-century Christian writers was most certainly a civilian, the God of Wilfrid was not. In the fourth-century Empire there had been a clear division between a professional army, now largely staffed by barbarians, and a civilian population; in seventh-century Northumbria there was no such distinction. The Christ of a barbarian people could not be a civilian, because among them there was no such person as an adult, male, free civilian, and no such concept.

Those who sought to convert the English to Christianity were generally well aware of the problem posed by a society in which the very notion of a free male, let alone of one who deserved honour in his native land, was inextricably bound up with violence—with bravery in war and with dexterity in the use of weapons. On 22 June 601 Pope Gregory the Great wrote to Æthelberht, king of Kent, only a few years after the king's baptism. The letter was accompanied by numerous gifts of different kinds, designed, so Bede says, to give glory in this world to a king who had acknowledged the glory of heaven (HE i. 32). In his letter Gregory explained how temporal power and honour were conferred on Æthelberht by God so that his power and glory might be used to spread the faith among peoples subject to his authority. If Æthelberht spread respect for the glory of God, God would ensure that his glory surpassed even that of his forebears. There were signs that this world was close to its end, but the honour won by Æthelberht would survive into the next world; and that would never end.

# Christianity, the Roman Empire, and the barbarians

There were advantages, even in the eyes of a monk, in being a barbarian Christian from a far north-western land. The Irishman Columbanus (d. 615) wrote a letter to Pope Boniface IV in which he recalled the papally sponsored mission of Palladius to his countrymen in 431. He described his fellow Irish as 'faithful disciples of the blessed apostles Peter and Paul', but he was quite clear that the Irish were not, and never had been, subjects of the Roman Empire. Two centuries after the legions had left Britain for good, this was still a matter for pride: unlike the Britons, they had never been conquered by Rome. The relationship between adherence to Christianity and subjection to Rome was a delicate issue. Columbanus also proudly declared that no Irishman had ever been an Arian heretic. When we consider the distribution of barbarian kingdoms led by Arian kings, as it had been in 500, the point becomes clearer. Arian kingdoms were arranged in a circlet around the western Mediterranean. Further north, things were different. In 500 the Franks, neighbours of the English across the Channel, were ruled by Clovis, subsequently famous as the first Christian king of the Franks. He was initially attracted to Arianism—one of his sisters even received an Arian baptism—but in the end Clovis chose to become a Catholic and thus a brother in faith to the Emperor in Constantinople. Neither the Irish nor, later, the English were in any danger of becoming Arians. By contrast, shortly before the Lombards invaded Italy in 568, their king switched from a pro-Catholic stance and an alliance both with the Emperor and with the Franks to full Arian adherence and hostility to the Empire and the Franks. It seems to have been easier to share the Emperor's religion the further one was from the Emperor himself. For the Goths, Arianism was their Catholic Christianity, as opposed to 'the Roman religion' of the Emperor and of their own Roman subjects. Those barbarians who lived around what the Romans had called 'our sea', and whose coastlines were vulnerable to attack by an imperial fleet, were the least anxious to align themselves with the Emperor in religion.

This phenomenon is an aspect of a deeper truth. In 400 the Latin culture of the Western Empire went up to the frontier; and there, almost always, it stopped. The Irish Sea was as much the frontier of a civilization as of an empire; and the peoples of the British Isles were therefore separated by the most deep-seated dividing line in western Europe. In the 430s, Prosper, a chronicler and theologian from Aquitaine, could contrast 'the Roman island', Britain, with 'the barbarian island', Ireland. Yet by 600 the Irish had long since adopted a Latin culture as well as the Christian religion, and had spread it to the islands between northern Britain and the full Atlantic Ocean. As the first monks had settled in the sandy deserts of Egypt, so the monks of the world's edge settled the deserts of the sea. There had been a profound change between the Christianity of the late fourth century—newly triumphant in the Empire, and much more closely identified with the Roman state under the Theodosian dynasty than it had been under Constantine—and the Christianity of 600, exportable across all boundaries. The same Prosper who contrasted Roman Britain with barbarian Ireland was also the person to perceive that, now that Rome no longer possessed the military might to keep the barbarians outside the Empire, a newly porous frontier might allow Christianity to spread outwards from Rome to the enemies of Rome. Prosper knew of one recent and especially notable example: the new Christianity of the Irish.

# The conversion of Ireland

The principal route by which Christianity spread beyond its base in Roman Britain may be described as a clockwise flow of men and ideas around the British Isles with some contributory streams: the principal flow went from Britain to Ireland, from Ireland to northern Britain, to the Picts beyond the old Antonine Wall, and finally from Iona, a Hebridean island now part of Argyll, back to the English settlers in what had been Roman Britain. This movement received two major impulses from the papacy: one almost at the beginning, when in 431 Pope Celestine sent Palladius to be the first bishop of the existing community of Irish Christians; the second when Gregory the Great sent the monk Augustine and his companions to England— they arrived in Kent in 597. External and internal influences were subsequently to become intermixed in the seventh century with the involvement in the English mission of the heirs of Columbanus, the Irish monk who had settled in Burgundy in 591. This initiated a subordinate and anti-clockwise current from Ireland to Francia and from Francia to England. Encouragements from outside were of great importance, but the main action was within the British Isles.

As far as we can tell, there was no clear chronological gap between the Christianization of one part of the British Isles and its extension to the next. In the late fourth century there were still powerful and rich adherents of the pre-Christian religion of Britain even in the most populous and most Romanized districts. At Lydney, in what is now Gloucestershire, a large and well-appointed temple was built to the British god Nodons about 360. It remained in active use as long as the Roman army remained in Britain. In Britain, as indeed in Rome itself, there were powerful men prepared to stay outside the Christian consensus encouraged by Theodosius I. While some Britons still worshipped Nodons at Lydney, some Irishmen had probably already turned to Christianity. They were the beginnings of that community of existing Christians who requested a bishop and whose wishes were answered by Pope Celestine consecrating Palladius as the first bishop in Ireland.

The Irish had also worshipped Nodons—Nuadu in Old Irish—and he appears in the later tales both of the Britons and of the Irish. That is an indication that, although there will certainly have been some differences between the Celtic religion of the Irish and the Britons, the two also had much in common. The extension of Christianity from Britain to Ireland can thus be given a context: there was a single and uninterrupted process by which Christianity was in competition with varieties of Celtic religion on both sides of the Irish Sea. Because of the military weakness of the Empire, the Irish had probably already gained power over the kingdom of Dyfed in south-western Wales and perhaps elsewhere. To an old pattern of trading connections across the Irish Sea, initially disrupted by major Irish raids from 360 onwards, we can add the connections between new Irish settlers in Britain and their homeland. The Irish Sea had been a frontier, as shown by the Roman forts at Cardiff and Holyhead; in the post-Roman period it became a highway. We may take one example to illustrate the change: inscriptions carved in stone with commemorations of single persons. In south-western Wales, in the kingdom of

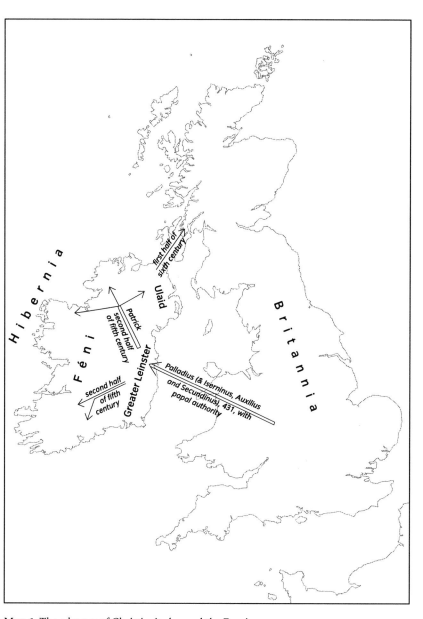

**Map 6** The advance of Christianity beyond the Empire, 431–550.

Dyfed, these were often in two languages and two alphabets: in Latin in the Roman alphabet and in Irish in the ogham alphabet. To judge by the form of Irish used, they belong to the fifth and sixth centuries; and, although the ogham alphabet was, as a whole, a new invention made to correspond very closely to the phonology of Irish in the fourth century, there is one clear sign that it was created by an Irish speaker who was familiar with the Latin language and its alphabet: it did not distinguish between long and short vowels. To commemorate a person with an inscription on stone was itself a Roman habit. In Roman Britain, as we have seen, such inscriptions tended to be put up by soldiers and government officials. In Dyfed, a kingdom now ruled by an Irish dynasty, we can assume that military force was controlled by the Irish. As the Romans had displayed their military occupation in stone, so now the Irish did the same, perhaps taking the habit straight from the last defenders of a Roman coastal frontier. The inscriptional habit had also spread within southern Ireland, most especially in a belt from the Corkaguiney peninsula in the West to central Leinster in the east. Here, however, the inscriptions were only in one language and one alphabet: in Irish and in ogham. The odd Roman name was used, such as Marianus (also found on the other side of the Irish Sea in the Meirion of Meirionnydd, Merioneth-shire), a symptom of a Roman influence which was not limited to Christianity; the name Marianus fell out of use in Ireland after the fifth century.

By the fifth century, therefore, the Irish Sea had become a highly porous frontier. Not merely did the Irish rule some parts of Britain bordering the sea, but western Britain, where they were settled, con-tained speakers of three languages: Latin, British, and Irish. There was no sharp break between the pre-Christian religion on either side of the sea. The presence of a Christian community in Ireland to which Palladius was sent in 431 is easy to explain. The ties between Britain and Ireland also explain why, although Palladius himself came with papal authority from the Continent, his followers and successors were predominantly Britons.

The eastern parts of Ireland, bordering the Irish Sea, were probably dominated in the early fifth century by two major alliances of Irish peoples: the Leinstermen and the Ulstermen (Laigin and Ulaid). At that date, Leinster appears to have extended as far north as the Boyne, and perhaps a little further. It thus included the far south-east, the lands on either side of the Wicklow Mountains, and also the rich plain to the north of the Liffey, which would be taken from Leinster by force about 500. This plain, known as Brega, had been the principal entry point for Roman artefacts. Palladius' mission appears to have been active in the greater Leinster, both Brega and the lands to the south of the Liffey. Its impact on Ireland was largely concealed, however, by two later developments, one political, the other within the history of the mission itself. The first change was a violent shift from a political order dominated in the east by the Leinstermen and the Ulstermen to the one revealed by the earliest contemporary annals in the late sixth century: power shifted westwards, away from the two great federations bordering the Irish Sea towards the Shannon basin, from which came a new dynasty, the Uí Néill. By the late sixth century, Irish politics were dominated by a two-part confederation extending all the way from Malin Head in the far north-west to the Old Man of Kinsale on the south coast of what is now Co. Cork. The northern part of this confederation was known as the Connachta, led by one Connacht dynasty, the Uí Néill; the southern part was known as the Éoganachta. The Uí Néill and the Connachta ruled much of the northern half of Ireland; the Éoganachta dominated Munster. The only province bordering the Irish Sea conquered by either section of this new confederation was Brega.

The second development which came to obscure the achievement of Palladius was the success of the Briton, St Patrick, in establishing Christianity in the far west of Ireland, in the lands controlled by the Connachta. The only place in Ireland which can be associated with Patrick from his own writings lies in what is now the north of Co. Mayo, bordering the Atlantic Ocean. But his activities were not confined to one part of Co. Mayo: his words reveal that he was active in several small kingdoms. Patrick's *Confessio*, written to justify his mission to British churchmen and to his own followers in Ireland, shows what he himself considered to be his greatest achievement. This was to have brought Christianity to the farthest edge of the inhabited world, beyond which there was only the Ocean. Patrick knew the Old Testament prophecies that foretold how the authority of the Jewish God would extend to 'the islands' (see Chapter 4 for the further implications of this idea); he knew also from the New Testament that the end of the world would not come until the Faith had been taken to the very ends of the world. In this north-western part of the known world he, Patrick, had accomplished this task.

These two changes—the rise of the Connachta led by the Uí Néill and the mission of St Patrick—came to be associated in later hagiography. The received account from the late seventh century maintained that Patrick had met the ancestors of the main dynasties of the Connachta, above all those of the Uí Néill, blessing some and cursing others. In combination, the blessings and the curses determined the internal balance of power among the Uí Néill as it existed c.700. Memories of Patrick were thus inextricably entwined with legends about the origins of Uí Néill power: it was he who had conferred legitimacy on the ancestors of the great Uí Néill kings. Palladius, on the other hand, seems to have worked in Leinster, powerful in his day but soon due to be eclipsed by the dynasties of the West. One of the traditional disciples of St Patrick, Secundinus, was the patron saint of the very early church of Domnach Sechnaill, Dunshaughlin in the modern county of Meath, the ancient Brega. Secundinus, however, was probably in origin a disciple of Palladius rather than of Patrick, and belonged to that earlier political order in which Brega formed part of Leinster. The best guess, therefore, is that the cult and reputation of Palladius declined and grew dim, to the benefit of the rival reputation of St Patrick, in part because Leinster declined and lost Brega to the Uí Néill.

For Palladius we have good contemporary evidence from the Continent; for Patrick, however, we have no such testimony; what we do have is a pair of writings by himself. He is the only major figure directly involved in the process by which the British Isles were brought under the sway of Christianity who speaks to us directly, in his own words. The two writings are the *Confessio*, occasioned by an accusation that a youthful sin had made him unworthy to be a bishop, and *The Letter to the Soldiers of Coroticus*, occasioned by a raiding expedition which had led off some of Patrick's converts into slavery. Both are texts of great emotional power. They reveal what sort of a man Patrick was, but they do not offer dates or detailed narrative. They enable us to understand Patrick rather than his career. I shall assume, however, that his phase of missionary activity was later than that of Palladius; that the mission to the far west was later than the mission to the eastern coastlands; and that the principal date given by the Chronicle of Ireland for his death, namely 493, cannot be taken as anything other than a best guess made some generations later, but is nevertheless likely to be approximately correct. While Palladius' mission may be situated in the 430s and perhaps the 440s, Patrick's belonged to the second half of the fifth century.

The glimpses of Patrick's mode of operation afforded by his *Confessio* suggest that he was an unusual missionary—unusual in his readiness to work in kingdoms where the king was not a Christian, and unusual also in his concern to approach the weak, even slaves, directly rather than via the powerful. The standard approach to missionary activity was cautious and practical. Before a bishop could be consecrated for a new territory, there had to be a viable Christian community which asked for a bishop; and viability included a measure of political security, and thus at least a benevolent neutrality on the part of the local ruler. This was the situation exemplified by Palladius' mission to the Irish, by that of Augustine to Kent, and by Aidan to Northumbria.

A problematic variant was the situation when a Christian overlord protected a missionary among a people subject to his power. In the eighth century, the difficulties inherent in such a situation were illustrated by the careers of the English missionaries in the lands east of the Rhine, by Willibrord among the Frisians and by Boniface in central Germany. In one of his letters, Boniface admits that he can go nowhere without the personal protection of Charles Martel, mayor of the palace and the effective ruler of the Franks. The normal protection afforded by a ruler to strangers, to merchants, and to envoys from other kingdoms was a help, but could not be relied on. The two Hewalds, two brothers from Northumbria who were religious exiles in Ireland, attempted to begin a mission among the Continental Saxons of northern Germany about 700. Saxony had local rulers, called 'satraps' by Bede, but no unified monarchy. The two Hewalds intended to seek the hospitality and protection of one such satrap, but they were killed by the local population before they could reach him. Their killers were afraid that, if the two Hewalds found the satrap, they might persuade him to impose upon them an alien faith (all too closely connected with the power of their neighbours, the Franks). Patrick's approach recalls that of the two Hewalds rather than that of Augustine of Canterbury. He himself imagines what cautious men were saying behind his back: 'Why does that man send himself off into danger among enemies who know not God?' (*Confessio* § 46).

Patrick seems to have exploited a particular feature of early Irish society: the high status it afforded to priests and persons of learning. The nature of the pre-Christian Irish druids is difficult to apprehend because of the ways in which their role was reinterpreted in Christian Ireland (quite apart from modern misconceptions). It seems, however, that they were the principal practitioners of the cult of the pre-Christian gods of the Irish, but that they were also expected to excel in learning. What is certain is that they formed a distinct social order whose leaders enjoyed high rank and prestige. One aspect of such social privilege was that a person went around with a relatively large company; and he was entitled to hospitality both for himself and for his company. Patrick reveals at one point the stratagem he used to gain political acceptance. 'Meanwhile I kept giving rewards to kings, besides which I kept giving a fee to their sons, who walk with me, and nonetheless they apprehended me with my companions' (*Confessio*, § 52, trans. Howlett). For a fortnight Patrick lay in chains facing death but was then released. This passage is most suggestive. To go about with a company including the sons of kings was to claim very high rank. To travel in that way from kingdom to kingdom—he gave rewards to kings, not just one king—was to claim the high-status mobility enjoyed by the privileged learned orders. During Patrick's career we may envisage an Ireland divided between Christian and non-Christian kingdoms. The temporary settlement may have been that all such kingdoms, Christian and pagan, should uphold the privileged status of all learned religious persons, whether Christian or not. There is a possible late echo of this situation when some legal texts of the seventh and eighth centuries go out of their way to deny such privileges to the druids, a denial which may not have been universal in the recent past.

Patrick was concerned with kings but also with judges and druids, with the power of the sword but also with the power of the word. He was also very closely concerned with women, even with slave women. His *Confessio* suggests that he was an enthusiastic supporter of female vocations to the ascetic life. He was especially proud of one woman of high birth and great beauty who came to him and declared that she had received a summons in a dream to be a 'virgin of Christ'. Mention of her, however, led Patrick straight to a recollection of the sufferings of such women at the hands of their families, and to the still graver suffering often imposed on women who lived in slavery.

Here one must remember two things: first, that Patrick had himself been captured by raiders when he was still a boy and had spent six years as a slave in Ireland before escaping; secondly, that while female slaves were extensively used in agricultural work, they were frequently sexually exploited by their masters. For a female slave to attempt to live a life of chastity was to risk at the very least, as Patrick wrote, 'intimidations and threats' (*Confessio*, § 42). In Patrick's writings one can sense how he was not merely a persuader of individuals but also, inescapably, had to confront a non-Christian social order.

# The conversion of Northern Britain

At the same time as Christianity spread from Britain to Ireland, it also spread to those British kingdoms between the two walls, the Antonine Wall and Hadrian's Wall. The British king Coroticus, who was denounced in Patrick's *Letter to the Soldiers of Coroticus*, was most probably king of Dumbarton, the royal fortress and capital on the Clyde. The letter regards Coroticus as a Christian king who has recruited a raiding expedition from Britons and also from non-Christian Picts. This offers a precious clue to a stage in the conversion of the British Isles: in the north the dividing line between Christian and non-Christian territory lay along an ethnic frontier separating Britons from Picts. It also throws doubt on the story told by Bede from oral reports, that a Briton, Ninian, bishop of Whithorn in Galloway, had converted the southern Picts, those south of the great ranges of mountains running east almost to the sea south of Aberdeen. The contemporary evidence of Patrick, brief though it is, counts for more than the later story told by Bede, who himself added the qualification 'as they say'.

Bede's story, however exaggerated it may have been, is founded on two truths. First, excavation has confirmed the British origins of Whithorn; and inscriptions in Galloway, notably at Kirkmadrine in the Rhinns, demonstrate the presence of post-Roman Christianity. Secondly, Britons did play a part in the conversion of the southern Picts, as shown by place name evidence. The leading part, however, was played by Columba and the monks of Iona, founded in 563. As has been pointed out above, Iona was Irish by foundation and lay within an Irish kingdom that extended from Co. Antrim across the North Channel to embrace Argyll; but its community came to include British, Pictish, and English monks. When it was founded, the most powerful ruler in Northern Britain was the Pictish king, Bridei son of Meilochon. Shortly before 563 he had inflicted a major defeat on Dál Riata. By the end of his reign, however, the roles had been reversed and a new king of Dál Riata, Áedán mac Gabráin, was attempting to detach outlying portions of Pictish territory. The near-contemporary *Amrae Choluim Chille*, a lament in Irish purporting (very probably correctly) to be a response to Columba's death in 597, portrays Bridei as the king approached by Columba; it also claims that the saint triumphed over 'the proud ones of the Tay' (the Tay being the great river of southern Pictland). Adomnán in his *Life of St Columba* recorded an approach by the saint to Bridei further north, close to Inverness. All this, together with Bede's description of Bridei as 'a most powerful king', indicates that Bridei was overlord of all the Picts, and that through Columba's efforts Christianity gained an assured foothold within Pictland between 563 and 580. If Bede's information, derived from a Pictish source, is to be believed, Columba personally converted Bridei. In the seventh century, Pictland emerged as a Christian part of the British Isles, where a Northumbrian royal exile, Eanfrith, became a Christian before 633 and apparently fathered a future Pictish king, Talorcan son of Enfret (Eanfrith).

# The conversion of the English

By Columba's death in 597 Christianity was politically dominant, though by no means universally accepted, among all the older peoples of the British Isles, Britons, Irish, and Picts. In English territory the reverse was true. There was some surviving Christianity among a subordinate British population, but that population was itself being Anglicized; and one element of becoming English was probably abandoning Christianity. This abandonment, however, was not universal even in Kent, where the local cult of a Romano-British saint, Sixtus, survived until the arrival of Augustine from Rome; and there must have a been a considerable British Christian population in those English kingdoms which were expanding territorially in the last part of the sixth century and the first half of the seventh. Some British territories were conquered by the first Christian kings of Northumbria: Elmet in West Yorkshire by Edwin (616–33) and Lothian by Oswald (634–42). In such areas British Christianity presumably continued uninterrupted until it again became politically suspect after the Synod of Whitby in 664. Even in the inner core of Bernicia, major places were known to the Irish by forms of their British names, not their newer English replacements: hence *Dún Guairi* rather than *Bebbanburg* for Bamburgh, *Medcóit* rather than *Lindisfarena ea* for Lindisfarne.

These were, however, all survivals associated with the Britons; and they were for the most part a defeated people, whose members living under English rule were politically subordinate and socially of relatively low status. Conversion, however, was, in part, a political process: seventh-century England was not a country where religious adherence was a merely private matter for individual choice separated from the public sphere; but it was unlike Patrick's Ireland in that learning and a priestly role did not regularly command high status. In Bede's set-piece debate in the council of the Northumbrian King Edwin (in part probably Bede's own imaginative reconstruction), it was the pagan priest, Coifi, who denounced the old gods as powerless. After all, he proclaimed, if they had been powerful, their priest should have had wealth, power, and honour far in excess of what he, Coifi, enjoyed. It is to be noted that the decision to convert was taken by Edwin after discussion with his advisers. The formal arrangements were no different than if they had been discussing whether to grant an estate or go to war.

Another piece of oral history related by Bede is likely to be more dependable. Edwin's early political patron was Rædwald, king of the East Angles, whom Bede presents as the most notable example of a failed conversion. Initially he had come under the influence of the first Christian king of Kent, Æthelberht, but when he returned to East Anglia he compromised. In his temple he had an altar to Christ, but he also offered worship to the old gods of his people. Bede had his account from Aldwulf, the current king of East Anglia, who had seen Redwald's temple in his youth. What is again notable is that this was the king's temple; which god was worshipped there was a matter for him. It may even be the case that grand temples came into fashion only in the wake of the emergence of the greater kingdoms and in the generation before conversion. When Edwin became a Christian, some of his nobles followed suit, whereas for many Northumbrians it would be years before they abandoned the old gods; yet the king's decision had changed the religious stance of the kingdom.

There were good reasons why, especially in seventh-century England, religious adherence should have been a matter for the political elite. First, many from their peasant populations had been British Christians. Yet the English had been outstandingly successful in imposing an English culture throughout their territories, both where Germanic immigrants were numerous and where they were rare. Part of the creation of England had been this imposition of language and culture. England was a society in which cultural norms had to be imposed from above. Secondly, in Bede's day, and probably also in the seventh century, it was claimed that all the royal kindreds with the exception of the East Saxons were descended from the god Woden. To have a pedigree which began with the god marked men out as royal; and this may have been another reason why a king's stance on which god should be worshipped should have been especially authoritative. On only one occasion is there a hint of a widespread rejection of Christianity: in Essex in reaction to the plague of 664. Yet, even there, one part of Essex remained largely unaffected, since there were at the time two kings who shared power, and one remained firmly Christian.

When in 597 the English elite looked beyond the bounds of their own kingdoms, they would have seen that the other peoples of the British Isles, and not just the defeated Britons, were now Christian. Across the Channel lay the powerful kingdoms of the Franks, sharing many elements of their culture and yet also Christian at the higher levels of society. But east, across the North Sea, Scandinavia contained peoples which would be pagan for centuries to come. When the Sutton Hoo ship-burial was laid out, probably about 625, some elements looked to pagan Scandinavia, others to the Franks or to more distant Christian countries. Yet by 630 East Anglia would have a Christian king who had been baptized when in exile in Francia, and who bore a name, Sigeberht, used by the Frankish Merovingian royal dynasty. At the level of kings and potential kings, English peoples were not isolated, since contenders for the kingship were regularly exiled. After Sigeberht, the East Anglians seem to have looked more to Francia than to Scandinavia: women of the royal kindred became nuns in monastic houses close to Paris, such as Chelles and Noirmoutiers-en-Brie, both of which belonged to the group of Frankish monasteries which claimed to follow the Rule of the Irishman, Columbanus.

The year when Columba died on Iona, 597, also saw the arrival of a mission to the English, led by Augustine but sent by Pope Gregory I, correspondent of Columbanus, when the latter was in Burgundy. Gregory the Great, as he is justly known, was subsequently venerated both by the English and by the Irish. His mission was born, however, of a disappointment. Ever since the conversion of Clovis, churchmen had hoped that Frankish political power would be used to foster Christianity among peoples subject to Frankish overlordship. From the 530s until the mid-seventh century that had included much of what is now Germany. Yet the old Rhine frontier of the Empire had remained, especially in the north, a stubbornly enduring boundary. Gregory of Tours wrote of the peoples from across the Rhine as of ferocious barbarians who would pillage Gaul. The Bructeri were a people originally belonging to the Frankish federation, settled on the east side of the Rhine close to the Ruhr. They remained non-Christian, and any sense that they were Frankish seems to have faded away. They were only converted c.700 by an English missionary, Swithberht, and were soon afterwards overwhelmed by the non-Christian Saxons. In the seventh century, Franks were increasingly seen as Christian and therefore no longer barbarian; the barbarians were the pagans across the Rhine.

The Franks may also have claimed an overlordship over part of southern England. Æthelberht, king of Kent, had married Bertha, daughter of Charibert I, king of Paris. It is unclear when the marriage took place, but it may have been as late as c.574, by which time Charibert was already dead, his kingdom was divided among his brothers, and they were embroiled in civil war. Bertha, however, remained loyal to her Christian faith: the marriage was agreed on the condition that she should be allowed to take with her a Frankish Bishop, Liudhard, to sustain the practice of her religion. Moreover, this was a period when Frankish material culture seems to have enjoyed an enhanced prestige in Kent. Yet neither Æthelberht nor his people had adopted Christianity; and even when he let it be known that he was interested in a possible conversion, Gregory the Great saw no sign that neighbouring Frankish bishops were anxious to lead any new effort. On the other hand, Gregory also knew that, if he were to send missionaries, they could achieve nothing without active Frankish support. He set about obtaining that support by letters written to kings, bishops, and, most important of all, Brunhild, widow of Sigibert I and grandmother of the current rulers of Austrasia and Burgundy. In Burgundy, the bishop of Autun was especially supportive and politically close to Brunhild; he received a papal pallium as a sign of gratitude.

Just as Pope Celestine had given his authority to the mission of Palladius to the Irish, so Gregory sent monks from his own monastery to England. It is even possible that Gregory was encouraged to send Augustine by the record of that earlier papal mission to the far north-west. There were, however, some inescapable yet drastic implications of the new initiative. It was to come via the Franks to the south-east of Britain, where Æthelberht, king of Kent, had acquired a military hegemony (and thus, perhaps, the prestige which would allow him to forsake the old gods of his people for the one God of Rome and the Franks). Gregory hoped that he could recreate provinces based on London and York. In the event, Canterbury replaced London, because that was the old Roman capital of Kent. However, very broadly, the Gregorian scheme was put into effect, using two old Roman cities in the east of the island as metropolitan sees. That, however, immediately implied that the Britons ought to be subject in ecclesiastical matters to sees situated in English territory, namely in the lands taken from them by pagan enemies. It is difficult to see what else Gregory could have done, and he seems to have been well aware of what he was doing: it would hardly have been possible to convert the English by proclaiming that the chief centres of ecclesiastical authority should be in the British west. Yet, it was not surprising that, when Augustine summoned the leaders of the British Church to participate in the new missionary effort under his leadership, they refused.

The mission enjoyed some success in the south-east in the favourable conditions created by Æthelberht's military overlordship. On the one hand, London was established as the episcopal see for the East Saxons in 604; on the other hand, the South Saxons, neighbours to the south-west across the Weald, as well as the Isle of Wight, remained non-Christian for the better part of a century. Moreover, Eadbald, Æthelberht's son and heir, remained a pagan, so that when

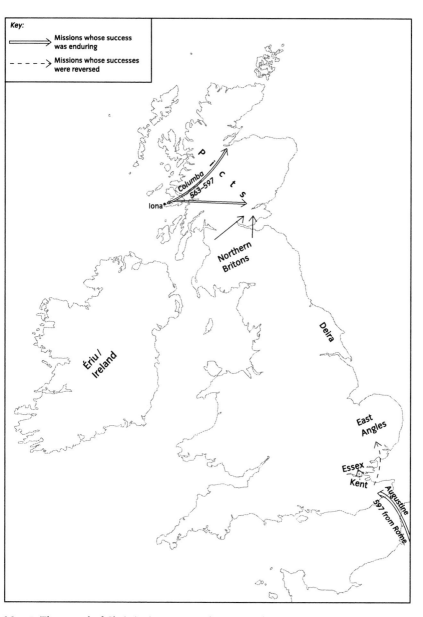

**Map 7** The spread of Christianity, 550–616: the Picts and the Gregorian mission to Kent.

Æthelberht died in 616 it looked as if Kent would revert to the worship of the old gods. However, when some of the missionaries had already departed for Francia, Eadbald changed his mind. Perhaps this was under pressure from Chlothar II, who had recently acquired an undivided rule over all the Frankish dominions: a representative of the new English Church had attended Chlothar's great council of Paris in 614. The whole episode illustrates how fragile the first beginnings of the Gregorian mission were.

Similarly fragile was the next major success for the Christian group in Kent. Edwin of Deira acquired power over the whole of Northumbria following the defeat and death of his rival, Æthelfrith of Bernicia, in 616. His victory was won on his behalf by Rædwald, king of the East Angles, that king who had erected an altar to Christ alongside the one devoted to the old gods. Yet Edwin sought a marriage with the sister of Eadbald, king of Kent, Æthelberg. According to Bede, Eadbald refused to give his sister in marriage to a pagan, 'lest the faith and sacraments of the heavenly king should be profaned by an alliance with a king who was entirely ignorant of the worship of the true God' (Bede, *HE* ii. 9). Faced with this pronouncement, Edwin promised that Æthelberg and her companions should have freedom of worship and suggested that he might himself wish to become a Christian. Æthelberg thus became Edwin's queen and was accompanied to Northumbria, as part of the arrangement, by Paulinus, consecrated bishop in 625. The conditions were essentially the same as those imposed by the Franks on Æthelberg's own father, Æthelberht, when he married Bertha. Moreover, Edwin was indeed baptized at Easter 627. Soon afterwards he persuaded his ally, Earpwald, king of the East Angles, to follow his example. Since Edwin was now the most powerful king in Britain, the prospects for Christianity seemed excellent. But Earpwald was killed by a pagan East Anglian shortly after his baptism; and Edwin himself fell in battle on 12 October 633, the victim of a rebellion (as Bede described it) led by Cadwallon, king of Gwynedd, and aided by a young Mercian prince, Penda. After his death Northumbria reverted to two kingdoms, Deira and Bernicia; and the new kings, although previously baptized, both openly rejected Christianity. Again, as with the Franks and as with Æthelberht's hegemony, the hopes occasioned by military overlordship proved vain.

As it happened, Christianity recovered lost ground very quickly. In

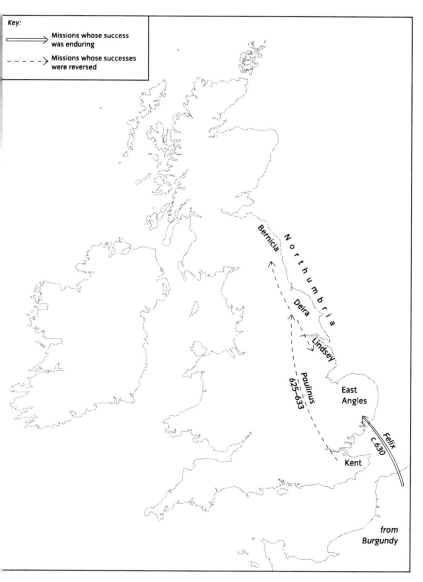

**Key:**

⟹ Missions whose success was enduring

⇢ Missions whose successes were reversed

Bernicia

N o r t h u m b r i a

Deira

Lindsey

Paulinus
625–633

East
Angles

Felix
c.630

Kent

*from
Burgundy*

**Map 8** The spread of Christianity, 616–633: from the death of Æthelberht of Kent to the death of Edwin of Northumbria.

East Anglia, Earpwald's death, in 627 or 628, was followed by three years of pagan rule; but then Sigeberht, mentioned earlier as an exile in Francia, returned to take the kingship. He acquired a bishop from Burgundy, Felix, who had probably belonged to circles close to the heirs of the Irishman Columbanus, which, by 630, were highly influential in Francia. From this date onwards, East Anglia remained Christian.

Of greater overall importance, however, was the Christian recovery in Northumbria. About a year after Edwin's death, and also after the deaths of his two apostate successors, Eanfrith in Bernicia and Osric in Deira, both at the hands of Cadwallon, king of Gwynedd, Eanfrith's younger brother Oswald succeeded in defeating and killing the British king. Oswald, like Eanfrith and also like his younger brother Oswiu, was a son of Æthelfrith, Edwin's rival. All three had been exiled when Edwin came to power in 616; and all three had been baptized while in exile. Eanfrith, the apostate king of 633–4, had been among the Picts; Oswald and Oswiu, however, had lived as exiles among the Irish, probably mainly in Dál Riata. Both of them spoke Irish as well as English.

After his victory over Cadwallon at Denisesburna, near Hexham, late in 634, Oswald became king of all Northumbria. There was no question of allowing a kinsman of Edwin to take power in Deira. One of Oswald's first actions was to request the abbot of Iona, Ségéne, to send a bishop for the Northumbrians. Ségéne, advised by his senior monks, sent Aidan, who established his see on the island of Lindisfarne in the core of Oswald's ancestral kingdom, Bernicia. Aidan was bishop of all the Northumbrians for some sixteen years (635–51); at first he was closely dependent on Oswald, whom Bede portrays as interpreting to his nobles what Aidan said in Irish; but after Oswald's death in 642, Aidan befriended Oswine, king of Deira from 644 to 651. He was not merely an ecclesiastical agent of Oswald or Oswiu. His relatively long episcopate was followed by those of Fínán, (651–60) and Colmán (661–4), both sent from Iona. Together they constituted what Bede called 'the episcopate of the Irish' (*HE* iii. 26), a period of almost thirty years, 635–64, during which Christianity put down firm roots in Northumbria. The leaders in this mission were monks of Iona— 'Columbans', *Columbienses*, as Ceolfrith, abbot of Wearmouth-Jarrow, called them. Yet other Irish, not owing allegiance to

Columba, also participated, such as Fursa in East Anglia and, later, Rónán in Northumbria.

The odd hint in Bede allows us to have some idea how the new religion was spread within a kingdom. The royal household was crucial because of the way it was integrated into the career of a nobleman. The household recruited 'king's thegns', aristocratic boys in their teens, to act as servants and as a standing military force. If they gave satisfaction, such thegns received a generous grant of land in their mid-20s, after which they would typically marry and cease to be normal inmates of the royal household. Instead of being called 'king's thegns', they were now known as *gesithas*, 'companions', even though, in reality, they no longer regularly accompanied the king. This arrangement gave the king immense influence over his nobility. His thegns formed part of his household and were thus in the daily presence of the king; they would also have been encouraged to seek his favour by the prospect of the crucial land grant at the end of their time as thegns. A *gesith* took to his estate his own experience of living in the presence of the king, and would hope to use the alliances and friendships made there to ensure that his own sons were chosen, in their turn, to be king's thegns. The halls of the *gesithas* can be seen in the Lives of St Cuthbert offering hospitality to the bishop in their local districts. Christianity could spread outwards from the royal household along the channels of aristocratic power. Oswald began with an advantage in that many of his thegns had shared his exile among the Irish. In the first two phases of the conversion, in the reigns of Æthelberht of Kent and Edwin of Northumbria, crucial advances had been made by marriage alliances; in this third phase, of Sigeberht in East Anglia and of Oswald in Northumbria, returned exiles initiated new and enduring conversions.

Bede reveals a second way in which the king's power aided the work of the missionary bishop, when he writes that Aidan used to have a chapel and a room in which to sleep in the various royal vills, and that he used such centres as bases from which to evangelize the neighbourhood. For the period of Edwin, Bede has a vivid story to illustrate his ideal of king and bishop working in harness. Edwin stayed for thirty-six days with his household, including Bishop Paulinus, at the royal vill of Yeavering in the heart of Bernicia. There the king could receive his food-renders, while Paulinus preached and baptized. Aidan, however, did not normally travel with the king; for one thing, he travelled like a good Irish monk, on foot, whereas the king rode; for another, he avoided the great feasts and exchanges of gifts by which kings and nobles were bonded together. Aidan's journeys, although they often went from royal vill to royal vill, operated according to a different calendar and in a different style from the corresponding journeys of the royal household. The physical support offered by the material underpinning of royal power was invaluable for Aidan; but he managed to distinguish what he was asking of the king's subjects as their bishop from the demands made by the king's servants. At this period, moreover, the king did not impose Christian observance, nor did he prohibit non-Christian worship. The first English king to issue such a prohibition was Earconberht, king of Kent (640–64), in other words about half a century after the initial royal conversion.

The main advance during Oswald's reign was in Wessex. Birinus was sent as a bishop by Pope Honorius, intending to preach in the innermost and most deeply pagan part of England, but he found that the Gewisse were as pagan as could be desired. Wessex was at this period a composite kingdom, liable on occasion to fall apart into its constituent parts. Birinus received a see at Dorchester-on-Thames in Oxfordshire and thus in the heart of one of these component parts, the Gewisse of the Upper Thames valley. Birinus had been consecrated on the orders of Honorius by Asterius, bishop of Milan but then resident in Genoa, in imperial Liguria. Northern Italy had its connection with the British Isles through Bobbio, the last monastic foundation of Columbanus, in the Apennines about forty miles from Genoa but within Lombard territory. Bobbio had been charged by the same Pope Honorius less than a decade beforehand with the task of preaching orthodox Catholic Christianity within a Lombard kingdom that was partly Arian, partly schismatic Catholic. There is thus a fair chance that Birinus' mission stemmed from the veneration felt by Honorius for Gregory the Great, and from the links between Rome, Bobbio, Luxeuil (Columbanus' principal monastery in Burgundy, which remained in close contact with Bobbio), and the regions of missionary work in north-western Europe.

Birinus' mission also benefited from an alliance made between the West Saxon king, Cynegils, and Oswald, now the most powerful king in all Britain. If Bede's information was correct, Oswald was present when Cynegils was baptized and acted as his godfather; moreover, he married Cynegils's daughter and, again according to Bede, 'both kings gave Dorchester to the bishop for him to make his episcopal see there' (*HE* iii. 7). Historians usually doubt whether Oswald could have given land so far from his own kingdom, but it is accepted that his double role as godfather and as son-in-law is genuine.

As in 633–4, so on Oswald's death in 642, some of the gains made under his overlordship were temporarily lost. Cynegils died in 643, a year after Oswald, but his successor, Cenwalh, remained a pagan. In 644 a cousin of Edwin, Oswine, was established as king of Deira, so reducing the kingdom of Oswald's successor, Oswiu, to the ancestral territory of Bernicia. Penda was now undisputed king of all Mercia; and he remained a pagan until his death in 655. By a roundabout route, however, Wessex was restored to Christianity. About 645 Cenwalh was imprudent enough to repudiate his wife, who happened to be Penda's sister. Penda took this as a hostile act and promptly drove Cenwalh into exile in East Anglia. There, however, he came under the influence of a strongly Christian king, Anna, and was converted and baptized. When he re-established himself in Wessex, *c.*648, he returned from exile as a Christian king. He also found himself a new bishop, a Frankish nobleman from the Brie region east of Paris, Agilbert, who was on his way home after spending a considerable period studying in Ireland. He is another example, in this case virtually certain, of the involvement of Columbanian monasticism in the conversion of England.

By 650, therefore, the gains of Oswald's reign had been restored, but the Midlands, from the Humber to north Oxfordshire, remained pagan, apart from British survivals. Penda's kingdom might be surrounded by Christian neighbours, but he was usually more than a match for them on the battlefield. The Irish monk Fursa, probably from Louth, had settled in East Anglia during the reign of Sigeberht and thus no later than *c.*640. About 648, however, he left East Anglia for Francia, because the incessant Mercian attacks made settled monastic life impossible.

On the other hand, Penda's reign saw both successes and reverses; and it looks as though he experienced striking reversals of fortune in the last five years of his life. Aidan died on 31 August 651, and Penda's incursions into Northumbria reached the region around Bamburgh and Lindisfarne, the heart of Bernicia, both before and after his death. Yet by 653 Oswiu and Penda were making a new and very short-lived alliance; furthermore, Oswiu was in a position personally to encourage another Sigeberht, this time king of the East Saxons, to seek baptism. Only part of the context can be reconstructed, but the starting point seems to be a killing regarded by Bede as especially deplorable. In the summer of 651 Bernicia attacked Deira, ruled by Oswine. The Deiran king was betrayed and killed about ten miles due west of the Roman town of Catterick. This was the end of the male line of the Deiran dynasty, after which Deira became, at best, a sub-kingdom of a united Northumbria.

In 653 a marriage was arranged between Penda's son, Peada, already sub-king of the Middle Angles, and Oswiu's daughter, Alhfled. The condition imposed on the bridegroom was more severe than those demanded of Æthelberht and Edwin: he was not to be given Alhfled until he was himself baptized. Expressions of a general interest were no longer enough. He was further encouraged to become a Christian by Alhfled's brother, Alhfrith, who was himself already married to Penda's daughter, Cyneburg. The Mercian and Bernician royal kindreds were often at war—and thus embroiled in a feud between dynasties—but they also often attempted to make peace through marriages. Three children of Penda married three children of Oswiu. Since Peada went to Northumbria to seek a wife, and since in the same year Sigeberht of Essex was persuaded, while in Northumbria, to accept baptism, 653 seems to have been one of the summits of Oswiu's power. Because of the marriage of Peada and Alhfled, four priests were sent to the Middle Angles, but not a bishop while Penda remained alive. As for Essex, however, Cedd, initially diverted from the Middle Angles in late 653, was consecrated bishop in 654 when he visited Northumbria to report his good reception to Fínán and Oswiu.

Yet the peace made with Mercia collapsed almost as soon as it was made. In 655 Penda led a combined army against Northumbria, with contingents from almost all of southern Britain, from East Anglia to Gwynedd. Moreover, when this expedition invaded Northumbria, Ecgfrith, another of Oswiu's sons and his eventual heir, was already a hostage in the keeping of Penda's queen, Cynuise. Contrary to all expectations, Oswiu defeated and killed Penda, probably by means of a surprise attack when Penda's great army was on its way home. After the battle of the Winwæd the lands that had belonged to the great overlordship Penda had created, extending from the Humber to the

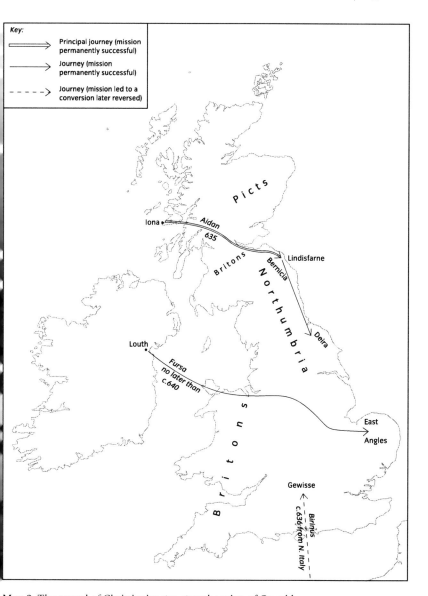

**Map 9** The spread of Christianity, 633–642: the reign of Oswald.

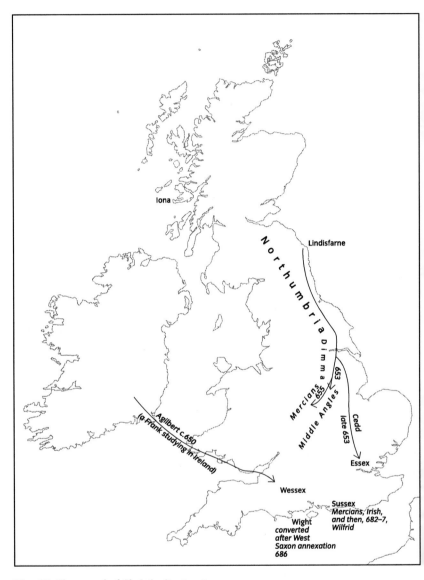

**Map 10** The spread of Christianity, 642–87.

Avon at Bristol, became formally Christian. Even when, in 658, the Mercians rebelled against Oswiu and set up another son of Penda, Wulfhere, as king, there was no revival of the royal paganism of Penda's day. Wulfhere, indeed, when he had regained a supremacy in southern England similar to Penda's, used that power to initiate the conversion of Sussex (between 658 and 674).

The episcopate of the Irish had secured the position of Christianity in England. If Cumméne, abbot of Iona, had visited England about 660, he could have entered Northumbria near Stirling, have continued some 400 miles to its southern frontier, crossed into Mercian-dominated territory, and then journeyed across the Midlands and down into Essex to Bradwell-on-Sea, one of Cedd's new churches, in an old Saxon-Shore fort built in the days of Roman power to keep the forefathers of the English out of Britain. Between Stirling and this Roman fort looking out over the North Sea, Cumméne would never have left those lands whose rulers had been converted by the efforts of his monks and their English disciples.

The power of the new religion is visible in the political events of the conversion period. Christianity spread from kingdom to kingdom through the families of kings, because through their marriages and their exiles they were most likely to experience the religious observance of their neighbours. When Christian married pagan, the pagan converted to Christianity; English royal exiles found themselves in Christian kingdoms from Francia to Dál Riata, and they too converted. Christianity was a missionary religion in a way that the pre-Christian religions of the British Isles were not. There is no hint of non-Christian counterparts to Augustine, Felix, and Aidan—or to Patrick, whose anxiety lest he might yet lose the fruits of his labours stands out from his *Confessio*. Patrick's God might be merciful to His sheep, but He perceived and recorded all the failures of His shepherds.

**Figure 4.1** The Lindisfarne Gospels. St Matthew. London, British Library, Cotton MS Nero D.IV, fo. 25v.

# 4

# The art of authority

Jennifer O'Reilly

The utter remoteness of the islands at the north-westerly limits of the Ocean and the barbarian nature of their inhabitants was a common-place or *topos* in the work of Roman poets and historians. They therefore regarded the partial conquest of Britain, the largest in the skein of islands at the furthest edge of the inhabited world, as a symbol of Rome's universal dominion and civilizing role. Christian commentators living in the Empire, however, adapted this secular image of the centrality of Rome in the light of the very different biblical tradition that Jerusalem was the centre of the earth. Old Testament prophecies had announced that the glory of the God of Israel would one day be revealed to all peoples, even to idolatrous gentiles throughout 'the multitude of isles' (Ps. 96: 1; Isa. 49: 1), 'from sea to sea . . . unto the ends of the earth' (Ps. 71: 8; 18: 5); the New Testament saw this fulfilled in the coming of Christ and in the continuing apostolic task of taking the Gospel from Jerusalem to all the world (e.g. Acts 13: 47, quoting Isa. 49: 6; Rom. 10: 18, quoting Ps. 18: 5).

When St Patrick evangelized beyond the frontier of the Roman Empire, he presented his mission to the Irish as a latter-day fulfilment of these Scriptural prophecies and of Christ's explicit final command that his disciples should teach all peoples (*omnes gentes*) and baptize them in the name of the Trinity (Matt. 28: 19–20, 24: 14), bearing witness 'even to the uttermost part of the earth' (Acts 1: 8). Patrick proclaimed: 'As we have seen it written, so we have seen it fulfilled: behold, we are the witnesses that the Gospel has been preached to the limit beyond which no-one dwells.'

Patristic writers (the Fathers of the Church) came to regard Roman imperial rule as a providential preparation for the coming of Christ and the triumph of a far greater and more truly universal dominion. From the combined traditions of imperial Rome and Judaeo-Christian Jerusalem there developed the concept that Rome, refounded from Jerusalem by the princes of the apostles, St Peter and St Paul, and sanctified by their martyrdom and the presence of their tombs, was the earthly centre of Christ's spiritual empire, even though the city ceased to be the capital of the Roman Empire. Papal initiatives in the spiritual conquest and successive conversions of the islands and peoples on the western periphery of the known world were, therefore, to have a key symbolic role in the development of this concept of Rome, but it was the ready response of Insular writers which gave it life. In a letter to Pope Boniface IV in 613, Columbanus described Peter and Paul as fulfilling the psalmist's prophecy : 'Their voice has gone out into every land and their words to the ends of the earth' (Ps. 18: 5); he acknowledged the papal successors of the holy apostles as the first deliverers of the Catholic faith to the Irish and recognized Rome as 'the head of the Churches of the world, saving the special privilege of [Jerusalem], the place of the Lord's resurrection'.

Over a century later, Bede made sophisticated use of the Roman, biblical, and patristic strands of the *topos* in his account of the various conversions and reconversions of regions and peoples within 'the multitude of the isles.' In the *Ecclesiastical History* he quoted Gregory the Great's claim that the Ocean and barbarous Britain, which had never been entirely subdued by Roman force of arms, had peaceably submitted to Christian preachers. Bede elsewhere presented Pope Gregory himself as fulfilling Christ's final command to the apostles to evangelize all peoples when in 597 he sent out Augustine and other missionaries from Rome to the new inhabitants of Britain who had not known Roman imperial rule. Bede quoted a letter of Boniface V applying the texts of Ps. 18: 5 and Matt. 28: 20 to the evangelizing work of Justus, the third Roman archbishop of Canterbury, when he sent him the pallium, the sign of his office, in 624 and authorized the consecration of more bishops, that the Gospel might be preached 'among all those peoples who are not yet converted'.

The memory of how the Gospel had also been taken from one part of the periphery to another, that is, from Britain to Ireland and then from Ireland and Iona to the Picts and Anglo-Saxons, was to be selectively accommodated within this Rome-centred model of conversion or spiritual conquest. Writers from various regions within the

Atlantic archipelago assimilated the layered *topos* of Rome and the ends of the earth, like other aspects of the literary heritage they had received with their Christianity from the Mediterranean world. But they also adapted and transformed it, and in a variety of ways and contexts which are of direct relevance in interpreting contemporary accounts of Insular art and building. This conceptual framework also offers some insight into the surviving evidence of Insular artistic responses to the Judaeo-Christian culture of the late Roman world and the role of interchanges between the Insular peoples in the formation of the repertoire of Insular art. The present chapter explores these themes by comparing contemporary descriptions and examples of the art of the Northumbrian Anglo-Saxon *Romani* with the art of the Insular Gospel books.

# The *Romani*, art, and building in the Roman manner

At the heart of the conversion and the art it inspired was the coming of the Latin Bible and of patristic exegesis, that is, of particular ways of interpreting the literal text and its underlying meaning which, for a literate elite, informed an entire world view. Insular writers refashioned Rome's stock image of conquering and civilizing the barbarous periphery, not simply to describe the Church's peaceable conversion of their island forefathers from paganism to the rudiments and external forms of the faith, but to persuade their own Christian contemporaries of the need for submission to a more thoroughgoing spiritual conquest. Obedience to God's will presupposed the authoritative interpretation of the divine word. In the developing Insular Christian culture of the seventh and early eighth centuries, the argument focused on the interpretation of the problematic biblical evidence for the date of celebrating Easter. Insular writers showed that the process of interpretation was inextricably bound up with core beliefs and a fuller realization of membership of the universal Church symbolized by Rome. Insular *Romani* dwelt not on the recent nature of papal sanctioning of the so-called Roman Easter in the early seventh century, but on Petrine Rome's role in safeguarding both the unity of the Church and the revelation of the full deposit of faith, handed to the apostles and divinely unfolded within the Church over time.

Insular *Romani* presented certain fellow islanders and fellow believers who obdurately clung to their own local customs on the dating of Easter, rather than follow universal 'Roman' practice, as being spiritually on the edge of the Christian world. This reuse of the old *topos* of Rome's centrality was not about ethnicity and geography: centre and periphery were here habitations of the mind. Thus at the synod of Whitby, Wilfrid criticized the Columban monks and implicitly those Anglo-Saxons who followed them, as well as the Picts and the Britons, 'who in these, the two remotest islands of the Ocean, and only in some parts of them, foolishly attempt to fight against the whole world'. It was essential for Wilfrid in 664, as for the Irishman Cummian exhorting Ségéne of Iona in similar terms to observe a Roman Easter over thirty years earlier, to show that their own remoteness from the physical centre of the Roman Christian world did not mean that they too were backwoodsmen. They supported the case for a particular interpretation of Scripture concerning the celebration of Easter by citing authoritative texts of the Fathers and decisions of Church councils, received from 'the centre', as well as the eyewitness experience of the delegation from southern Ireland (631) and of Wilfrid (c.653), who had travelled to Rome and seen how things were done in the chief of cities.

The desire to demonstrate familiarity with Rome as the touchstone of orthodoxy by acquiring and emulating things Roman is evident in the written and archaeological record of Wilfrid's prodigious artistic patronage. He brought in stonemasons and craftsmen and used Roman building types and architectural decorative motifs from the Continent; he built aisled and columned churches of dressed stone at Hexham and at Ripon and a crypt incorporating inscribed Roman stones. At York he restored the stone church founded by the Roman mission, which his biographer implies had fallen into ruin under the Columbans, and for Ripon he obtained endowments including lands confiscated from the Britons, while the site itself had earlier been given by King Alhfrith to Columban monks, who had abandoned it rather than accept 'the catholic Easter and the other canonical rites of the Roman and apostolic church'. Wilfrid's biographer presents him as the vanquisher of those 'whom the Apostolic See does not receive into communion', and quotes the *acta* of Pope Agatho's synod (679) where Wilfrid had later undertaken to sign a confession of the Catholic faith 'on behalf of the whole northern part of Britain and Ireland, together with the islands inhabited by the Angles and Britons, as well as by the Irish and Picts.' He embellished his churches with altar plate, furnishings, altar hangings of gold and Tyrian purple, and ornaments of precious metalwork, including a cross of gold at St Peter's, Ripon, described in his Latin epitaph there as a *tropaeum* or victory trophy. The accounts read like entries from the contemporary Roman *Lives of the Popes,* where the founding and embellishing of churches in Rome on an imperial scale of patronage were prominent amongst the deeds recorded of successive popes and helped visually to identify Papal Rome with ancient tradition.

Rosemary Cramp has demonstrated the general *imitatio* of Rome implicit in the layout of St Peter's at Wearmouth founded *c.*673 and St Paul's at Jarrow, *c.*681, in the proportions of their high basilican churches, which recall those of Roman churches such as Santa Maria in Cosmedin, and in specific features such as the *porticus* (in this context meaning a covered way). Bede records that Benedict Biscop sought out masons in Francia, *c.*671, 'to build him a stone church in the Roman style he had always loved so much', and also glaziers, 'craftsmen as yet unknown in Britain', who taught the English their skills. The Anglo-Saxons drew not only on the city of Rome but on the common vocabulary of Roman building types and ornament used by the Western Church. The archaeological evidence documents their use of Roman techniques and materials—dressed and mortared stone, poured concrete, painted plaster, lathe-turned baluster shafts, coloured window glass, porphyry, stone inscriptions, and a range of architectural ornamental motifs, including vine-scroll, as well as the remarkable development of figural sculpture in relief on free-standing monuments.

There was, however, regional diversity. Although the existence of Irish *Romani* long pre-dates the synod of Whitby, churches in Ireland were typically of wood: later stone churches often simulated features of hallowed wooden buildings. Nor can the large-scale use of stone at Hexham, Ripon and Wearmouth–Jarrow be taken as typical of the early Anglo-Saxon Church. Furthermore, the work of Bede cannot be cited without qualification as evidence that the Anglo-Saxon *Romani* identified orthodoxy on Easter with building in stone. Certainly,

Bede's account of the development of ecclesiastical authority and unity in the second phase of conversion or spiritual conquest after the synod of Whitby documents increasing Roman cultural influences, including building in stone. As Gaul had influenced Romanizing Northumbrian patrons, Wearmouth–Jarrow in turn became a Romanizing centre of influence for the Picts. When King Nechtan adopted the Catholic time of keeping Easter, in order to make the change (from Columban practice) 'with greater authority', he sought help from the English, who 'had long since based their religious practices on the example of the holy Roman and apostolic Church'. He asked Ceolfrith of Wearmouth–Jarrow for further information on Easter and the tonsure, but also for masons to be sent to build a church of stone 'after the Roman fashion', and vowed that he and his people would always 'follow the customs of the holy Roman and apostolic Church, so far as they could learn them, remote though they were from the Roman people and their language'. In responding to Nechtan's three requests, Ceolfrith distinguished between the Roman celebration of Easter, derived from a spiritual interpretation of Scripture and bound up with orthodox belief, and the Roman tonsure. He explained how he had strongly recommended to Adomnán of Iona (who followed the Roman Easter) the form of tonsure which imitates Christ's crown of thorns as a fitting outward sign whereby 'we, who desire to be saved by Christ's Passion, wear with Peter the sign of the Passion'. But Ceolfrith stressed that difference over the form of tonsure, which arises from historical circumstances, 'is not hurtful to those whose faith in God is untainted and their love for their neighbour sincere'.

Similarly, Ceolfrith's disciple, Bede, shows that building in the universal Roman manner could fittingly proclaim the most recently converted peoples at the ends of the earth to be members of the universal Church, but warns that it could never provide or replace the irrefutable proof of membership demonstrated by love of God and neighbour. Bede's account of the Whitby synod itself, for example, honours Aidan's memory and is framed by a laudatory treatment of the community at Lindisfarne, whose church, though built 'after the Irish method, not of stone but of hewn oak', was later enshrined rather than replaced. Bede pictured Cuthbert heroically advancing to a battlefield beyond Lindisfarne and conquering a remote, demon-haunted island further out in the limitless ocean, where he 'built a city fitted for his *imperium*'. Bede subverted the Roman *topos*, however, by specifying that Cuthbert's *civitas* on Farne was built not of cut stone or bricks and mortar, but of turf and boulders with a roof of rough-hewn timber and straw, and that the saint stuffed the cracks in the planks of the oratory walls with mud and straw. Though Cuthbert was English and, by this stage, observed the Roman Easter, he was 'more concerned with the splendours of his heavenly than his earthly abode'. The *civitas* on Farne did not by its outward form evoke any earthly city; rather, the life of the holy man lived within it was patterned on the life of the heavenly city to come.

The surviving art of Lindisfarne also challenges stereotypical contrasts of English and Irish, *Romani* and Columban, Roman and barbarian. Like Wearmouth–Jarrow and Hexham, Iona and Lindisfarne testify to the seventh-century cult of the Virgin, which had been promoted in Rome before the formal establishment of the four Marian feasts by Pope Sergius (687–701). It has been suggested that paintings acquired from Rome by Benedict Biscop for Wearmouth may have inspired the depiction of the Virgin and apostles on St Cuthbert's wooden coffin reliquary at Lindisfarne; the pose of the Virgin and Child provides the closest surviving comparison for that in the later Columban Book of Kells. Bede's prologue to the *Life of Cuthbert* testifies to close relations between his community and Lindisfarne. The scene of Christ in majesty on Cuthbert's coffin lid, like that in the Codex Amiatinus, a highly Romanized biblical manuscript produced at Wearmouth–Jarrow, has a similar though not identical reconciliation of two Mediterranean types of the Evangelist symbols. The Lindisfarne Gospels, like other Insular Gospel books, has ornament derived from native metalworking traditions, but its script is more formally developed and its Italian Vulgate text, laid out in columns, compares with that in the Codex Amiatinus. It also uses touches of gold and has a set of finely individualized Evangelist author portraits with inscriptions transliterated from Greek, implying late antique influence; the figure of Matthew is demonstrably from the same antique Evangelist portrait type which underlies the scribal portrait in the Codex Amiatinus (Figs. 4.1, 4.3).

Bede gives a glimpse of the extensive range of Mediterranean figurative art brought into Northumbria through Wearmouth–Jarrow. The spoils from the fifth of Benedict Biscop's six journeys to Rome included paintings of the life of Christ which were placed all round the walls of Jarrow's chapel of the Holy Mother of God. There was also a set of scenes 'very skilfully arranged to show how the Old Testament foreshadowed the New'; Moses raising the brazen serpent, for example, was paired with Christ exalted on the Cross (cf. John 3: 14). This typological way of reading Scripture, sanctioned in the New Testament, was one of the interpretative techniques of patristic commentators, and was widely adopted in early Christian art. Bede's description is valuable evidence of Jarrow's familiarity with the concept of art as visual exegesis. He also alludes to the patristic argument that the tradition of the Church is not only passed on in written form: since God in becoming man became visible, the contemplation of visual images can lead the faithful towards an understanding of the divine. In 679 Benedict Biscop brought back scenes from the Gospel and the Apocalypse with which he decorated the south and north walls of the church at Wearmouth. Bede observed that they enabled even the illiterate to contemplate the face of Christ and his saints; picturing more clearly the Incarnation and seeing the Last Judgement brought before their very eyes, they were prompted to affective penitential meditation. The images of the Virgin and apostles arranged on a wooden entablature from wall to wall are likely to have been icons—a reminder that Rome, which was within the orbit of the Byzantine world and had a significant Greek population well before the long line of Greek and Syrian popes began in the later seventh century, was an important repository and clearing house of art and influences from the eastern Mediterannean.

# Jerusalem

The concept of a spiritual world dominion emanating from its earthly centre in papal Rome was further enlarged by the biblical metaphor of the people of God being drawn from the ends of the world to its centre at Jerusalem, the earthly symbol of the *heavenly* city. Petrine Rome, founded from Jerusalem, came to share symbolically in some of Jerusalem's associations of centrality. Rome not only continued the apostolic task of taking the Gospel to all peoples but, like Jerusalem at Pentecost, drew all peoples to itself. The liturgy, buildings, and art of papal Rome assimilated features of Jerusalem, particularly through allusions to the temple and the enshrined site of Christ's burial and resurrection.

Jerusalem was in turn, often through the influence of such Roman intermediaries, made present at the ends of the earth in Insular art and buildings and descriptions of churches. This process of *imitatio* did not require the literal imitation or detailed description of a particular architectural or pictorial image, but the suggestion of some identifying feature or aspect of the image through which its significance could be both appropriated and transformed for a new context. There are hints and evocations of the temple (and therefore of the heavenly Jerusalem it foreshadowed), or of Christ's tomb, in widely differing descriptions and survivals of Insular sites. Examples include not only Paulinus' stone church at York (square in shape, like the sanctuary of the temple and the new Jerusalem) or Wilfrid's layout of the stone crypt at Ripon, but also Cogitosus' account of Brigit's church at Kildare, Adomnan's depiction of Columba's Iona, and Bede's account of Cuthbert's hermitage on Farne.

Wilfrid's biographer describes the Romanizing splendours of Hexham as without rival in scale north of the Alps, but also claims that the plans and construction of Hexham and Ripon were divinely inspired, like those of Moses' tabernacle and Solomon's Temple. Bede was careful to avoid any suggestion that the two Old Testament sanctuaries prefigured actual church buildings. In common with patristic tradition, he interpreted both tabernacle and temple as divinely ordained symbols or *figurae* which can apply to Christ himself, to the universal Church and the individual believer, and to the heavenly life of the New Jerusalem. He shared his vision of the Church more closely with Acca, who succeeded Wilfrid at Hexham (709–32), and to whom Bede dedicated his spiritual interpretations of the biblical accounts of the building and rebuilding of the temple.

Christian allusions to the tabernacle and temple were often combined with New Testament architectural metaphors of the community of Christ's body (that is, the Church) as a living building, with an inviolable foundation and cornerstone in Christ and a building fabric made up of the living stones and pillars of the faithful (1 Cor. 3: 11; Eph. 2: 19–22; 1 Peter 2: 4–10). Such interpretations were well known, and themselves inform a number of Insular works of art. The apostles figured as pillars of the Church (Gal. 2: 9) in arcaded Roman portrait-bust reliefs on stone pillars and cross shafts, as at

Easby. Visualizations of the tabernacle–temple metaphor in manuscripts show considerable exegetical complexity, and range from the massive inscribed plan of the tabernacle in the Codex Amiatinus to the house-shaped shrine format of the living Church depicted in the Book of Kells (fo. 202ᵛ), and the inscribed diagram of the heavenly Jerusalem in the Book of Armagh, whose inscriptions harmonize the apocalyptic vision of the new Jerusalem and the biblical descriptions of its prefiguring in the tabernacle and the temple.

# The cult of the Cross

In his account of the Holy Places, which circulated in Northumbria during the reign of Aldfrith (685–705) and was adapted by Bede, Adomnán depicted a plan of the great pilgrimage complex enclosing Golgotha and Christ's sepulchre. He saw the historic location of Christ's passion and resurrection in Jerusalem as the literal fulfilment of the prophecy: 'God our king before the ages has wrought our salvation in the centre of the earth' (Ps. 73: 12). The churches founded in Jerusalem by Constantine to commemorate the site of Christ's crucifixion and resurrection at the centre of the earth had a symbolic counterpart in the Constantinian church of the Holy Cross, known as the *basilica Hierusalem*, founded near the Lateran in Rome to house a relic of the True Cross. The veneration of the Cross in Jerusalem and imperial Constantinople was simulated in the papal development of the cult in seventh-century Rome, aspects of which were reflected in the early eighth-century cult of Oswald's cross. A cross-slab in reused Roman stone at Jarrow has an inscription: 'In this unique sign life is given back to the world.' It refers to the saving power of the Cross but the opening words, *In hoc singulari signo*, specifically recall accounts of Constantine's victory under the sign of the Cross in 312, with momentous results for the Church, which Bede also evokes in his description of Oswald setting up a wooden cross before battle against the British King Cadwallon in 635.

It announced a military victory over the enemy, but also signalled a spiritual conquest begun not directly from Rome but by teachers 'from the land of the Irish' who 'proclaimed the word of God with great devotion in all the provinces under Oswald's rule', later defined by Bede as 'all the peoples and kingdoms of Britain, divided among the speakers of four different languages, British, Pictish, Irish and English'. Oswald's cross, though of wood and 'hastily made', and possibly influenced by wooden crosses he could have seen on Iona during exile, is described as a *vexillum* and a *tropaeum*, the Roman terms for a battle standard and victory trophy but here, Bede stresses, denoting a heavenly triumph. The story is not simply of a new Constantine, but of the extension to the ends of the earth of Christ's spiritual empire, more lasting than the might of imperial Rome, whose monumental remains now littered the landscape. Bede claims that the Cross was the first sign of the Christian faith in Anglian Bernicia and was set up 'close to the wall with which the Romans once girded the whole of Britain, from sea to sea'.

# The Ruthwell Cross

Beyond Hadrian's Wall a century or so after Oswald's victory, the Anglo-Saxons were to erect magnificent signs of the Cross in stone at Bewcastle and Ruthwell, each over five metres in height, which demonstrate mastery of the Roman skill of relief sculpture and possibly the influence of Jarrow. Some have viewed the Ruthwell Cross on the Solway Firth as an ensign of Romanizing Anglian triumphalism over Celts in a frontier territory of the Bernician kingdom. In the tradition traced here it proclaims a larger victory.

The cross-head surmounting the shaft features two Evangelists, identified by their symbols as Matthew and John; presumably Mark and Luke and their symbols occupied the original transom. The psalmist's words were often applied to the universal mission of the four Gospel writers, two of whom were apostles, two of whom had received their testimony of Christ from Peter and Paul : 'There is no speech or language where their voices are not heard. Their sound has gone out into all the world, and their words to the ends of the earth' (Ps. 18: 4). The New Testament, followed by biblical commentators including Bede, associated diversity of languages, denoting diversity of peoples, with the unifying effect of the Gospel. St Jerome had influentially observed that before the resurrection of Christ, the peoples of the world from India to Britain, from the frozen North to

**Figure 4.2** (a) The Ruthwell Cross. Christ recognized by beasts in the desert. (b) The Ruthwell Cross. Inhabited vine-scroll: the Tree of Life.

the burning South, had lived like brutes in discord. But now, 'the voices and writings of all nations proclaim the passion and the resurrection of Christ'. Alluding to the patristic idea that the name and title of Jesus inscribed on the title-board of the Cross in the sacred languages of Hebrew, Greek, and Latin (Luke 23: 38; John 19: 20) was a sign announcing Christ's universal sovereignty, Jerome explained that Christ is 'now the one cry of the world', not only for 'the Jews, the Greeks and the Romans, peoples which the Lord has dedicated to his faith by the title written on his cross', but also for barbarians.

At Ruthwell, the Cross proclaims the Gospel in sacred and barbarian languages: it 'speaks' through Latin texts written in the Roman alphabet but also in Old English verse, written in the first person and incised in runes. Éamonn Ó Carragáin has argued that the subject matter and Latin captions or *tituli* of the series of deeply cut figural panels on the two broad sides are closely influenced by the Roman liturgy of the catechumenate and concepts of Christ's presence in baptism and the Eucharist, and are theologically complemented by the heroic vernacular account of the death of the incarnate Christ, which is told in the borders of the narrow sides of the monument.

In a single unifying image the sculptural decoration of the narrow sides reveals Christ to be the Tree of Life, that is, the axis at the centre of the world joining heaven and earth and providing spiritual food and healing for all. The Tree rises the height of the towering shaft on both sides and is shown in the form of a rooted vine-scroll filled with diverse creatures feeding on its fruit. It regenerates a Mediterranean image of the incorporation of all the faithful members of the Church into the sacramental and the glorified body of Christ (John 15: 1–5; 6: 56). The form and iconography of the Ruthwell Cross, its Christology and use of the written word show the Anglo-Saxons to be a people engrafted into the universal Church and familiar with its Romanized culture but also highly creative in adapting its conventions and integrating elements from their own tradition (Fig. 4.2).

The Bewcastle and Ruthwell monuments feature an otherwise unknown image of Christ offering a blessing with two beasts at his feet, which differs from the imperially derived image of Christ trampling defeated beasts in fulfilment of Ps. 90: 13. The version at Ruthwell has an inscription which is so arranged that the sacred name and title, *Jesus Christ*, appear immediately over Christ's head like a caption, customarily abbreviated as *Ihs Xps* ('Saviour' and 'Messiah'). The words incised down the sides further show him to be both Judge and Saviour of the world, and recognized as such by beasts and dragons in the desert (*Ihs Xps iudex aequitatis bestiae et dracones cognoverunt in deserto salvatorem mundi*). Verbal similarities have been sought in biblical images of the desert, such as Isa. 43: 20, and Jerome's Life of St Paul the Hermit, where St Antony marvels to find that although far from any great city, the desert beasts 'speak of Christ'; one of them, half-man, half-beast, voices their knowledge that Christ came for the salvation of the world and that 'his sound went forth into all the earth' (Ps. 18: 5). An Insular version of such an epiphany, transposed to the shore of the North Sea, has suggested a visual parallel to the Ruthwell image: in the *Life of Cuthbert* a monk observes two otters who humbly prostrate themselves at Cuthbert's feet and receive his blessing, evidently recognizing Christ in the holy man.

The Ruthwell Cross attests Christ's spiritual dominion at the world's edge and particularly his presence in the monastic desert. The scene of Christ and the beasts is positioned directly above an inscribed panel of the monastic desert saints, Paul and Antony, who are elsewhere portrayed not in Anglo-Saxon sculpture but on the great Pictish cross-slab at Nigg, *c.*800, and on later Irish high crosses. The lifelong Lenten fast of monastic life 'in the desert', in imitation of Christ, is a recurring theme in hagiography. The monk disciplines the carnal within himself, and the wilderness is transformed into a renewed and peaceable creation which anticipates the heavenly paradise. The two inscribed panels at Ruthwell have some affinity with Bede's accounts of Anglo-Saxon saints in the Columban tradition. In what is described as a custom of Lindisfarne, Cedd and his brother had undertaken Lenten penitential fasting, vigil, and prayer at a remote Deiran site 'which seemed better fitted for the haunts of robbers and the dens of wild beasts than human habitation'. They conquered this wilderness, and transformed it from the stains of former crimes into a place suitable for laying the foundations of the monastery of Lastingham. Bede's comment directly applies the desert image: 'as Isaiah says, "In the habitations where once dragons lay, shall be grass with reeds and rushes" [Isa. 35: 7; cf. 43: 20], that is, the fruit of good works shall spring up where once beasts dwelt or where men lived after the manner of beasts.'

# The Codex Amiatinus

Central to the complex artistic and other cultural changes accompanying the process of conversion and the reception of the Latin Bible and its exegesis was the Insular production of manuscripts. In *c.*678 Ceolfrith journeyed to Rome with Benedict Biscop. They returned, accompanied by John, the archcantor of St Peter's, Rome, with many treasures, including a pandect or single-volume copy of the whole Bible, which was a rarity in the early medieval world. The monastery of St Peter and St Paul at Wearmouth–Jarrow was to produce three great pandects during Ceolfrith's abbacy (688–716). Two were placed in the monastic churches and Ceolfrith took the third and largest, the Codex Amiatinus, on his final pilgrimage to Rome in 716, not simply as a diplomatic gift for Pope Gregory II but 'as a gift to St Peter, the prince of the apostles'. On the dedication page Ceolfrith offered it in gift exchange, 'desiring that I and mine may ever have a place amidst the joys of so great a father, a memorial in heaven'. He described himself as 'abbot from the furthest ends of the English', sending pledges of his devotion 'to the body of the sublime Peter, justly venerated, whom ancient faith declares to be head of the Church'. The ancient *topos* of Rome conquering, civilizing, and Christianizing the barbarian periphery was here elegantly used as a foil to the magnificent *Romanitas* of the Anglo-Saxon book, now taken to the centre from which the faith had been received.

It is the earliest extant Latin Bible, written on a magisterial scale (over 1,000 folios or 2,000 pages, 505 × 340 mm) in formal Roman uncial script. Its prefatory illustrations and diagrams reflect the art of late antiquity, for example in the use of gold and the illusion of spatial depth in the depictions of the scribe and the tabernacle. Although influenced by one or more books deriving from the sixth-century monastic library of Cassiodorus in Vivarium, southern Italy, the Codex Amiatinus is not simply a copy of any of the books which are now known from Cassiodorus' description of his library. The Amiatinus has a one-volume format, like Cassiodorus' 'big book' which contained the Old Latin biblical text, as partially revised by Jerome. This book reached Northumbria—Bede records seeing its illustrations of the tabernacle and temple—and may well have been the pandect 'of the old translation' brought back by Ceolfrith. The text used in the Codex Amiatinus, however, is Jerome's 'new translation' (the 'Vulgate'). It is written in columns rather than as a solid block and is laid out, according to Jerome's recommendations, in sense units, as Cassiodorus had done in another of his bibles, which was divided or bound in nine volumes (*novem codices*). A nine-volume bible is depicted in the scribe's book cupboard in the frontispiece of the Amiatinus (Fig. 4.3), and it is likely that all or part of Cassiodorus' *novem codices* also reached Northumbria.

The *History of the Abbots of Wearmouth and Jarrow* does not say

**Figure 4.3** The Codex Amiatinus. The *armarium* of the Scriptures. Florence, Biblioteca Medicea Laurenziana MS Amiatinus I, fo. V.

that the new translation used in Ceolfrith's three pandects replaced the old translation of the pandect he had earlier brought back from Rome. Rather, it suggests that Ceolfrith ensured his monastery had complete copies of the Old Testament and the New in both the old translation and the new, which had radical implications for the study of Scripture.

Cassiodorus had voiced a major patristic theme when he argued that the divine authorship and authority of both Testaments, and consequently the unity and harmony of their constituent books, is reflected in the harmony underlying the diversity of inspired biblical translations and variety of exegesis made by orthodox commentators through the ages. He likened the different divisions and groupings of the biblical books made by Augustine, Jerome, and the Septuagint to the work of the four Evangelists who, 'though their manner of speaking is divergent', are united in the one faith. The three classifications are set out in the Codex Amiatinus as opulent diagrams. In each the titles of the canonical books of the Old Testament as well as the New are listed within cruciform or lozenge-shaped frames which are suspended from roundel depictions of the Trinity and accompanied by classically framed captions. These striking whole-page images present an orderly digest of information and a symbolic interpretation of its theological significance.

A sumptuous purple, arcaded page lists the titles of all the biblical books as they appear in the Amiatinus. A further large diagram depicts the harmony of the Old and New Testaments by symbolically showing that the Mosaic Law, spiritually interpreted, is contained within the Gospels. The diagram displays the titles of the books of the Pentateuch (the Law or five books of Moses) in five linked golden circles which are prominently arranged in the shape of the Cross and set within one large purple circle. Each title is accompanied by its interpretation drawn from Jerome's description of the five books of the Law in his famous letter 53, which briefly reviews every book of the Bible in order to show that Christ the divine Wisdom is concealed throughout, beneath the literal letter of Scripture, and that the Mosaic Law is 'the prefiguring of the law of the Gospel'.

These multiple listings and images of the complete *bibliotheca* of Scripture in the opening pages of the Codex Amiatinus provide a thematic context in which to read the frontispiece portrait of a scribe seated before an *armarium* or book cupboard filled with nine volumes, whose inscribed titles constitute yet another grouping of all the books of Scripture. The frontispiece offers in pictorial form the kind of exegesis Jerome was drawing on when, in letter 53, he used the term 'an *armarium* of the Scriptures' to describe a Christian commentator. It was a metaphor of classical and biblical origins which could refer both to the divine library of orthodox belief constituted by all the books of Scripture, and to the inner library of the individual believer who, guided by the fathers, knows not only the literal text of the sacred books but also how to interpret their spiritual meaning.

Above the scribal portrait is an epigraph: 'The sacred books having been burned by enemy fire, Ezra, zealous for God, restored this work.' Isidore of Seville summarized the tradition that the Old Testament priest and scribe Ezra edited the Hebrew scriptures salvaged after the Babylonian Captivity; their translation into Greek in the Septuagint and into Latin by Jerome marked stages in the providential bringing of the divine word to the Hebrews, the Greeks, and the Romans. Bede richly elaborated this tradition to show that Ezra, whom the British writer Gildas had described as 'the library of the Law', was the inspired restorer and editor of the literal text, but also renewed its meaning. Bede's commentary on Ezra presents him as a prophetic figure of all orthodox teachers who share in Christ's work of showing how the New Testament is contained within the Old, the Gospel within the Law.

The epigraph in the Codex Amiatinus highlights the fact that the Hebrew text restored by Ezra (and made accessible through Jerome's translation) is contained in this very book. The haloed scribe sits before the *armarium* of the Scriptures in the pose of an antique Evangelist portrait. Whether or not it was intended to commemorate Jerome or any other particular teacher occupied in the continuing evangelical task, the iconography conveys the patristic idea that the Holy Spirit who inspired the original biblical authors and their editor continues to work through those who faithfully interpret the divine word. The scribal frontispiece and the illustrations which follow it make clear that Wearmouth–Jarrow not only possessed exemplary editorial and scribal skills in producing the text of this monumental Latin Bible, but was in union with the community of the faithful throughout the ages in interpreting the Scriptures handed down from the apostles. It was this assurance, and not just the outward appearance of *Romanitas*, that Ceolfrith brought from the furthest ends of the English in 716 to offer at the tomb of St Peter, 'whom ancient faith declares to be head of the Church'.

It was over a hundred years since Columbanus had told Gregory the Great of his veneration of the authority of Jerome and had assured Boniface IV of the orthodoxy of his people and their devotion to Scripture:

> For all we Irish, inhabitants of the world's edge, are disciples of Saints Peter and Paul and of all the disciples who wrote the sacred canon by the Holy Spirit, and we accept nothing outside the evangelical and apostolic teaching . . . but the Catholic faith, as it was delivered by you first, who are the successors of the holy apostles, is maintained unbroken.

# The Insular Gospel books

Of all the books in the library of Scripture, the Gospels epitomized the faith of the Church, handed down through the testimony of the apostles and taken to all peoples. An enthroned Gospel book had symbolically presided over the ecumenical councils of the early Church in which orthodox belief, centring on the Trinity and the identity of Christ, had been defined and defended. Archbishop Theodore emulated the custom when he convened an assembly of the 'bishops of the island of Britain' at Hatfield in 679 to recognise the decrees of all five universal councils from Nicaea in 325 to Constantinople in 553, as well as the Lateran council of 649, and to subscribe to a Trinitarian confession of the faith:

> Having the most holy Gospels before us . . . we united in declaring the true and orthodox faith as our Lord Jesus Christ delivered it in the flesh to the disciples . . . and as it was handed down in the creed of the holy fathers and by all the holy and universal councils in general and the whole body of the accredited fathers of the catholic Church . . . We glorify our Lord Jesus Christ as they glorified him, adding and subtracting nothing.

The credal confession was witnessed by John, archcantor of St Peter's, who was to take a copy of the proceedings back to Rome in preparation for the forthcoming sixth ecumenical council.

In Rome the four Gospels were displayed over the altar in the oratory where Wilfrid had prayed for aid to teach the Gospel among the nations (cf. Matt. 28: 19). Under the instruction of the archdeacon of Rome on that first visit, Wilfrid studied each of the four Gospels, together with the Easter rule. Later, 'for the good of his soul', he ordered 'the four Gospels to be written out in letters of purest gold on purpled parchment and illuminated' with a gold case set with precious gems, which he presented to his foundation of St Peter's at Ripon. It was 'a marvel of beauty unheard of in our times'. The description recalls late antique uncial books, clearly distinguishing Wilfrid's book from another category of illuminated manuscripts known as Insular Gospel books, produced in Ireland and Britain during the seventh and eighth centuries. These books are generally regarded as the most characteristic expression of Insular art, yet most of them appear to belong to a different world from the one in which antiquity and *Romanitas* were evoked.

It is difficult to ascribe precise dates and places of origin to Insular Gospel books or even to place some of them in sequence. Dating has sometimes reflected assessments of whether a manuscript looks more or less 'progressive' than the Lindisfarne Gospels, which shows unusually clear Mediterranean influences and once seemed to offer a fixed point because of its presumed connection with the translation of the relics of St Cuthbert in 698. A great deal of evidence has been lost, scribes and manuscripts did not necessarily remain in the place of production, and different elements in a manuscript could be derived from sources of various date and background.

# The Book of Durrow

There are sub-groups and individual variants among surviving manuscripts and their texts, but the features which readily distinguish Insular Gospel books from others are already present in the Book of Durrow. It is the earliest complete example, though its dating to the third quarter of the seventh century is currently questioned. Northumbria and, increasingly, Iona or Ireland have all been proposed as the place of origin. Unlike the Codex Amiatinus, it could never be mistaken for a Mediterranean book. Its script is the distinctive Insular half-uncial which was first developed from antique forms in Ireland and in the Celtic part of Britain; its page layout differs from the regularity and restraint of antique uncial manuscripts. Some of its decorative intrusions on the text, such as the enlargement and highlighting of certain initial letters and the *diminuendo* or tapering size of the following letters, are features already accomplished in the Irish psalter known as the Cathach, dating from the early seventh or even late sixth century. At the opening (*incipit*) of each of the four Gospels in Insular Gospel books, the first letters are magnified and decorated, with the rest of the initial word and several of the following words written in display letters, usually arranged in successive lines in a descending hierarchy of size and type, and radically reducing the remaining area of text on the page (Fig. 4.4). Patrick McGurk described the practice of also magnifying and decorating the *chi-rho* (Xp) abbreviation of the name of Christ at the beginning of Matt. 1: 18, already present in Durrow, as an Insular symptom with no surviving antique precedent. The form of the display letters is distorted by their embellishment with motifs found in Celtic and Anglo-Saxon metalwork, which migrated to vellum more readily than to stone.

The full-page decoration in the Book of Durrow, confined to the beginning and end of the book and the two pages before the *incipit* of each of the four Gospels, does not hint at the naturalistic and narrative riches of the Graeco-Roman pictorial tradition and carries a very restricted range of subject matter, notably framed canon tables which list the Gospel concordances, carpet pages of abstract ornament in which the Cross may be the focus of the design or concealed within it, and stylized renderings of the symbols of the four Evangelists. Durrow's depiction of the symbols as full-length creatures, unaccompanied by the Evangelists, is a striking feature of Insular books and those produced in areas of Insular influence: it occurs in the Echternach, Trier, and Cambridge–London Gospel books and in the Book of Kells; in the Lindisfarne, St Gall, and Lichfield Gospels this symbol type is combined with pictures of the Evangelists. The portrayal of the unaccompanied full-length symbols as terrestrial creatures (that is, unhaloed and wingless) in the Book of Durrow and the Echternach, Trier, and Cambridge–London Gospels is very rare elsewhere.

The decorated pages of Durrow simulate techniques and motifs used in precious metalwork, including cloisonné, enamel, millefiori, glass studs, spiral bosses, and pierced panels, and may similarly carry

**Figure 4.4** The Book of Durrow, *Incipit* of Mark's Gospel. Dublin, Trinity College MS A.4.5 (57), fo. 86.

connotations of prestigious commissions and gift objects. Close parallels have been drawn with treasures deposited in the Sutton Hoo ship-burial in the early seventh century, particularly the Germanic shoulder clasps, purse lid, and great gold buckle and, more generally, with the escutcheons of the Celtic hanging bowls. Recent discussions have again made comparisons with Irish material, including the Moylough belt shrine, and noted the common availability of motifs on both sides of the Irish Sea. But the chequered cross pattern of the Sutton Hoo clasps has clear affiliations with the Roman Christian world, and the Frankish and east Mediterranean items in the hoard also help suggest a more complex background for the Book of Durrow's decoration than the direct transposition of native metalworking motifs into the new medium and context of a book. Insular metalworkers themselves assimilated Roman motifs, and not only for ecclesiastical commissions such as altar plate, reliquaries, and book covers.

Ornamental motifs ultimately derived from these augmented Germanic and Celtic La Tène traditions already occur together in the Book of Durrow, though within separate compartments. This suggests there was considerable earlier interchange between the various Insular metalworking cultures underlying the decorative repertoire of the Gospel books, as well as interchange between media. The stylized delineation of limb joints on some of the Evangelist symbols in Durrow and other books has been compared with designs on Pictish carved stones. The discovery of Anglo-Saxon moulds and fragments of artefacts in the seventh-century metalworking deposits at Dunadd emphasizes the likely role of Dál Ríata in the amalgamation of Celtic and Germanic styles. The importance of Ireland in the formation of the English Church in the seventh century, and especially of Columban influences among the Picts and in Northumbria and its southern outreaches, suggests Columban monasticism and its royal patrons as an important agency in the long cultural interchange between the Insular regions which had been intensified by the processes of conversion and reached an extraordinary creative synthesis in the Insular Gospel books. Durrow itself is generally regarded as a Columban book. It has been suggested that an early non-Roman liturgical lection system may underlie the selection of some at least of the Gospel passages which received decorative highlighting in Insular Gospel books.

The quality of Durrow's design, and the fact that the major features of Insular Gospel books are already in place, argue that it comes from an existing Insular tradition of Gospel book production. Several features, including the frontispiece cross-carpet page and some of the other interlaced ornament in Durrow, suggest the influence of eastern Mediterranean books and their covers. The pattern on the cloak of St Matthew's symbol of a man has been compared with the Sutton Hoo clasps, but there is a closer parallel in an Armenian Gospel book (Figs. 4.5 a–b). Like Durrow, it has a restricted palette and shows the human figure frontally but with feet in profile. It depicts two standing, bearded Evangelists shown frontally and with their feet in profile; they wear cloaks of bell-shaped outline which are filled with geometric patterns, one of chequered rectangles. The book is tenth-century but probably preserves earlier eastern Mediterranean traditions which could have been available to Insular artists. Some Insular books have additional full-page pictures, most notably the Book of Kells, which assimilates but visually transforms a wide range of Mediterranean iconography and motifs such as the equilateral stepped cross, lions, peacocks, angels, and vine-scrolls. In short, although the Insular Gospel books differ from manuscripts produced in Wearmouth–Jarrow and Canterbury which self-consciously display *Romanitas*, they do reveal the influence of the Roman world, particularly of motifs and iconic images from eastern parts of it where local artistic traditions of abstraction and stylization had long interacted with the figurative traditions of Graeco-Roman art.

# The spiritual interpretation of Scripture

One of the most telling signs of Mediterranean influence in the art of the Insular Gospel books is the use of visual techniques analogous to the rhetorical devices employed by patristic and Insular commentators to illuminate the continuing spiritual significance hidden within the literal text of Scripture. St Augustine, in his influential work *On Christian Doctrine*, warned that understanding the meaning of the sacred text cannot be achieved by learning and reason alone. Many passages do not have obvious application to Christ and the Church, to the inner life of the individual reader, or to the heavenly life: to find

**Figure 4.5** (a) The Book of Durrow. Symbol of Matthew. Dublin, Trinity College MS A.4.5 (57), fol. 21v.

**Figure 4.5** (b) Armenian Gospel book. Evangelist portraits. Baltimore, Walters Art Gallery MS W.537, fo. 114v.

such spiritual meaning in the divine word is an act of discernment requiring grace and, for most people, authoritative guidance in reading the signs. Patristic commentaries presuppose that the apparent contradictions and obscurities in Scripture were intended by the divine author to stimulate certain kinds of reader to seek beyond a fundamental or 'carnal' level of understanding. Meditating on the mystery could lead to the apprehension at a more profound level of truths more openly expressed in other parts of Scripture. Properly interpreted, the very difficulties in the literal text could act as *sacramenta* or signs to its concealed spiritual meaning. Exegesis of such signs was also often expressed in the riddling language of paradox, metaphor, and wordplay, and made use of numerology, etymology, and the verbal or visual associations of a text with other Scriptural passages.

This rhetorical repertoire of the Fathers was assimilated by Irish writers in the century before the age of Bede. The work of Adomnán suggests that biblical learning on Iona was particularly rich. Hiberno-Latin Gospel commentaries show a readiness of response to certain aspects of the tradition which is of considerable interest in trying to understand features of Insular Gospel books such as the elaborate highlighting of the text at the four Gospel openings and Matt. 1: 18, and the decorative presentation of the listing of names in Christ's genealogy and of numbers in the canon tables. The Insular Gospel books do not illustrate the text literally and do not provide visual aids for teaching doctrine. Their approach reaches a climax in the Book of Kells where certain passages of the text have the decorative density of carpet pages; the words, hidden and rendered almost illegible by the distortion and ornamentation of the letter forms, ambiguous spatial relationships, and multiple outlining, become abstract images. Such veiling and metamorphosis of the text provides some broad visual parallel to the concept that the literal text of Scripture conceals a hidden meaning. But there are also more particular parallels, as the example of the Evangelist symbols may show. The ancient traditions of decoration and stylization on which Insular artists drew, when combined with the rhetorical traditions of the spiritual interpretation of Scripture, were extraordinarily well suited to the creation of powerful iconic and arcane images in a sacred liturgical Gospel book which itself constituted a major image of the Word.

# The authority of Scripture and the symbols of the Evangelists

The Church's defence of the divine inspiration of Scripture had early focused on the existence of four Gospels which, of all the Gospels written, were alone regarded as authoritative. Even the most scholarly attempt to reconcile the manifest differences between the four, Augustine's *On the Harmony of the Gospels*, also made use of *symbolic* demonstrations of their underlying harmony. The four winged creatures who attend the divine throne in Ezekiel's cosmic vision of God's majesty (Ezek. 1: 4–26) are evoked in St John's apocalyptic vision of the four winged beings who worship the Lord enthroned in glory, the Creator of all things (Rev. 4: 6–8). They were interpreted by the Fathers as signs or *figurae* of the four Evangelists, Matthew, Mark, Luke, and John, whose four testimonies form the different facets of a single Gospel. Early exegetes combined this image of the fourfold Gospel with pre-Christian cosmological concepts of a fourfold ordering of all time, space, and matter, which is evident in the four divisions of the day and seasons of the year, the four winds or cardinal directions, the four elements and their properties. The underlying quadriform unity and measure of such cosmic order was seen to reflect the divine wisdom of its Creator. To those who looked with the inner eye, these cosmological and biblical quaternities overwhelmingly demonstrated that divine authority underlay the fourfold form of the Gospel in which Christ was revealed. What at first sight constituted a difficulty, namely the existence of four apparently conflicting Gospels, was therefore read as a sign pointing to a spiritual truth: the four Gospels together comprise the fullness of faith handed down by the apostles to peoples throughout the four corners of the world.

The tradition of defending orthodox belief contained in the Gospel against those who try either to increase or diminish its fourfold nature was profoundly shaped by a series of patristic texts which were used as prefaces in Insular Gospel books and expounded in Hiberno-Latin Gospel commentaries. The first such 'text', the Eusebian canon tables, is composed of lists of numbers, corresponding with numbered sections of each Gospel. The lists are arranged in ten tables to show the sections of text common to all four Gospels, the sections common to three or two Gospels, and, finally, the sections unique to each Gospel. Carl Nordenfalk noted that Eusebius did not compare all possible combinations of the Gospels, but restricted the tables to ten because the ancient world regarded ten, the aggregate of the first four numbers, as a perfect number, containing within itself 'all other numbers, proportions and harmonies'. Like other Christian exegetes, he used this numerological image of cosmic harmony to demonstrate the fulness and harmony of Scripture: when spiritually interpreted, the Decalogue (the ten commandments of the Law, epitomizing the Old Testament) can be seen to contain the fourfold Gospel.

Columbanus alludes to this tradition when he describes the spiritual life as the fulfilling of 'the words of the ten commandments in the Gospel's completeness, which resides in the number four'. The Irish scholar Ailerán (d. 665) wrote a numerological poem on the Gospel canons which visualizes the Evangelists' four symbolic beasts—the man, the lion, the calf, and the eagle—in harmonious discourse. In each of nine cryptic stanzas the creatures in various combinations—first all four, then in threes, then in pairs—tell through riddling clues the number of times they utter the Lord's praises together 'with one voice' in any particular canon table and, in the tenth stanza, how many times each 'speaks' of him alone. The image finds a visual counterpart in the diverse animated groupings of the Evangelist symbols depicted above the canon tables in the Book of Kells.

The Eusebian canon tables act as a visual exegesis in Insular Gospel books, most elaborately of all in Kells, where the cross, the *chi*, the lozenge, and Eucharistic motifs set amidst the rich profusion of Insular ornament serve as further signs of the identity of Christ about to be revealed in the Gospels. The canon tables symbolically proclaim the harmony of the Gospels and the divine authority of the whole of Scripture even when, as in the Book of Durrow and the Lindisfarne Gospels, cross-references written in the margins of the Gospel text render the canon tables superfluous or, as in the Book of Kells, the absence of any marginal numbering of the sections of Gospel text makes the tables unusable. In both Lindisfarne and Kells the Eusebian canon tables form monumental decorative sequences framed beneath architectural arcades, a pictorial convention for marking the entrance to the sacred text which derived from Mediterranean practice (Figs. 4.6 a–b). Most Insular *de luxe* Gospel books, including the Book of

Durrow and probably the now incomplete Book of Kells, also included a copy of Jerome's letter, *Novum Opus*, as a preface. This means that, like the Codex Amiatinus, they contained Jerome's dedication of his revised Gospel text to his papal patron, and his explanation of how the accompanying Eusebian canon tables avoid the serious error of other concordances which fail to take account of the complete Gospel text or to show the diversity as well as the unity of the four Gospels.

In the Lindisfarne Gospels the *Novum Opus* facing the frontispiece cross-carpet page is decorated on the scale of a Gospel *incipit*; it is headed 'Prologue to the ten canons', which themselves span some sixteen pages. The opening of Jerome's introduction to his commentary on Matthew's Gospel was also used as a preface (*Plures fuisse*) in Vulgate Gospel books, including the Lindisfarne Gospels, and was widely quoted by Hiberno-Latin commentators. Jerome affirmed the four canonical Gospels as the measure of orthodoxy, and emphasized both the individual character of each of the Gospels and their authors and their essential harmony. He harmonized the visions from the Old Testament and the New, the creatures of Ezekiel's vision (each of which had the face of a man, a lion, an ox, and an eagle) with the four creatures in the apocalyptic vision (the first like a lion, the second like a calf, the third with the face of a man, and the fourth like a flying eagle). He did not focus on the differences between the two texts' literal descriptions of the beasts, but on what both texts signify. In his commentary on the Book of Ezekiel, Jerome again linked the four creatures to the Evangelists and their Gospel openings, but also related the image of the four Gospels going out over all the earth to various cosmological quaternities—the four elements, seasons, and directions—whose diverse constituents similarly form a unity.

Columbanus told Gregory the Great that he had read the first six books of Jerome's commentary on Ezekiel, and asked the pope to send him a copy of his own recent tracts on the subject. Gregory's homilies, delivered in Rome in 593, reinforce Jerome's pairings of the beasts in Ezekiel's vision with the Evangelists, and the idea that each Gospel, as characterized in its opening lines and by the nature of its appropriate symbolic beast, reveals a particular aspect of Christ's identity: the man signifies Christ's humanity, the lion his kingship, the calf or ox his priesthood, and the eagle his divinity. Gregory's mysterious description of Christ who became a man at his birth, a sacrificial ox in dying, a lion in rising again, and an eagle in ascending

Figure 4.6 (a) The Lindisfarne Gospels, Canon Table I: material common to all four Gospels. London, British Library, Cotton MS Nero D.IV, fo. 11.

to heaven was quoted by Hiberno-Latin commentators, and may have influenced the development of the iconography of the beasts: the magnificent lion in the Echternach Gospels and the ascending eagle in the Cambridge–London Gospels, for example, probably functioned not simply as Evangelist symbols but as Christ-bearing images.

**Figure 4.6** (b) The Book of Kells. Canon Tables VI–VIII. Symbols paired Mtt-Mk, Mtt-Jn, Mk-Lk, Lk-Jn. Dublin, Trinity College MS A.I.6 (58), fo. 5.

The pairing of the Evangelists with their symbols (generally in the order Matthew—man, Mark—lion, Luke—calf or ox, John—eagle) constituted a spiritual interpretation of the Gospel openings. For example, St Matthew has the symbol of a man, because his Gospel opens with the account of Christ's genealogy and Incarnation. St

John alone of the Evangelists was seen to fly straight to Christ's divinity in the opening words of his Gospel, just as the eagle alone of all creatures can fly and gaze unblinkingly on the sun. The ninth-century Irish writer Eriugena was drawing on this ancient exegesis when he described John as a spiritual eagle who, on swiftest wings of high contemplation, transcends all vision and flies beyond what can be thought or spoken; he pictured John entering into the mystery of the Trinity and directly receiving the revelation: 'In the beginning was the Word . . . and the Word was made flesh' (John 1: 1–14).

# Four-symbol pages: the Book of Kells

The individual beasts often appear singly before their appropriate Gospels in Insular Gospel books, and all four symbols are sometimes shown grouped around the Cross either as a frontispiece, as in the Book of Durrow, or before each Gospel, as was probably the case in the Lichfield Gospels and the Book of Kells. In Kells each of the three surviving four-symbol pages shows the four creatures in the angles or at the cardinal points of a cruciform design; but each page is decoratively distinct, enclosing the symbols within four rectangular, circular, or triangular fields. Each page differently adapts the early Christian convention of using a golden cosmological cross to represent the glorified Christ. The scheme may suggest both the harmony of the fourfold Gospel in revealing Christ and the individual character of each Gospel's testimony, which was also displayed in the physical differences of their respective symbolic beasts and epitomized in the magnified and ornamented opening words of each Evangelist which these whole-page images preface. Patristic and Insular exegetes showed that in witnessing to Christ's humanity and divinity, his priesthood and kingship, the four Gospels together constitute a portrait of his identity, and in evoking his incarnation, passion, resurrection, and ascension they represent the whole Gospel story of salvation.

   In the example in the Trier Gospels from the eighth-century Echternach scriptorium, the four beasts of the rare Insular terrestrial type are inscribed with their names from the apocalyptic vision and stand in the four quarters of the design around an interlaced cross whose arms extend to meet the frame (Fig. 4.7 a). The Anglo-Saxon artist clarified the meaning by inserting a portrait-bust of Christ at the centre of the cross and personifications of the winds or directions beyond the four corners, figural features derived from the Mediterranean art of late antiquity. Furthermore, this pictorial frontispiece, which unambiguously presents Christ in a cosmic setting and and at the centre of the fourfold Gospel, directly faces a textual preface, *Plures fuisse*, Jerome's expository text on the Evangelists and their symbols. The cross-symbol pages in Kells have none of these additional clues to their interpretation, but are arguably derived from the same exegetical tradition.

Jerome interpreted the triple *Sanctus* eternally chanted by the four heavenly beasts in the apocalyptic vision, 'Holy, Holy, Holy, Lord God Almighty, who was and who is and who is to come' (Rev. 4: 8), as an image of the four Gospels acclaiming the whole Trinity; it is crucial to his demonstration of the orthodoxy of the fourfold Gospel. The closing vision of the seventh-century Irish hymn *Altus Prosator* draws on such patristic interpretation in describing the praise of the Trinity in the 'eternal threefold exchanges' offered by the four creatures and the heavenly host. In the probably late eighth-century compilation known as the Irish Reference Bible, the fourfold ordering of the world's three continents is interpreted as a figure of the fourfold Gospel and the Trinity to which it testifies. The commentary notes that the Gospels have a single source but each was composed in one of the four parts of the world; in turn, the Gospel, whose characteristics are figured in Scriptural and cosmic quaternities, is taken to the four corners of the world. The commentary shows familiarity with features which were given visual expression in early schematic maps, now known only through Carolingian and later copies, in which the quadrangular world is set cornerwise like a lozenge within a square, with the various cosmic quaternities of time, space, and matter inscribed at the four corners and four cardinal points of the design.

The four-symbols page prefacing St John's Gospel in the Book of Kells suggests the Christian appropriation of such a world view (Fig 4.7 b). The rectangular design is divided into four not by an upright cross but by crossed diagonals with a prominent rhombus at the centre; the four corners and four cardinal points of the frame are also decoratively emphasized. In the context of a Gospel book, the

**Figure 4.7** (a) The Trier Gospels. Four-symbols page facing the preface *Plures fuisse*. Trier, Domschatz, Cod.61, fo. 1v.

quadriform design may be read as depicting a stepped cross which diagonally spans the universe depicted by the frame, with the lozenge at the centre of this *chi*-shaped cross forming a cosmological symbol. There is no portrait-bust or other representation of Christ in human form: there is no attempt to instruct viewers in what they do not already know. For those familiar with the signs and with what the four winged creatures at the cardinal points represent, however, Christ is here symbolically revealed in his fourfold Gospel, as in his

Figure 4.7 (b) The Book of Kells. Four-symbols page prefacing John's Gospel. Dublin, Trinity College MS A.I.6 (58), fo. 290v.

fourfold creation, and those very concepts are renewed. The image immediately precedes a glorious double opening which shows St John in contemplation with pen poised seated in a quadriform design, facing the opening words of his Gospel: 'In the beginning was the Word . . .' Strongly quadripartite cross-carpet pages preface St John's Gospel in the Lindisfarne Gospels and the Augsburg Gospels, and it has been noted that a particular mathematical harmony underlies the measurement and ratios of their design. Like the Kells cross-symbol page, they offer some broad visual parallel to the frequent exegetical linking of St John's opening identification of Christ as the Word, the Creator-Logos 'without whom nothing was made' (John 1: 1–3), and the Old Testament description of the divine Creator who made all things 'in measure, and in number, and in weight' (Wisd. 11: 21).

# The individual Evangelist and symbol: St Luke and the Lichfield Gospels

The Gospel section of the Book of Armagh, *c.*807, develops the experimentation in visual exegesis characteristic of the Insular Gospel books' depiction of the symbols. On the four-symbol page Luke's calf is inscribed *vitulus* (cf. Rev. 4: 7) but is drawn, like the remaining symbolic beasts on the page, with the four wings peculiar to the creatures as described in Ezekiel's vision (Ezek. 1: 6). Their wings just touch (Ezek. 1: 11), or extend into each other's compartment within the quadripartite design (Fig. 4.8). On the page prefacing Luke's Gospel a similar full-length calf is shown alone but with small medallions on its wings depicting the faces of the man, lion, and eagle, which suggests the harmony of Luke with the other three Gospels. The allusion to Ezekiel's vision (where each beast has the faces of all four creatures) again harmonizes the two visions of the beasts in the Old Testament and the New. The Book of Kells folio 27$^v$ shows Luke's symbol as a calf (not an ox, as in Ezek. 1: 10), but with two pairs of wings and small horns, which offers a visual counterpart to Jerome's harmonization in the *Plures fuisse* of the description of this creature in the Old and New Testament visions as *bos* and *vitulus* respectively.

The calf with splayed-out legs and with horned head turned towards the viewer, which appears twice in the Lichfield Gospels and in the Evangelist portrait of Luke in the Lindisfarne Gospels, hints at a significance which is heavily spelt out in a didactic context elsewhere. The mysteries of the Gospel were symbolically handed on in a catechetical ceremony, the *traditio evangeliorum*, to which Bede testifies. It involved reading out the four Gospel *incipits* and expounding the way in which the individual Gospels are epitomized in their

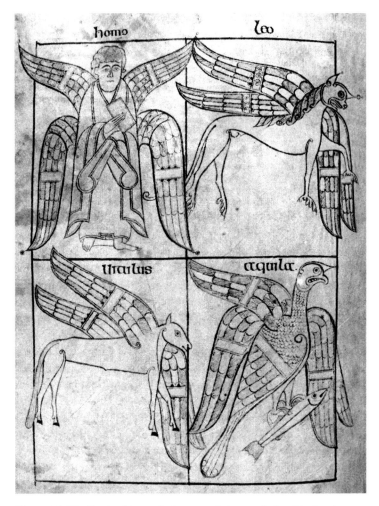

**Figure 4.8** The Book of Armagh. Four-symbols page facing Matthew's Gospel. Dublin, Trinity College MS 52, fo. 32v.

opening words and related to their respective Evangelist symbols. The text of the ceremony in Gallican sacramentaries, including the Bobbio Missal, describes Luke's symbol as *vitulus* and explicitly identifies its two horns with the Old and New Testaments and its four hoofs with the four Gospels; in the late eighth-century Frankish Gellone Sacramentary the initial letter of Luke's name in this text is formed from the disembodied horned head and legs of a calf, and points like a bizarre *nota bene* sign to the relevant passage.

Another kind of contrast to the Insular Gospel books is offered by the St Augustine Gospels, a sixth-century Italian uncial book brought to Anglo-Saxon England early, possibly with the Gregorian mission. Facing the chastely unadorned opening page of St Luke's Gospel, the Evangelist is pictured like a classical philosopher, enthroned in an elaborate Roman architectural setting with lapidary inscription, and with a half-length figure of a winged ox in the arch above him. Luke is flanked by twelve tiny scenes unique to his Gospel, beginning with Zachariah at the altar.

The visual language of the Insular Gospel books is very different from both of these Continental manuscripts. In the Lichfield Gospels a drum roll of decoration in the form of a portrait page, a four-symbol page, and then a cross-carpet page announces the framed and ornamented *incipit* of Luke's Gospel, pp. 218–21. The first of the three prefatory pages presents the Lucan symbol of the full-length horned calf, its body arched over the haloed head of a figure who holds two crossed rods or staffs like sceptres (Fig. 6.1). There is only the barest outline of a throne framing the figure. The stylized image, composed of two-dimensional abstract shapes of patterned symmetry, is a radical departure from the norms of Mediterranean figural art. The antique convention of the author portrait has here been transformed to show, not a scribe at work or an earthly author inspired by his muse, but an evocation of the aspect of Christ's identity particularly revealed in Luke's Gospel, which exegetes saw figured in Luke's symbolic calf and epitomized in the first event the Gospel describes. The opening scene in Luke's Gospel introduces the incarnation of Christ by describing Zachariah, the last of the priests of Aaron's line, making an offering at the altar in the temple. From the time of Origen commentators had noted that, read in the light of the Epistle to the Hebrews (chapters 5, 7–10), this scene in Luke prefigures Christ's role as both the new High Priest and the new sacrifice, which superseded the Aaronic priesthood and its blood offerings. Luke's symbol, a sacrificial calf, alludes to this sacerdotal mystery.

Patristic and Insular exegetes interpreted the miraculous budding of Aaron's dry rod, by which he had been designated the first High Priest (Num. 17: 8), as a further image of Christ, and specifically a prefiguring of the Cross which at the Crucifixion was revealed to

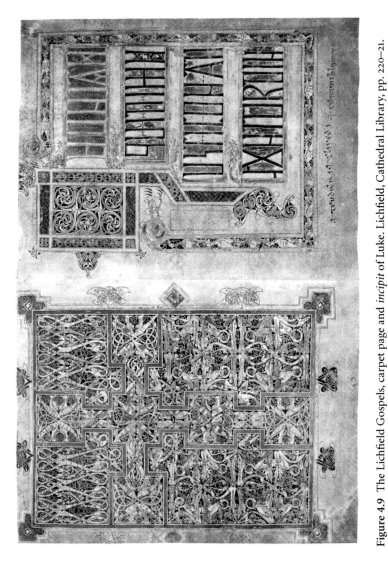

Figure 4.9 The Lichfield Gospels, carpet page and *incipit* of Luke. Lichfield, Cathedral Library, pp. 220–21.

be the Tree of Life. This linking had been given pictorial expression in the canon tables of the sixth-century Syriac Rabbula Gospels, which carry an elaborate cycle of Old and New Testament scenes depicting the harmonized reading of the fourfold Gospel as the fulfilment of the Law. The Lucan scene of Zachariah at the altar is here directly paired with the figure of the High Priest, Aaron, who is holding his budding rod and has the sign of the Cross already delineated in the twelve stones of his priestly breastplate. The Lichfield Gospels image alludes to the same traditional understanding of Luke's presentation of Christ's priestly and sacrificial identity, and to the harmony of the Old Testament and the New, but in a more abstract idiom. The enthroned Lichfield figure ceremonially displays a budding green rod which branches in the shape of a crosier; the other rod flowers in the form of the Cross. Their crossed stems form a prominent *chi* across his breast. His haloed head is framed within the large lozenge shape formed by the rods, and by the wings and splayed legs of the symbol of the calf above.

This hieratic figure positioned at the outer entrance to Luke's Gospel text communicates a sense of the numinous and visually epitomizes the testimony of Luke's Gospel regarding Christ's priesthood and Passion. The four-symbol page which now follows on p. 219 has the function of setting Luke's distinctive testimony within the harmony of the fourfold Gospel. All four winged creatures are shown 'full of eyes' (Ezek 1: 18, Rev. 4: 8) and Luke's symbol is again depicted as a horned calf, which in this context may have been read as alluding to the harmony of the Old Testament and the New. In the cross-carpet page which follows on p. 220 the sign of the Cross, denoting the glorified Christ, is conspicuously revealed in the dominant outlined image of the Cross which spans the page (Fig. 4.9). It is also concealed in the profusion of ornament, made up of the interlaced bodies of birds and quadrupeds, outside that outline; the page offers a visual analogy to the exegetical concept that the identity of Christ is both proclaimed by and hidden within the literal text of Scripture. On the facing page the opening words of Luke's Gospel are framed, magnified, and decoratively distorted, which does not facilitate their literal reading but presents the words as angular, rune-like signs of the mystery they enshrine. If such a four-page decorative sequence as survives for Luke originally announced all four Gospels in the manuscript, and if its now missing prefatory texts and canon tables were decorated on the same scale, the Lichfield Gospels would indeed have been a very splendid book. Concepts from the Mediterranean world of late antiquity have here been so assimilated to an Insular visual tradition as to be almost unrecognizable to the casual eye.

## The Crucifixion in the Durham Gospels: an image of orthodoxy

In the earliest extant fragment of an Insular illuminated manuscript (Durham A.II.10), the final verses of Matthew's Gospel (Matt. 28: 16–20) are written in an ornate minuscule script, different from the majuscule script used for the rest of the Gospel. In the Lichfield Gospels the last two verses of Matthew are centred and occupy a whole page which is decoratively framed. It is obviously difficult to interpret the meaning of these and other examples beyond saying that the passage seems to have been important. In the Durham Gospels, however, there are clues to suggest how it may have been read there. On folio 38 the text of Matt. 28: 17–20 is isolated and arranged to fit within a cruciform decorated frame, exactly corresponding in outline with the framed Crucifixion scene on the verso, indicating that text and image may be related (Figs. 4.10–11).

Christ is shown alive, wearing a long robe and with his arms extended on the Cross in a priestly gesture of prayer. This visualization is ultimately derived from Crucifixion images of the kind surviving in the Rabbula Gospels, icons from Sinai, and Byzantine-influenced works in Rome; but here, stripped of narrative detail and spatial depth, it has been dramatically transformed into a linear design of abstract shapes on the same plane as the frame. The two human figures of the spear-bearer and sponge-bearer below the horizontal bar of the Cross, and the two angelic beings above it, symmetrically flank the central axis. The cross-bar is abnormally low so that the four terminals of the cross suggest the four cardinal directions of its reach. The Cross and the body of Christ span earth and heaven.

The image puts into arresting visual terms a common patristic linking of St John's account of the Crucifixion and of Christ's Second

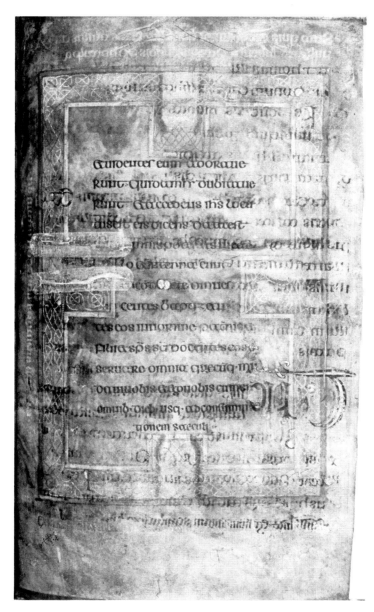

**Figure 4.10** The Durham Gospels. Framed text of Matt. 28: 17–20. Durham, Cathedral Library MS A.II.17, fo. 38r.

Coming in judgement at the end of time. St John describes the wounding of Christ as a fulfilment of the prophecy, 'They shall look on him whom they pierced' (John 19: 37; Zach. 12: 10). He specifies that Christ's side was pierced only after his death, yet the Durham picture shows Christ both wounded and alive, a pictorial device for conveying John's spiritual interpretation of the Crucifixion as the triumph over death. The identifying *titulus* written on the cross above Christ's head simply says: 'This is Jesus, the king of the Jews.' The wording is from Matt. 27: 37, which does not have the detail of the three languages of the title-board. Its meaning is infinitely extended, however, for the reader who sees that the *titulus* is here flanked by two additional letters, *alpha* and *omega*, the first and last letters of the Greek alphabet, (looking like A and W), and by the words *initium et finis* ('the beginning and the end'). These additions allude to the apocalyptic vision of the Lord at his Second Coming, 'when every eye shall see him, even those who pierced him'. Though recognizably the same person who was pierced, he appears in the vision 'clothed with a garment down to the foot', is adored by the angelic host, and proclaims his eternal divinity with the words: 'I am Alpha and Omega, the beginning and the end, which is, and was, and which is to come, the Almighty' (Rev. 1: 7–8, 13; cf. John 19: 37). The Durham Gospels' image simultaneously presents Christ crucified and exalted in glory. It is a powerful devotional icon in which Christ's gaze draws the present beholder to 'look upon him who was pierced' and recognize his true identity now. The image also speaks by means of inscriptions surrounding the frame. The epigrammatic upper text, for those who can puzzle it out, further discloses Christ's twofold nature.

The picture is clearly not a literal or didactic illustration of the end of Matthew's Gospel text highlighted on the recto, which culminates in Christ's final command to his disciples to go and 'teach all peoples, baptising them in the name of the Father and of the Son and of the Holy Spirit, teaching them to observe all things whatsoever I have commanded you. And behold, I am with you always, even to the end of the world' (Matt. 28: 19–20). Rather, the Crucifixion picture of Christ as both human and divine, Saviour and Judge, distils the very essence of the Gospel which is taken to all peoples. Christ's words in Matthew's text include a Trinitarian baptismal formula, which therefore appears in baptismal liturgies. Because it implicitly proclaims Christ's divinity, it was also important in exegesis and early councils.

**Figure 4.11** The Durham Gospels. The Crucifixion. Durham, Cathedral Library MS A.II.17, fo. 38v.

The Council of Chalcedon (451), in acknowledging Pope Leo the Great's important articulation of orthodox belief in the humanity and divinity of Christ (which was cited by seventh-century popes and councils), characterized Leo as preserving those final instructions of Christ to his disciples to teach and baptize all peoples, 'teaching them to observe all things whatsoever I have commanded you'.

The Durham image affirms orthodox belief but also points to its spiritual implications. Patristic and Insular commentators interpreted the piercing of Christ's side and the issue of water and blood, uniquely described in John 19: 34, as the opening of the source of the sacraments of baptism and the Eucharist, through which Christ sustains the faithful until he comes again. Bede describes how the resurrected Christ had assured his disciples 'that by his hidden presence he would fulfil what he had promised: "Behold, I am with you always, even to the end of the world" [Matt. 28: 20]'. Bede adds, 'For after we have been buried in death with Christ through baptism [Rom. 6: 4] . . . it is necessary for us, in this wilderness [i.e. in this earthly life], to have the Lord's guidance. May he lead us to the heavenly kingdom.'

The inscription around the sides and lower edge of the picture is in the first person plural. It describes how Christ, overcoming the author of death, 'renews our life if we suffer along with him'; it recalls how 'He rose from the dead and sits at the right hand of God the Father, so that when we have been restored to life, we may reign with him'. This evokes a chain of Pauline texts, including the fundamental concept of baptism as a sharing in Christ's death in order to share in his risen glory (Rom. 6: 3–4). The inscribed image prompts meditation not simply on the historical moment of baptism but on the continuing process of inner conversion and repentance begun at baptism, the daily crucifixion or dying to the world which is a central theme in the works of Cassian and in other literature of the monastic life. The Prologue to the Rule of St Benedict addresses those mindful of the coming Judgement and desirous of the heavenly life : 'faithfully observing his teaching in the monastery until death, we shall through patience share in the sufferings of Christ that we may also share in his kingdom.' Columbanus repeatedly exhorted his monks and others to have perseverance 'up to the end' and to become sharers in Christ's passion: 'if we suffer together with him, together we shall reign' (2 Tim. 2: 12; Rom. 8: 17).

Like the inscriptions of the Durham Crucifixion, Columbanus' spiritual counsel to follow the example of the crucified Christ is combined with an explicit declaration of doctrinal orthodoxy on the twofold nature of Christ revealed in the mystery of the Cross, as that had been repeatedly expounded by Leo the Great and affirmed by Gregory the Great. Leo had preached that the Cross of Christ set up for human salvation was both a mystery or *sacramentum* 'whereby the divine power takes effect' and an *exemplum* stirring devotion. The power to follow the cross by *imitatio* was supplied by Christ's continuing hidden presence with the faithful:

If we unhesitatingly believe with the heart what we profess with the mouth, in Christ we are crucified, we are dead, we are buried, on the third day we too are raised. Hence the Apostle says, 'If you are risen with Christ, seek those things which are above, where Christ is, sitting on God's right hand . . .' [Col. 3: 1–4]. In order that the faithful may know that they have the means whereby to spurn the lusts of the world and be lifted to the wisdom that is above, the Lord promises us his presence, saying, 'Behold, I am with you always, even till the end of the world' [Matt. 28: 20].

Inscriptions, *tituli*, epigraphs, and the interpenetration of text and image have been a frequent feature of Insular works of art discussed here. The placing of the inscriptions around the Durham Gospels' Crucifixion picture adapts the classical rhetorical device of *ekphrasis*; the texts do not provide a literal description of the visual image but direct the viewer's reading of it and imprint its significance on the mind's eye by eliciting a response. It is an early and particularly elaborate example of a practice sometimes seen on Byzantine icons and the Roman works they influenced; the Durham Crucifixion's inscriptions are not, however, in Roman capitals or the uncial emulated in the Codex Amiatinus and Wilfrid's Gospel book, but in Insular majuscule.

The image of the Durham Gospels, without its inscriptions, became the characteristic form of the Irish iconography of the Crucifixion in vellum, metalwork, and stone. It went through a further process of reduction, for example on the eighth-century Athlone gilt-bronze plaque, where Christ's priestly robe and the wings of the cherubim are covered with Celtic spiral ornament, interlace, and fret patterns, and the *titulus* of the Cross is replaced by three interlinked spirals (Fig. 4.12). For a viewer unaware of St John's account of the opening of Christ's side or its traditional exegesis there is nothing in the image which will provide that information. The Durham Gospels'

**Figure 4.12** Athlone Crucifixion Plaque. National Museum of Ireland.

Crucifixion looks very different from works which display *Romanitas* in their script and style; however, through its iconography, inscriptions, and juxtaposed text it demonstrates concern with central issues of Christological orthodoxy which were defined and defended in the series of ecumenical councils and in the Lateran council attested at the Council of Hatfield. The text from Matthew which the Crucifixion picture highlights was quoted by Insular writers not only to show that the Gospel in reaching the islands at the ends of the earth had truly been preached to all peoples, but that they had received the same faith Christ had handed down through his apostles and their spiritual descendants throughout the ages.

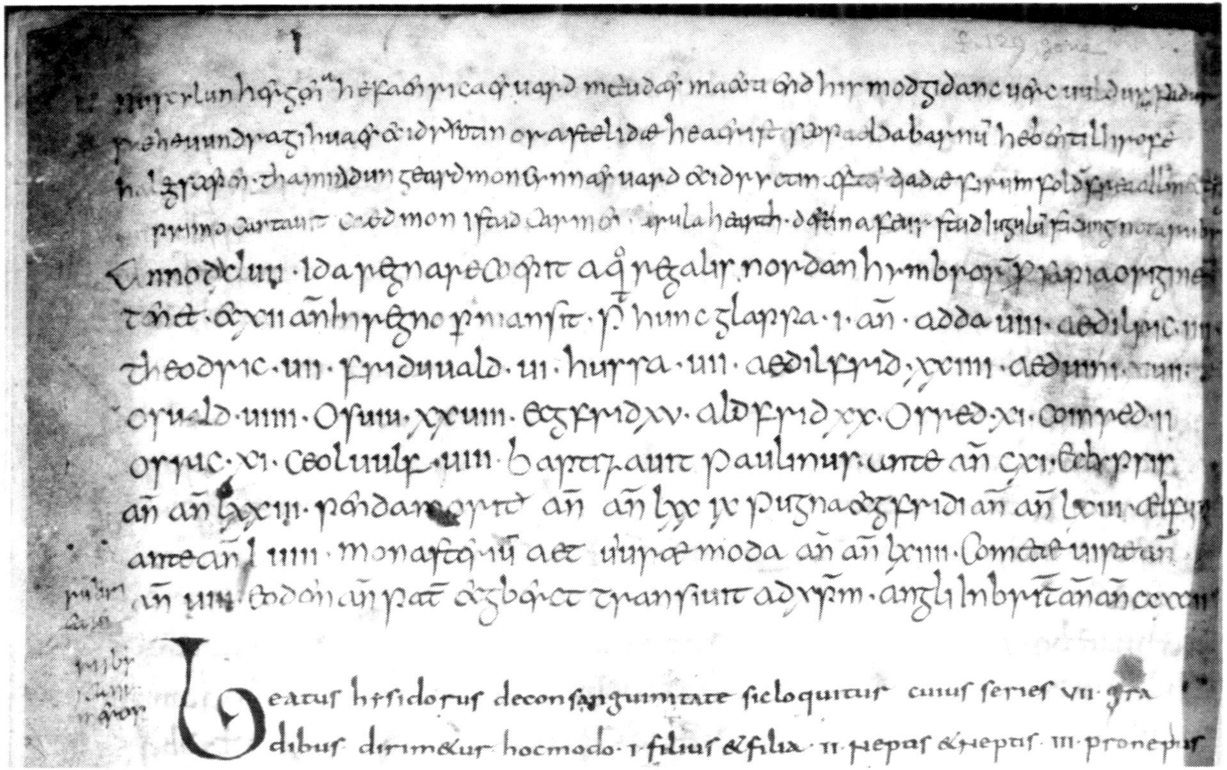

Figure 5.1 Moore MS of Bede.

# Latin and the vernacular languages: the creation of a bilingual textual culture

Andy Orchard

The period between the time that the Romans left and the continuing conflicts against the Vikings around 900 proved one of the most fertile and productive in literary and linguistic terms that the British Isles have ever known. A complex nexus of competing influences inspired a rich and fruitful cultural exchange that the repeated introduction of Latin letters and Christian ideas only served to stimulate further; and the shock waves started by the successive importation of literacy and Latin book learning were still being felt as the ninth century drew to a close. Bede, writing in 731, famously characterized contemporary mainland Britain as an island of five languages, 'according to the number of books of Divine Law'. But if Bede's appeal to the sacred parallel of the Pentateuch is wholly in keeping with his pious perspectives, and if the language of the Picts is for us still more of a mystery than it must have seemed even to Bede, his inclusion of the tongues of the Britons (we should now say Welsh), the English, and the Irish (we should now include all the Gaelic languages) still rings true today. To Bede, writing in Latin, it is the sad demise in the British Isles of his last-named language, Latin, 'which through study of the Scriptures is made common to all', that would surely have seemed the most shocking and least likely outcome of the intervening centuries.

Certainly, the influence of Latin, and in particular of the Latin alphabet, can be detected even in the earliest written sources from the British Isles. As with the runic alphabet, it seems likely that the creation of ogham letters (which, like runic letters, exhibit predominantly straight strokes well suited to inscription on wood or stone) was a response to the Latin alphabet, in this case by one or more persons bilingual in Latin and Irish. Such an argument is wholly consistent with the large numbers of material finds from the Roman Empire (most likely via Roman Britain) in central eastern Ireland, which although formally never part of that Empire nonetheless could not escape its considerable influence. The ogham alphabet was used for writing Irish and Pictish from at least the fifth century on; inscriptions are particularly common in Ireland and south Wales. There are only thirty-nine inscriptions all told surviving from Pictland (which is to say that area of Scotland under Pictish control in the seventh, eighth, and early ninth centuries), and eight of these are solely in the Roman alphabet: mostly these are in Latin, with a scattering of Pictish names and titles. Two monuments (at Dupplin and Newton) combine the runic and ogham alphabets, and the remainder solely exhibit ogham. In Wales (but not in Ireland) bilingual inscriptions carrying texts both in Irish in ogham and in Latin in Roman letters are also found. Such monuments seem to bear witness to the status of the vernacular in these areas, as well as to the considerable cultural interchange across the Irish Sea. Though part of the ogham corpus is apparently pre-Christian, assuredly not all of it is so: ogham forms for 'abbot', 'bishop', and 'priest' are recorded, and serve as a reminder of the extent to which literacy and Christianity went hand-in-hand. An early cross-slab, from Papil, Shetland, depicts figures carrying book satchels, and (again, like runes) ogham was not restricted to its epigraphic functions, appearing in manuscripts from an early date. As in the case of the runic letters added to the Latin alphabet in

Anglo-Saxon England, the 'original' twenty letters of the ogham alphabet were successively augmented by 'additional letters' (*forfeda*), representing native sounds not catered for in other ways; it has rightly been noted that these *forfeda* have a distinctly bookish quality about them, and are indeed far easier to write than to carve.

Like ogham, the angular form of the earliest runic alphabets appears to have been originally designed to be carved on wood, in its avoidance of curved or even horizontal strokes that might get lost in the grain. Runes were used up until the ninth century (and beyond) by a variety of peoples: by a host of Germanic tribes on the Continent (the so-called *Germani*), by the Goths, the Frisians, and the Scandinavians, as well as the Anglo-Saxons. Certainly, the runic alphabet came to the British Isles from Continental Europe, and probably originated in an area where Germanic peoples had contact with the Roman Empire, since several runes (one need think only of ⟨f⟩ [ᚠ], ⟨r⟩ [ᚱ], and ⟨b⟩ [ᛒ], for example) have forms very similar to their Latin equivalents. The earliest surviving runic inscription from the British Isles is found on the ankle-bone of a roe deer from Caistor-by-Norwich (presumably used as a gaming piece), dated to the fourth or fifth century. The inscription itself, **raïhan** ('from a roe deer'), may seem superfluous and baffling to modern eyes, but then so are a number of other runic inscriptions (one might compare the assertion on the so-called 'Brandon antler' inscription, datable no more closely than some time between the seventh to ninth centuries, that it 'grew on a wild animal'); it hardly seems necessary (or indeed desirable) always to attribute such enigmatic texts to the realms of magic or cultic practice, since the primary value of runes as a practical writing system in the days before widespread use of the Roman alphabet seems paramount.

During the pagan period of Anglo-Saxon England (up until about the mid-seventh-century), runes are found widely scattered throughout the south and south-east, East Anglia, and the east Midlands; across the country, some early coins from this period also bear runic inscriptions. Although after this time runes are recorded in the southeast and east Midlands, such finds are sporadic; by contrast, runic inscriptions apparently flourished in the north and north Midlands in Christian times. The further use of runes in manuscripts for a variety of purposes (whether indicating a sound, a rune name, or being used as an extension of or alternative to the Roman alphabet) should again highlight the fact that runes are far from restricted to the pre-Christian past; indeed, it has been argued that the particular form of runic alphabet found in Anglo-Saxon England from the mid-seventh century on was directly influenced by the developing Roman-based scripts used to write both Latin and the vernacular, and that rather than the gradual evolution of different letter forms, we should think instead of a conscious reform of the runic alphabet in Anglo-Saxon England. Certainly, runic letters were themselves incorporated into the Roman alphabet to represent certain characteristically Anglo-Saxon sounds, notably 'thorn' ⟨þ⟩ (which rendered the 'th'-sound in its various forms) and 'wyn' ⟨ƿ⟩ (which represented the 'w'-sound); such innovations need to be set against other attempts to render these and other sounds by variant versions of Latin letters, including using a 'crossed d' or 'eth' ⟨ð⟩ to represent the 'th'-sound, using 'u' or 'uu' for the 'w'-sound, and using a combined form of ⟨a⟩ and ⟨e⟩ called 'ash' ⟨æ⟩ to represent a vowel that fell between these two sounds. Occasionally, one even finds Latin inscriptions written in runes, or bilingual inscriptions in both Latin and the vernacular: a number of the most famous artefacts from the period (such as the Franks Casket and the Ruthwell Cross (see Fig. 4.2), both apparently dating from the seventh century) are of just this type.

# Latin and the vernacular in sub-Roman Britain and early Wales

To the legions leaving mainland Britain for the last time to shore up a crumbling Continental empire, the loss of Latin in the British Isles might well have seemed inevitable, but for the relics of empire left on those shores in sub-Roman Britain, the late imperial education system evidently soldiered on for some time. The widespread three-tiered pattern of instruction common throughout the Continent was firmly established in Roman Britain, with students first learning the rudiments of language with a 'teacher' (*magister*) before passing on successively to a 'grammarian' (*grammaticus*) to gain a basic acquaintance with the best Latin authors (especially Virgil), and (for the chosen few) finally to a 'teacher of rhetoric' (*rhetor*) to learn the polished principles of public speaking and debate. The same system can be inferred to have been experienced (at least in part) by (for example) Gildas, Patrick, and Columbanus, as we shall see. The passion for Latin in the British Isles is attested early: in the first century Tacitus notes that in Britain 'those who once spurned the Latin language craved eloquence', and Martial boasts of a British readership for his poems, while early in the second century the poet Juvenal notes that 'eloquent Gaul has taught the Britons to be advocates', and Plutarch mentions that one Demetrius, a Greek *rhetor*, was successfully plying his trade in Britain. In this context it is perhaps unsurprising that among the examples of writing surviving from mid-fourth-century Britain are an inscription quoting Virgil in a matter-of-fact manner and a letter inscribed in lead by one Vinisius, describing someone with the British name 'Bilcunus' (which would mean 'good dog' or some such) as a 'dog of Arius' (*canem Arii*), so providing the earliest attested bilingual pun from Britain.

There also survive appreciable numbers of Latin inscriptions from the earliest period that bear witness to the high levels of Latin literacy to be found on mainland Britain at the time. Indeed, the Latin education available in sub-Roman Britain seems to have equipped several to shine on a wider stage: Faustus (who died in 490) went on to become bishop of Riez and write a handful of surviving theological tracts ('On grace', 'On the Holy Spirit', 'On the reason for faith'), as well as a small number of letters, while more (in)famously Pelagius (*c.*350–*c.*430) received at once the signal compliment of being singled out for his linguistic talents by Jerome (the translator of the Latin Vulgate Bible) as a 'most Latinate man' and of being reviled for his theological views as a 'beefy dog . . . weighed down by Gaelic porridge' by the same Jerome. Pelagius was condemned as a heretic in 418 for his views on the subject of free will (though they would not perhaps seem so offensive today), but his other writings, notably an elegant, thoughtful, and (above all) beautifully written commentary on the Pauline Epistles, show that, at least as far as his British background and education were concerned, it was Jerome's first assessment which is the most just.

While on his own admission Patrick (whose precise dates within the fifth century are still a matter of hot debate) missed out on the higher levels of rhetorical training available in sub-Roman Britain (he was, after all, abducted by Irish pirates at an early age), his surviving writings are nonetheless steeped in a deep and ready knowledge of the Bible, as well as being imbued with a subtle (and likely biblically inspired) artistry that can seem no less effective than the polysyllabic tub-thumping of more highly trained authors. Throughout his works, especially in his so-called 'Confession' (*Confessio*), Patrick wears his 'rustic' language (the term is his) almost as a badge of pride; but his evident skill as a wielder of words surely points up the contemporary premium on the power of the written (and spoken) word.

Not every educated Briton, however, was forced to leave home (one way or another) to make his literary mark: perhaps the most celebrated of the stay-at-home scholars was Gildas, principally known for his extraordinarily stylized and sustained invective against a range of targets including no fewer than five sub-Roman-British princes, the so-called *De excidio Britanniae* ('On the destruction of Britain'), composed around the middle of the sixth century. In this work, which bears all the marks of wide reading and a sophisticated Latin rhetorical training, Gildas (who notably refers to Latin as 'our language' [*lingua nostra*]) rails against the vices of certain sections of the aristocracy, and grimly attributes the invasion of the foreign pagan hordes to their louche living and lascivious ways. In the fifth and sixth centuries the pagans were Saxons, who soon swarmed over what was to be England; but it is ironic to note that the descendants of these same Saxon invaders, suitably converted, would themselves invoke the name and reasoning of Gildas in the face of their own infidel attackers, as Alcuin did in the late eighth century (when it was the Vikings) and Wulfstan in the early eleventh (when it was the Vikings again).

After Gildas, and likely as a direct result of the Saxon invasion, British Latin is largely silent. A brief and skilful Latin prayer by one Moucan (whose name betrays his Welsh origins) preserved in the mid-eighth century in the so-called Book of Cerne is almost the only text that can be ascribed with confidence to a named author from Wales until the time of Asser, bishop of St David's and Sherbourne, who in 893 composed his great biography of Alfred the Great (*De rebus gestis Ælfredi regis*). That the authenticity of the work has recently been called into question partly on stylistic grounds is itself a (misdirected) testimony to its literary sophistication, which not only includes combines reminiscences from well-known classroom authors such as Aldhelm and Caelius Sedulius but even includes a quotation in praise of Alfred first penned to commend the Emperor Justin by the little-known sixth-century North African poet Corippus. It is worth noting that Asser cites the Bible in the so-called Old Latin version, which had been largely superseded in the West by Jerome's Vulgate. The Old Latin was the version used by (for example) Pelagius and Gildas, and Asser's continued use of it into the late ninth century, offers striking testimony to the essential conservatism of the British Church.

Although the transplantation of Breton and the Bretons to Armorica highlighted the ways in which language now divided the inhabitants of Britain from those of Gaul, it is worth noting that Brittany bears witness to a similarly broken stream of Latin writings during the same period. The earliest of these pre-dates Gildas (it can be placed between the years 509 and 521), and comprises a brief but fascinating letter to two clerics bearing Breton names, Lovocat and Catihern, from three Romano-Gaulish bishops, Licinius of Angers, Melanius of Rennes, and Eustochius of Tours. Evidently the Bretons in question were part of the wave that fled Britain as the Saxons arrived, and the fact that the bishops felt obliged to chastise the newcomers for their practices (including apparently assigning prominent roles to women during the Mass) may reflect at least some aspects of the parent British Church. As in mainland Britain, there follows a gap in the written record of Latin until the ninth century, when a constellation of named (and unnamed) Bretons were producing (mostly hagiographical) Latin works. Among the more celebrated Breton Latin writers whose work has survived were Clemens of Landévennec, Bili, Ratuili, Wrdisten of Landevenec, Wrmonoc, and Lios Monocus.

But if the roster of named British-, Breton-, and Cambro-Latin authors in the years before 900 is distinctly short, there also survive several important anonymous texts from the ninth century which demonstrate that Latin learning was still alive, if not exactly thriving, perhaps the most important of which is the so-called 'History of the Britons' (*Historia Brittonum*), the earliest recension of which has been dated to 829/30. Other scattered Latin texts in both prose and verse surviving in two ninth-century manuscripts, the so-called *Liber Commonei* (Oxford, Bodleian Library, Auct. F.4.32) and the 'Cambridge Juvencus Manuscript' (Cambridge, University Library,

Ff.4.42), add to the picture, which can be sketched out still further by a charming (probably ninth-century) text, 'Concerning strange tales' (*De raris fabulis*), which was evidently used to teach Latin. In this curious text, which has obviously been added to over the years, we follow a young monk through his daily routine, acquiring lots of useful Latin words and phrases along the way, and again stressing the importance of the Latin language in the British Isles at this period.

Accounts of early Welsh literature have usually begun with Gildas, not simply since he seems to have been a speaker of the vernacular (to judge from his bilingual puns), but also because he seems to give a description of bardic praise poets in his withering attack on the hapless King Maelgwn (Maglocunus) of Gwynedd:

> when your ears' attention is caught it is not God's praises in the sweetly modulating singing-voice of Christ's apprentices that are heard, or the music of ecclesiastical melody, but rather your own, which are nothing, in the mouths of grasping barkers stuffed with lies and likely to spatter anyone at hand with foaming spit, grinding away like those possessed.

Given that Maelgwn himself was evidently a highly educated man (Gildas tells us that he was the student of a 'polished teacher' (*magister elegans*)), it is not, perhaps, beyond question that the panegyrics Maelgwn was wont to hear were (at least in part) addressed to him in Latin: a later tale of the tenth or eleventh century records that he was surrounded by bards proficient in many languages, although it is in Welsh that the great bard Taliesin utterly silenced them with his skill. Taliesin himself is the Welsh poet *par excellence* to whom poems attached themselves and about whom legends grew. It is, then, sobering to recall that Taliesin appears only third in a famous passage in the *Historia Brittonum*, where the author names the famous poets of almost three centuries before: 'At that time Talhaern, "father of inspiration" [*tat aguen*], was famed in poetry; and Neirin, and Taliessin, and Bluchbard, and Cian, who is called the "sheaf of song" [*guenith guaut*] together at the same time were famed in British poetry.' Of these illustrious names, only Aneirin (given here as Neirin) and Taliesin are now much more than that; but it must not be forgotten that the *Historia Brittonum* itself is not so much history as pseudo-history, and its assertions need to be treated as such.

Nonetheless, the earliest candidates for inclusion in a list of early Welsh poetry are: those separate elegies on dead warriors that make up the *Gododdin*, attributed to Aneirin, together with their associated 'lays' (*gwarchaneu*); a (select) number of panegyrics attached to the name of Taliesin; a praise-poem for Cadwallon of Gwynedd (who died in 634); an elegy on the seventh-century prince Cynddylan; and a fragment of a poem on the battle of Strathcarron (which occurred in 642). All of these poems, however, survive only through their preservation in much later (thirteenth- and fourteenth-century) manuscripts; and while the older view that such poems enjoyed a lengthy oral transmission seems unlikely for a range of reasons, evidence for earlier manuscripts containing verse remains elusive: in a (ninth- or perhaps tenth-century) poem in praise of Tenby (*Edmic Dinbych*), the poet describes how 'the writings of Britain were the chief object of care' (*yscriuen brydein bryder briffwn*), but contemporary care seems not to have ensured ultimate survival. The present state of preservation of some of these poems, especially certain of the individual elegies that make up the *Gododdin* which are found in vastly different variant versions within the same manuscript, certainly seem to attest to a long and complex transmission history that may well have included both oral and written stages. The widely circulated notion that no Welsh text was written down before the ninth century now seems (to some, at least) unnecessarily pessimistic, despite the absence of direct manuscript evidence before that date: some at least of the evident copying errors in the later manuscripts seem to suggest, both in terms of language and orthography, a lengthy written transmission.

Apparently dating from a later period than the *Gododdin*, there also survives a haunting series of elegiac verses attached to the names of Llywarch Hen and Heledd. Although in each case the poems focus on figures and events from the late sixth century, the poems themselves are generally held to date from the mid-ninth century. A case has been made that these verses are the residue of fully-fledged sagas combining both prose and verse, such as are found commonly in Irish and (much later) Norse, and certainly they seem to scream out for some contextualizing comment. All of these verses from the earliest period are notable for their frequent use of decorative devices such as alliteration, rhyme, assonance, and verbal repetition, which are used not only within lines but also to link lines and stanzas together. In part, such devices may have served a mnemonic function (and so perhaps have helped in the poems' preservation), but there can be little doubt that they are mostly intended as aural ornamentation, underlining the fact that these are poems primarily aimed at the ear, rather than the eye. By contrast with the comparative wealth of early Welsh poetry, prose is all but absent in this period, bar a few brief and fragmentary texts and glosses, where Welsh survives essentially as a direct result of its transmission alongside Latin. The first inscription in Welsh (at Tywyn) can be dated around the turn of the ninth century, and is decidedly unusual at this early date: rather than the standard epigraphic alphabet, it uses half-uncial forms close to those found in contemporary manuscripts.

The earliest datable Welsh manuscript is the so-called *Liber Commonei*, which can be dated to the year 817 or soon after. To the same period can be dated a marginal note recording the purchase of the so-called Lichfield Gospels (Lichfield Cathedral MS 1) by one *Gelhi filius Arihtiud*. Important in this context are the Welsh poems (comprising nine religious and three secular stanzas (*englynion*) preserved as marginalia in a manuscript of the Latin works of the fourth-century Spanish poet Juvencus that was apparently written in ninth-century Wales by a scribe with a clearly Irish name (Núadu). The manuscript is heavily glossed in Latin, Irish, and Welsh, by a number of hands, so testifying to the importance of Juvencus as a much-studied school text in the British Isles. Some of the Welsh glosses were written by the same hands that wrote Irish glosses; the fact that the former are sometimes bungled seems to argue for itinerant Irish scribes working in Welsh monasteries, copying misunderstood Welsh glosses into the manuscript and adding Irish ones of their own. Even the celebrated *englynion*, so prized by scholars of Welsh literature, contain what look like copying errors, and the same scribe also wrote a marginal poem in Latin hexameters concerning one Féthgna, perhaps to be identified with Bishop Féthgna of Armagh (who died in 872): the very fact that the oldest Welsh poetry in a (?near-)contemporary hand was written in a Latin manuscript, perhaps by an Irishman of the late ninth or early tenth century, bears potent witness to the fruitful cultural exchange not only between Latin and vernaculars, but also between vernaculars in the British Isles before 900.

# Latin and the vernacular in early Ireland and Scotland

By contrast with the great gap in the Latin written record in Britain after Gildas, Hiberno-Latin literature, the Latin of Ireland, explodes into view, fully formed, by the seventh century. Early inscriptions and other kinds of text (such as the so-called Springmount Bog tablets of around 600, which bear the traces of copied Latin psalms) bear witness to the fact that Latin was being written in Ireland before that time, while the poems and letters written in Latin by Irishmen abroad at each end of the seventh century surely testify at some level to the high standards of education they must have enjoyed before leaving home. While it is impossible to be sure how much of their learning was acquired on the Continent, the works of such skilled and sensitive Latin writers as Columbanus of Luxeuil and Bobbio (who died in 615) and Cellanus of Péronne (who died in 706) certainly betray a comfortable and confident command of literary Latin that was likely learned over a considerable period. From Ireland itself during the seventh century there survives a wealth of beautifully written and highly competent Latin writings in a variety of styles and genres. There are notable contributions in theology by (for example) Cummian (whose letter on the Easter controversy can be dated between 632 and 635), the 'Irish Augustine' (whose marvellous work 'On the marvels of sacred Scripture' (*De mirabilibus sacrae scripturae*) can be dated precisely to the year 655), and Ailerán Sapiens (who died in 665 and wrote a treatise on the ancestors of Christ). A large number of other anonymous Irishmen contributed to this seventh-century wave of exegetical activity, including the authors of the tracts 'On the twelve abuses of the world' (*De duodecim abusiuis saeculi*) and 'The book on the order of creation' (*Liber de ordine creaturarum*), in which (as in so many Irish writings of the time) the influence of Isidore, whose works were evidently much studied in Ireland from the mid-seventh century on, is clear: Irish authors apparently sought inspiration not simply from Britain, but from Visigothic Spain.

Successive decades at the end of the seventh century saw sophisticated and well-written hagiographical texts composed by (for example) Cogitosus (whose 'Life of Saint Brigit' (*Vita S. Brigitae*) was

202 | ANDY ORCHARD

written around 680), Tírechán (whose *Collectanea* on St Patrick was
composed around 690), Muirchú (whose 'Life of Saint Patrick' (*Vita
S. Patricii*) was written around 695), and Adomnán (who died in 704
and wrote a well-constructed 'Life of St Columba' (*Vita S. Colum-
bae*)). As in the field of biblical exegesis, a number of anonymous
authors were inspired to write hagiographical texts that largely
focused on the same trinity of saints. Likewise, the so-called
'Antiphonary of Bangor', which dates to the last decade of the seventh century, includes a collection of strikingly original Hiberno-
Latin hymns in a number of different forms. Some are alphabetical,
some are macaronic (including Irish, Greek, and even Hebrew words
alongside Latin), some are obviously earlier than others: but the sheer
variety and vitality of the texts is both unmistakable and remarkable.

A number of the seventh-century Hiberno-Latin texts to have survived have a distinctly bizarre and outlandish quality, and show a
high level of sophistication and command of Latin. So, for example,
the works of Virgilius Maro Grammaticus (who appears to have
flourished—and that is certainly the right word—around the middle
of the seventh century) comprise nothing less than an exuberant
discussion of the Latin language itself, while the extraordinary text
now known simply as the *Hisperica famina*, which exists in several
versions, shows an alarming tendency to coin new Latin words from
old, as well as producing new 'Latinisms' from Greek, Hebrew, and
Irish (a translation of the title along the lines of 'Latinacious speaki-
fications' may convey something of the flavour and the punning
quality of the text).

After this first burst of activity in Ireland, however, there is a sharp
decline in surviving Latin texts composed in Ireland before 900: a
notable exception is the eighth-century treatise on Latin grammar
composed by Malsachanus, again highlighting the importance of
Latin letters in Ireland at the time. Perhaps also to be dated to the
same period is the extraordinary work purporting to describe the
'Voyage of Saint Brendan' (*Nauigatio S. Brendani*) to the 'Land of
Promise' (*terra repromissionis*), which proved enormously popular in
later centuries and was translated into a number of European vernaculars. Irishmen had been leaving home and writing works abroad
since at least the time of Columbanus, but from the eighth century on
there are records of many Irishmen who left their native land and
made a name for themselves in foreign courts and ecclesiastical

centres. At that time, two such travellers (so-called *peregrini*), Frigulus and Sedulius Senior, both composed exegetical works on the Gospel of Matthew, while at the end of the eighth century Josephus Scottus and Columbanus of Saint-Trond both produced creditable Latin metrical verse. If the seventh century produced an impressive array of Hiberno-Latin authors at home, then the efforts of their ninth-century countrymen abroad were no less prodigious: so, for example, the treatises on astronomy and geography by Dícuil and the copious writings in the fields of biblical exegesis, grammatical commentary, and poetry by Sedulius Scottus are justly celebrated, but are simply part of the massive production of Irish *peregrini* in this period. Most learned of all (both in Latin and Greek) was John Scottus Eriugena (who died in 877), whose massive and massively impressive output of biblical exegesis, natural philosophy, poetry, translations from Greek, and commentaries on a range of authors and texts reveals a hugely keen and capable mind. Again, not all of the Irish *peregrini* who wrote Latin texts in this period deigned to sign their works, and there survive large numbers of texts in a variety of genres which can be ascribed with more or less confidence to Irish hands.

Only ten manuscripts older than the year 1000 have survived in Ireland, whereas more than five times that number are still extant because they were taken out of the country. Comparable figures for Wales are still more desperate: there are no manuscripts at all surviving in Wales itself that date from before 1000, and only about ten or so manuscripts and fragments are still extant outside Wales, the majority of them preserved in England. Scottish-Latin texts are entirely restricted to inscriptions before the eleventh century, but considerable activity in and around Iona should indicate that the area of modern Scotland cannot have been entirely a Latin wasteland, and close cultural contacts between Gaelic speakers in Ireland and Britain (both termed *Scotti* in Latin) only serve to blur the picture. Although the bulk of Irish manuscripts from the earliest period are unglamorous, often crowded affairs, their primarily functional nature itself testifies to the sheer exuberance and excitement in the written word that many of the seventh- and eighth-century texts demonstrate, whether written in Irish or in Latin. Nor are all the manuscripts entirely plain, though the extraordinary artistry of the justly famed eighth-century Book of Kells (whether it is Irish, Northumbrian, or even Pictish in origin) is entirely atypical.

Although there are scattered glosses in the written record else-where, it is a salutary fact to recall that our knowledge of Old Irish (the language of the seventh, eighth, and ninth centuries) relies almost entirely on three heavily glossed Latin manuscripts all of which now survive in Continental libraries. The interlinear 'Würz-burg glosses' were entered into a Latin manuscript of the Pauline epistles (Würzburg, Universitätsbibliothek, MS M.p.th.f.12) evidently prepared for the purpose: the book is best considered as a classroom text. The 'Milan glosses' (found in Milan, Biblioteca Ambrosiana, MS C.301) offer an extended commentary on the Psalms, and refer to the authority of one Máel Gaimrid, once in the present tense; presumably this figure is to be identified with the abbot of Bangor of the same name (817–39). The same Máel Gaimrid is cited as an authority in the third of these heavily glossed manuscripts, this time a weighty tract on Latin grammar by the sixth-century scholar Priscian (Sankt Gallen, Stiftsbibliothek, MS 904). Indeed, both the Milan and Sankt Gallen manuscripts appear to come from the same intellectual milieu, and both can be associated with the circle of Sedulius Scottus, one of the best-known mid-ninth-century Irish *peregrini* active on the Continent. Several of the glosses seem to demonstrate copying errors, implying that they derive from one of more exemplars, and bearing witness to a vigorous glossing tradition, perhaps over several generations. It seems certain that the chance survival of this extensive body of Old Irish owes much to its transmission alongside Latin, and highly likely that such manuscripts would not have survived in Ire-land, where the conditions for preservation seem poor; it is even possible that one or all of the three was actually produced on the Continent, part of the ferment of intellectual activity associated with Irish *peregrini* throughout the ninth century.

The Sankt Gallen manuscript of Priscian also contains some of the earliest surviving vernacular Irish verse to have survived in a con-temporary (or near-contemporary) witness. One such famed mar-ginal poem was evidently composed with the Viking threat in mind:

> Bitter is the wind tonight,
> It ruffles the deep sea's grizzled locks;
> I do not fear a crossing of the clear waves
> By a band of greedy warriors from Scandinavia.

But if, as has been suggested, these lines were written in the manuscript not in Ireland itself but by one of the Irish *peregrini* on the Continent, they nonethless reflect the extent to which these *peregrini* may have carried their learning and literature with them, as likely in their memories as on the written page. In another well-known marginal poem, again preserved in a Continental manuscript, an Irish scholar celebrates his cat, who, significantly, carries a Welsh name (*Pangur*): Wales would have been on a commonly used route to the Continent for many Irishmen. Bizarrely enough, at least three other marginal Irish jottings in later manuscripts mention cats that have gone astray, so offering an endearing sidelight on the home life of at least some Irish scribes. The Sankt Gallen manuscript also contains a rueful comment on Priscian's assertion that 'Virgil was a mighty poet' (*Magnus poeta Virgilius fuit*); someone has added in Irish, 'and he isn't easy, either'. Elsewhere in the margins of the same manuscript the word *latheirt* is written twice, once in ogham; since the word in question elsewhere seems to gloss the Latin word *crapula* ('drunkenness', 'hangover'), one wonders in what state the scribe must have been who wrote the original Irish.

Many of the vernacular writings from the earliest period of Irish literature shadow those of Hiberno-Latin, or otherwise betray signs of Latin influence. The earliest datable vernacular poem, the so-called *Amra Choluim Chille*, is an elegy on Columba written by one Dallán Forgaill shortly after the saint's death in 597. The poem itself is a highly skilful piece, and surely bears witness to a thriving vernacular poetic before that date, but it also shows clear signs of Latin learning: one passage says of Columba that 'he made known books of law, / he loved books like Cassian, / he won battles of gluttony, / he followed the books of Solomon'. Not only are 'books' mentioned in three out of four lines, but included in this first explicit Irish reference to the Church Father Cassian is an implicit allusion to Cassian's famous inclusion of the vice of gluttony (*gula*) at the head of the eight deadly sins. Moreover, the poet actually includes the correctly inflected form of this Latin word at this point in his poem; nor is it the only Latin word in this brief extract. Other vernacular poetry has been attributed to the second half of the sixth century, and although much of it is anonymous, certain poets (such as Colmán mac Lénéni) are named. The basis for assigning such an early date to these poems is partly linguistic but partly, it must be admitted, a matter of faith: as with most of the earliest Welsh poems, most are preserved in much later manuscripts. The 'linking alliteration' (*fidrad freccomail*) that is the hallmark of this early verse seems both a mnemonic and an ornamental device, and serves to connect consecutive stanzas in an unbroken sequence. The basic verse scheme is accentual: poetry that counts syllables rather than stresses seems to be a later innovation, but one which certainly caught on; the history of Irish poetry for much of the medieval period is dominated by syllable-counting stanzaic forms.

As in Hiberno-Latin from the same period, vernacular grammatical, metrical, and exegetical texts all survive, alongside a wide range of religious writings. One such fascinating text is the so-called 'Alphabet of Piety' (*Apgitir Chrábaid*), attributed to Colmán moccu Sailni, abbot of Lann Elo (Lynally), who died in 611. The interest of this beautifully crafted spiritual primer lies partly in its mixture of verse and prose (and especially metrical prose): 'linking alliteration' is just one of several ornamental devices employed. From about a generation later is the so-called 'Cambrai Homily' (composed around 630), which is generally regarded as the earliest vernacular homily to have survived from the British Isles, but which again shows great assurance in its stylish handling of Latin source material. Such texts indicate that the intellectual primacy of Ireland in the seventh century (when both Bede and Aldhelm bear witness to a significant 'brain-drain' of Anglo-Saxon students across the Irish sea in search of learning) was not simply restricted to Latin learning. Later texts testify to a growing confidence in Irish as a language alongside Latin well suited to spiritual, literary, and intellectual endeavour.

Important in this regard is the so-called 'Primer of the Poets' (*Auraicept na nÉces*), dated some time before about 750 and beginning with a charming tale of the invention of Irish from all the best bits of other languages after the fall of the Tower of Babel. Though clearly modelled on Latin grammatical tracts, it is the sheer pride in vernacular Irish that shines through this remarkable work, which shows just how much an interest in language itself (especially Latin, but not forgetting the other 'sacred languages', namely Hebrew and Greek, and, of course, Irish) was prevalent at the time. Legal texts in both languages are found from the seventh century on: the earliest datable such text in the vernacular is 'Caín Fhuithirbe', composed some time between 678 and 683, which focuses on the relationship between kings and the Church, while the great eighth-century lawbook *Senchas Már* comprises no fewer than forty-seven separate tracts on a great variety of topics; in Latin there survives an equally eclectic collection, the seventh-century 'Irish Collection of Canons' (*Collectio Canonum Hibernensis*), compiled by Ruben of Dairinis (d. 725) and Cú Chuimne of Iona (d. 747). The hugely popular Hiberno-Latin account of the Voyage of St Brendan can be paralleled in a number of vernacular ecclesiastical voyage tales (*immrama*). It can be shown that in legal texts some of the most striking early Irish rhetorical sequences (*roscada*) long held to be fossilized examples of ancient lore are in fact directly derived from Christian-Latin texts such as the *Hibernensis*; parallel and equally flamboyant sequences of rhetoric (*retoiric*) in literary prose seem now to have originated during the sixth century in imitation of Latin verse. In short, while it was once the vogue to stress the gap between vernacular Irish literature and parallel developments in Hiberno-Latin, it has become increasingly clear that there are marked benefits in considering the two together.

# Latin and the vernacular in Anglo-Saxon England

Christianity has always been (like Islam and Judaism) a religion of the book, and the symbolic power of the written word was routinely exploited by missionaries in and from the British Isles. In Tírechán's seventh-century *Collectanea* on Saint Patrick, the saint is depicted appearing in Ireland 'with written tablets in his hands', and by the ninth century he was credited with writing 365 alphabets (though quite what that means is still a matter for dispute); an extant letter by the Anglo-Saxon Boniface, attempting to convert the Germans, asks for a gold-lettered copy of the Epistles of Peter to impress the illiterate pagans. Likewise, Augustine and his companions presumably established a school at Canterbury soon after their arrival in 597: its primary aim would have been simply to train a native clergy capable of reading the Latin Bible and performing the liturgy; at all events, by the 630s it was well-enough established that (according to Bede's testimony a century later) King Sigeberht of East Anglia was able to set up a school in his kingdom with teachers sent from Kent, and there soon followed the first English bishop, Ithamar of Rochester (644), and the first English archbishop, Deusdedit of Canterbury (655–64). By contrast, in contemporary Northumbria, King Oswald (634–42) looked west for his learning, a direct result of his exile among the Scots of Dál Riada (where he was converted), and his close ties with Iona; at all events, it was to Irish monks that he turned in establishing an educational system in his realm. These twin strands of influence, westwards from Ireland and eastwards from Continental Europe (and still further East from Constantinople), would continue to play a part in English education throughout the seventh century, culminating in the career of Aldhelm, abbot of Malmesbury and bishop of Sherborne (who died in 709 or 710), who was taught initially by an Irishman at Malmesbury and then by two scholars from much further afield, in the most famous school of its time, at Canterbury.

The latter school came about by chance, when, after a long and distinguished career in Tarsus, Constantinople, and Rome, the hapless Greek monk Theodore (602–90) was selected by the pope to be the next archbishop of Canterbury, and insisted on bringing with him his friend and colleague Hadrian (who died in 709 or 710), probably a native of North Africa, and a man thoroughly steeped in Latin learning. The school they established and ran together at Canterbury was evidently a wonder: more than a generation later the Venerable Bede, writing in Northumbria, records (not, perhaps, without a hint of envy) that its English students were highly proficient in both Greek and Latin. The most celebrated student of the Canterbury school whose works have survived is also perhaps one of its least typical: Aldhelm, who was first trained at Malmesbury by an Irishman and apparently thought himself well-educated enough up until that point, records his amazement at going to Canterbury in his mature years and realizing how much he still had left to learn. According to his testimony and that of Bede, the curriculum at Canterbury evidently included law, astronomy, and (most wonderful of all to Aldhelm) the study and composition of Latin metrical verse. Aldhelm himself left an enduring literary legacy, writing extensively in Latin in both prose and verse; and although it is unclear how much weight to attach to the witness of the twelfth-century historian William of Malmesbury that Aldhelm was a celebrated poet in Old English too (William claims that Aldhelm was one of King Alfred's favourite poets), there survives a short poem partly in Old English, partly in Latin (with a dash of Greek thrown in), which opaquely celebrates this 'first English man of letters'. Most likely this poem was composed long after Aldhelm's death: for all his obscurity to generations of modern students and scholars, it is clear that Aldhelm's stylish and stylistically challenging writings were studied and imitated in Anglo-Saxon England across more than three centuries.

The generations of Anglo-Saxon authors that followed Aldhelm were immediately influenced by him, especially in the twin areas of Latin prose style and Latin verse composition. So, for example, in prose, Aldhelm's stylistic and philosophical influence can clearly be seen in the extraordinary (and probably eighth-century) anonymous work now known as the *Liber monstrorum* ('book of monsters'), which in three sections dealing in turn with humanoid, bestial, and serpentine creatures catalogues some 120 'monsters' from nature, legend, and (most importantly) classical literature. Steeped in Latin learning, the author combines both classical and patristic traditions in a highly skilful way, effectively endorsing Christian authors at every turn, while at the same time acknowledging the seductive charms of secular literature; at all events, the message to young scholars seeking to study classical texts (especially Virgil) is clear: here be dragons. Similar deep familiarity with the works of Aldhelm is apparent in the Life of St Guthlac (*Vita S. Guthlaci*) penned by one 'Felix', who flourished between 713 and 749, of whom we know little bar his name (which may in any case not be the name he was born with, being simply the Latin word for 'happy', 'lucky', or 'blessed'). It is important to note that in composing his Life of Guthlac, the hermit of Crowland (in Lincolnshire) who exchanged his early life as a successful soldier and mercenary for that of a fenland hermit, Felix demonstrates not only the influence of Aldhelm but also of the Northumbrian Bede.

Aldhelm's influence on succeeding generations of Anglo-Latin poets is still more pervasive, and can be felt not simply at the level of style and diction (Aldhelm is certainly the most imitated pre-Conquest Anglo-Latin poet whose works have survived), but even at the level of genre. Taking as his model the extraordinary riddles of Symphosius (probably a North African poet whose works were brought into Anglo-Saxon England by Hadrian), Aldhelm had written from a strictly Christian and didactic perspective his own set of

100 *Enigmata* ('riddles', or perhaps better 'mysteries'). Symphosius had chosen as his subjects a banal and bizarre series of objects ('tile', 'key', 'chain'; 'gouty soldier', 'tightrope walker'); by contrast, Aldhelm, in depicting the subjects of his *Enigmata*, combined a keen naturalist's eye ('wallwort', 'woody nightshade', 'bivalve mollusc', 'pond-skater'), with the primary concerns of a dedicated churchman ('chrismal', 'candle', 'organ', 'creation') and, above all, teacher ('alphabet', 'writing-tablets', 'book cupboard'; 'Scylla', 'elephant', 'unicorn'). Among later Anglo-Saxons who wrote *Enigmata* based in part on those of Aldhelm were Tatwine, archbishop of Canterbury (d. 734), and Boniface, missionary to the Germans and archbishop of Mainz (d. 754). In both cases, the choice of subjects chosen for inclusion is telling: whereas Tatwine, who also composed a textbook on Latin grammar, selected for the most part bookish or pious objects to describe ('lectern', 'altar', 'prepositions that take two cases'), Boniface (*c.*675–754), whose interests were largely pastoral, instead composed a linked series of *Enigmata* on the vices and the virtues.

Boniface, indeed, can be said to be in large part responsible both directly and indirectly for exporting Aldhelm's works and influence to the Continent, whence a number of them were brought back to Britain centuries later, after the Viking raids had subsided. Indeed, the whole Bonifatian mission to convert the Germans shows just how precarious a hold on Latin learning there was among Anglo-Saxons, and how much it relied not only on the efforts and excellence of so very few but on constant and constantly renewed access to books. The steady decline in Latinity shown by the 150 or so surviving letters of the Bonifatian correspondence over a period of around a century from the last quarter of the seventh century to the last quarter of the eighth effectively foretells the disastrous decline of Latinity in Anglo-Saxon England during the ninth century, as the Viking depredations intensified. In microcosm, one can see the same process at work in the writings of Boniface himself, who lived to be nearly 80 and wrote a series of increasingly desperate letters from his isolation and exile on the Continent, begging for books. Boniface's horrific martyrdom at an advanced age at Dokkum, apparently attempting in vain to ward off pagan weapons with a (presumably Latin) book, offers a potent metaphor for the plight of English letters as the ninth century ground on.

But if the efforts of Aldhelm and Boniface demonstrate the swift progress in developing a Latin literate culture in Southumbria, there were equal and parallel achievements north of the Humber during the same period. Benedict Biscop (who died in 689), who had accompanied Theodore from Rome, founded the famous monastery at Monkwearmouth—Jarrow, of which he was first abbot, after extensive travels on the Continent, including five trips to Rome and a period as a monk at the renowned monastery at Lérins. The books he brought back from these foreign forays doubtless provided the backbone of an extensive collection at Monkwearmouth—Jarrow that allowed the most renowned of its students, Bede (c.673–735), to become one of the most prolific, learned, and influential Anglo-Saxons without ever straying far or often from its walls. Bede's recorded output is prodigious by any measure, and although modern scholars have tended to focus on his *Ecclesiastical History of the English People* (*Historia ecclesiastica gentis Anglorum*), completed in 731, it is clear that Bede's own main concerns lay elsewhere: nearly two-thirds of his surviving texts deal with issues of Scriptural interpretation, and it is these that Bede foregrounds in his own assessment of his work. Alongside his historical and hagiographical writings, Bede also composed a quantity of Latin verse, together with a whole series of textbooks on (for example) chronology, cosmography, grammar, and rhetoric. In all these works, as in his *Historia ecclesiastica*, it is Bede's burning Christian piety that shines through, whether he is quoting from Church Fathers such as Augustine, Ambrose, Gregory, or Jerome, or carefully purging the works of Late Latin grammarians of their pagan poetic examples and substituting instead (and surely at great effort) comparable excerpts from Christian Latin verse. Like Aldhelm, Bede too had an interest in vernacular Old English poetry, whether in his description of how the illiterate cowherd Cædmon was first moved to compose Old English poems on Christian themes, or in the short Old English poem he is said to have recited (and perhaps composed) shortly before his own death. At any rate, it is the popularity of Bede's Latin writings (alongside which they circulated) that have ensured that *Cædmon's Hymn* and *Bede's Death Song* survive in more manuscripts than any other extant Old English verse.

That Bede was not the only highly educated Northumbrian whose Latin writings have survived from this period is clear, for example, from several anonymous Saints' Lives, including one of Pope Gregory the Great (*Vita S. Gregorii*), produced at Whitby during 680–704, and another (*Vita S. Cuthberti*) of Saint Cuthbert, who died in 687; a third, a Life of Abbot Ceolfrith (*Vita S. Ceolfridi*), evidently produced at Monkwearmouth–Jarrow shortly after his death in 716, shows that Bede did not have the monopoly on Latin learning there. All these Lives, like that of Bishop Wilfrid (who died in 709) produced by Stephen of Ripon some time between 710 and 720, show a high level of Latinity closer to the limpid, biblically derived style of Bede than the more complex and self-conscious style of Aldhelm, which evidently had its origins at least in part in the word order and word formation so characteristic of Latin metrical verse.

Again, like Aldhelm, Bede was enormously influential on later Anglo-Saxons, and his immediate impact was felt first in his native Northumbria. Perhaps the most learned and distinguished of those who happily acknowledged their intellectual debt to Bede was Alcuin (*c.*735–804), who was born about the same time that Bede died, and who was trained at York by Archbishop Ecgberht (who died in 766) and (especially) by Archbishop Ælberht (767–78). It was the latter who established at York a school perhaps without parallel in contemporary Europe for the range and depth of its learning, and who bequeathed to Alcuin a formidable library, which his student lovingly catalogued in verse. It was while *en route* to Rome to collect the *pallium* (part of the archiepiscopal vestments) for Ælberht's successor that Alcuin met Charlemagne and received an invitation to join the imperial court. So it was that the most learned of contemporary Anglo-Saxons ended his days abroad as abbot of Tours, after spending more than two decades on the Continent as one of Charlemagne's most trusted advisers. Like those of both his actual and spiritual teachers, Ælberht and Bede, Alcuin's own interests were commensurately broad: he wrote widely both in poetry and prose, and seems to have regarded himself primarily as a teacher; certainly, his personality shines through his many surviving letters and verses to his students, many of whom rose to high rank in the church. Like many exiles and emigrés, Alcuin retained to the end of his life a deep affection for the land of his birth: several of his letters (nearly 300 survive) mention England in general and York in particular, as the ageing Alcuin struggles to come to terms with the increasingly persistent Viking raids.

Just as in Southumbrian learning one can trace a notable decline once Boniface took a whole generation of the learned aristocracy off to the Continent to convert the Germans, so too Alcuin's departure to serve as chief adviser to Charlemagne marks a clear decline in Latin learning in the schools of Northumbria. Damning evidence is offered by some verses on the life of Saint Nynia, an early missionary of Whithorn (*Miracula S. Nyniae*) sent to Alcuin by a group of students: errors of grammar and prosody abound, and the whole piece is little more than a cut-and-paste selection from popular school texts. More technically proficient (though still barely of literary merit) is a poem on the abbots of an unidentified monastery composed by one Æthelwulf and dedicated to Bishop Ecgberht of Lindisfarne (803–21); Alcuin's own influence on these verses seems clear, and it seems possible that the monastery in question was Crayke, a dependency of Lindisfarne barely a dozen miles north of York.

That Latin learning in England should have fallen off so dramatically after the turn of the eighth century is scarcely surprising given the increased number and intensity of Viking raids: Lindisfarne itself was famously sacked in 793, and there is a palpable decline in manuscript production as the eighth century wears on. It has been noted that fewer than three dozen manuscripts (and slightly more than three dozen manuscript fragments) survive which were both written or owned in England before about 825 and preserved there during the ninth century; figures of a similar order obtain for manuscripts and manuscript fragments written or owned in England before about 825 but preserved in Continental libraries during the ninth century. It is clear, moreover, that a significant number of pre-ninth-century Anglo-Latin texts known today only survive thanks to their Continental transmission. Moreover, one can see striking signs of the extent to which standards of 'correct' Latinity had slipped in England in the surviving series of twenty-two single-sheet charters produced around the middle of the ninth century at a time when the principal scribe at Canterbury was an old man evidently too blind to see his own frequent and gross mistakes.

Such, then, was the root of the situation that Alfred famously described as being prevalent on his accession in 871:

There were very few this side of the Humber who were able to understand their services in English, or translate even a single document from Latin into English, and I reckon that there were not many the other side of the Humber; there were so few that I cannot think of a single one south of the Thames when I first came to the throne.

Some have sought to see this bald statement as some kind of rhetorical exaggeration, but surely further validation is found in the fact that Alfred himself was apparently obliged to seek scholars far and wide to implement his programme of educational reform: Grimbald the Frank from Saint-Bertin, John the Old Saxon, and Asser from St Davids in Wales were all recruited to join four scholars from Mercia (the part of England at that date least affected by Viking depredations), namely Werferth, Plegmund, Æthelstan, and Werwulf. Under Alfred's programme, Latin would be taught to those that seemed most apt or were intended for holy orders: learning to read English was the priority. And so began a revolution in vernacular English letters, the impact of which would be felt long after 900, when successive waves of Vikings had left or simply settled, and had long been assimilated into their new home.

Any estimation of the Old English literature composed before 900 is to a large extent blighted by the dearth of manuscript evidence: only around two dozen manuscripts and manuscript fragments containing Old English survive that can be dated (in whole or part) securely before that date, and although such a figure far outstrips what can be said for any other of the vernacular languages of the British Isles, it seems a slender basis upon which to build. The texts that these manuscripts contain are suitably eclectic: various scribbles on mainly Latin manuscripts, Latin–Old English glossaries, glosses to the Latin Psalter, fragments of the *Old English Martyrology*, the earliest version of the *Anglo-Saxon Chronicle*, and sundry texts associated with Alfred's programme of educational reform. To be sure, we know of other texts that must have been recorded in this period and still survive, albeit for the most part in (much) later copies; such texts include the law codes of Æthelberht of Kent (d. 616) and Ine of Wessex (688–726), as well as a good number of charters and wills. Old English is used for the boundary clauses of several early Latin charters, but significant vernacular charters only really begin to appear around the eighth century; vernacular wills are not in evidence before the ninth century. We are told that Bede himself translated part of Isidore's treatise 'On the nature of things' (*De natura rerum*) into Old English, but not a scrap of it survives.

The search for pre-Alfredian prose has generally restricted itself to a handful of texts which seem Mercian in origin, since it was Mercia that was least affected by the Viking raids. The texts in question are a curious selection: the *Old English Martyrology* (a series of brief extracts on individual saints, following the order of the year), the *Life of Chad*, and the *Letter of Alexander to Aristotle*. Of Alfred's own prose, we have perhaps five texts: the *Laws of Alfred*, the *Prose Psalms* (a rendering of the first fifty psalms), the *Pastoral Care* (a version of the *Cura pastoralis* of Gregory the Great), the *Soliloquies* (adapted from Augustine's *Soliloquia*), and the *Consolation of Philosophy* (based on the *De consolatione philosophiae* of Boethius). It is surely no coincidence that most of these texts are derived directly from Latin sources, nor that other texts written as part of the same impetus for educational reform, namely the *Dialogues* by Bishop Werferth of Worcester (based on the *Dialogi* of Gregory the Great), the *Old English Bede* (a rendering of Bede's *Historia ecclesiastica*), and the *Old English Orosius* (a version of Orosius' *Historia contra paganos*) should follow the same pattern. Only the first section of the *Anglo-Saxon Chronicle*, which presumably formed part of the same grand Alfredian scheme, is free of obvious Latin sources, but here too the length and style of individual entries seems to indicate that here and there earlier sources (presumably this time in Old English) have been incorporated. The best example is found in the entry for 755 (*sub anno* 757), which tells the tale of the dynastic rivalry and feuding over the West Saxon crown by Cynewulf and Cyneheard. The entries to this point have been notably terse and matter-of-fact, but here the *Chronicle* springs to life, with a vivid description of conflicting loyalties and deeds of great courage; many commentators have suspected that the Chronicler is here drawing on a pre-existing account, though opinions differ as to whether this precursor was a poem or a piece of prose wrought after the fashion of (much later) Norse sagas.

It is important to stress that Alfredian prose is not the simple and functional vehicle of tentative expression that one might suppose of the earliest extant English prose. Alfred himself employs a wide range of rhetorical devices evidently drawn from both written (which is to say Latin) and oral (which is to say native) traditions: if he begins his *Preface to the Pastoral Care* with a standard opening imitated from Latin epistolary style, he also employs a number of patterns of alliteration, doublets, wordplay, and other techniques familiar from vernacular Old English verse. To divide up his *Preface*, Alfred even uses a technique found also, for example, in some early Welsh poetry, where it is described as 'incremental repetition': the repetition of words and phrases at the beginning of successive stanzas (or, in this case, paragraphs). The same technique is used in several Old English poems (notably the *Wife's Lament*, for which no Latin source has been detected); and although one can trace similar rhetorical devices in Latin too (where it would be described as a form of anaphora), there seems no particular need here to suppose that Alfred, who is after all decrying the state of Latin learning, is doing anything other than adopting rhetorical techniques from the native poetic tradition. Certainly, we know that Alfred himself was very interested in vernacular verse from an early age: Asser tells the story of how as a young boy Alfred had been inspired to have read to him and so learn by heart a 'book of English poetry' with a beautiful initial that his mother owned.

Among the earliest Old English verses extant are some engraved on two artefacts dated around 700, the Ruthwell Cross (see Fig. 4.2) and the Franks Casket. The verses on the Ruthwell Cross are highly significant for their evident relationship to a much longer poem, a marvellous vision of the Cross (the so-called *Dream of the Rood*), which is preserved complete only in the Vercelli manuscript of around 1000. The 300-year pedigree of at least that part of that poem has inspired much speculation as to the antiquity of a number of other poems that only survive in manuscripts dating to the turn of the millennium (which is to say almost all of them), but the general difficulty of dating the highly artificial language of Old English verse, full of dialect forms and archaisms, has confounded most commentators. The verses on the Franks Casket, which is apparently made of the bone of a stranded whale, seem to celebrate the poor creature who provided the raw materials somewhat in the fashion of the Old English *Riddles* (and indeed of the Anglo-Latin *Enigmata*, at least some which would have been current at around the same date). Other Old English poems of undoubted early date include *Cædmon's Hymn* (which, whether or not one believes it to have been the actual poem produced by Cædmon rather than a back-translation of Bede's Latin, survives in two very early manuscripts as well as a good many later ones), *Bede's Death Song* (whether or not it is Bede's own composition), and the so-called *Leiden Riddle* (an Old English version of one of Aldhelm's *Enigmata*, preserved in a Continental manuscript by a scribe clearly unfamiliar with the language, and probably copying from an eighth-century exemplar). All three of these poems survive in both (early) Northumbrian and (later) West Saxon versions, and bear witness to the apparent ease with which poems could be altered (and updated) in transmission. A fourth poem at least as old as the eighth century is the so-called *Proverb from Wynfrith's Time*, which survives in a ninth-century Continental manuscript preserving part of the Bonifatian correspondence, and may already have been old when an eighth-century monk included it in his (Latin) letter to a likely missionary. One notes that all four of these earliest Old English poems preserved in manuscript owe their survival to a combination of circumstances, including their association with a known, named, and celebrated figure from the early Anglo-Saxon Church (in these cases Aldhelm, Bede, and Boniface: all, of course, were also well known Anglo-Latin authors), as well as their transmission in manuscripts not only primarily written in Latin but transported to the Continent. That this combination of factors evidently increased the chances of survival seems self-evident, but offers no clues about how much Old English poetry not transmitted in this way may have been produced: it is simply impossible to estimate how much has been lost.

Once one moves away from Old English poems which survive in pre-900 contexts, however, the deep waters of speculation threaten to close over the head. The use of linguistic criteria to date Old English poetry has a long and sorry history, and has mostly focused on the troubled question of the date of *Beowulf*, undoubtedly the finest Anglo-Saxon poem to have survived. There is no current critical consensus: recent estimates range from a supposition that *Beowulf* existed in written form before 750 to an assertion that it is no older than the manuscript that contains it (the date of which is also disputed, as the outer limits of the traditional date around the turn of the eleventh century are probed). As ever, the whole issue of assigning a date is itself made problematic by questions of dialect origin, and although a recent thorough survey of the metre of Old English verse asserts for *Beowulf* a date no later than 725 if Mercian, and no later than 825 if Northumbrian, that view too has yet to win the day. Fresh work has shown that the poet of the Saint's Life *Andreas* (which survives only in the Vercelli Book) was likely drawing both on *Beowulf* and on the poems of Cynewulf in composing his work, and that Cynewulf himself (who apart from Cædmon, Bede, Aldhelm, and King Alfred is the only person whose name is associated with the composition of Old English verse) probably consciously echoed

*Beowulf* in his own poems, while *Beowulf* may be echoing vernacular biblical verse; but such relative chronology, promising though it seems for future research, fails to offer new absolute dates. A more or less traditional view (supported by several metrical analyses) would hold that of the longer Old English poems to have survived, it is the biblical poems, notably *Genesis, Exodus,* and *Daniel,* that probably represent the earliest phase of composition, with *Beowulf* roughly contemporary or perhaps a little later, and Cynewulf later still. Whether any or all of these poems can be securely situated earlier than the tenth century must remain for the moment a moot point, but certainly the lengthy Christian-Latin poems on biblical themes (especially those by Juvencus, Caelius Sedulius, and Arator), which seem to have inspired both the vernacular biblical poets and Cynewulf (especially in the area of style), were curriculum texts taught and studied in Anglo-Saxon schools throughout the period. Once again, there seems to have existed a close and fertile inter-relationship between Latin and the vernacular at this time.

# Conclusion

At the end of the sixth century, which is to say at the very beginnings of recorded written Irish, Columba could be justly praised in the *Amra Choluim Chille* as 'learned', in terms drawn both from the Latin (*docht,* derived from Latin *doctus*) and vernacular (*suí*) traditions. Some indeterminate time later, in a poem surviving only in a single manuscript dating from the turn of the eleventh century, Aldhelm, the first Anglo-Saxon whose extensive writings in Latin survive, is also justly celebrated both in Latin as a 'good author' (*bonus auctor*) and in Old English as a 'noble poet' (*æþele sceop*). The juxtaposition of Latin and the vernacular is in both cases apposite, and underlines the fruitful interaction that occurred throughout the British Isles. The introduction of Latin and Latin learning was indeed a revolution, first in its initial guise as the language of the Roman Empire and the gateway to the wider world of secular letters, and then as the language of Christian culture and Christian learning. But, far from stifling vernacular languages and cultures in the British Isles, Latin could well be said to have provided the necessary stimulus and vehicle for their development and (in the case of written records) their very survival. A consistent and repeated pattern in the extant written record of the British Isles is the chance survival of more or less parasitic vernacular texts preserved alongside Latin in manuscripts transported out of their country of origin and away from the Vikings. But whatever damage these raiders caused to manuscripts, scriptoria, and libraries, the Vikings too were, even as the ninth century drew to a close, beginning to succumb to the twin influences of Christianity and Latin letters. To Bede's five languages of the British Isles, these raiders and invaders were to add a sixth, Norse, one that was to prove both stimulating and productive in both literary and linguistic terms wherever its influence was felt, and one whose mighty vernacular literature is mainly preserved from the post-Conversion period, when descendants of the Vikings chose to write it down in a Latin alphabet adopted from the Anglo-Saxons. If the year 900 marks a convenient end to the first wave of learning and literature in the British Isles, it also signals the beginning of a new phase of language and letters, in which the sons and daughters of Vikings would play a noble part.

**Figure 6.1** The Lichfield Gospels. The portrait of the evangelist, St Luke, shows him with his symbol, a calf, and with crossed rods, evoking at once the rod of Aaron, the first priest under the Mosaic Law, and Christ's Cross. The document in the margins, written in highly competent Insular minuscule at Llandeilo Fawr in Carmarthenshire, probably in the second half of the ninth century, records the purchase of their freedom by four sons of Bledri, for which they gave four pounds and eight ounces of silver (silver valued by weight was a normal medium of exchange in the west and north of the British Isles). Lichfield Cathedral Library, p. 218.

# 6

# Texts and society

Robin Chapman Stacey

In 709 Bishop Wilfrid of Hexham, formerly of York, died as he had lived: with conspicuous attention to property and to the material wellbeing of his supporters. Shortly before his death, he caused the monastic treasury at Ripon to be formally opened and, in the presence of abbots and other clerical worthies, publicly divided his gold and silver and jewels into four portions. One portion he assigned to the churches of Rome, and one to the poor. To the abbots of his main monasteries at Ripon and Hexham he granted the third part of his wealth so that they might purchase the goodwill of the bishops and kings with whom they came in contact—a goodwill that had frequently eluded the imperious, and hence perpetually controversial, Wilfrid during his lifetime. The remainder of his legacy went to members of his 'retinue': those retainers, secular and clerical, who had followed him into exile whose service he had not previously rewarded with grants of land. After naming his successor at Ripon, Wilfrid then travelled to the other monastic houses subject to him, making similar bequests and granting lands and treasure to his supporters. It was while on this testamentary tour that he suffered a renewed bout of an illness from which he had long suffered and, shortly thereafter, died.

The manner of Wilfrid's passing affords us a valuable glimpse into the complex relationship between the written and the spoken word that had developed in Britain over the century or so since Augustine's arrival at Canterbury. As the above account makes clear, Wilfrid's will was oral rather than written. Its authority stemmed not from its existence as a document or its inscription in literate form, but from the fact of its having been publicly performed by the ailing Wilfrid himself in the venues most closely associated with him as bishop. And yet we owe our knowledge of this oral will to a written text, a life of Wilfrid written by Stephen, a monk at Ripon, shortly after the bishop's death. For while there were many in Britain who did not mourn Wilfrid's passing—including most likely the reigning Archbishop of Canterbury, in whose side the good bishop had been a most considerable thorn—his supporters and dependants felt differently. With their protector gone, the monks in his houses faced an uncertain future in their scramble for power and patronage. Particularly worrisome was the competition presented by the cult of another, less arrogant and more visibly well-behaved Northumbrian saint, Cuthbert, whose fame already threatened to eclipse what Wilfrid's communities were hoping to achieve for their patron. An anonymous saint's life of Cuthbert, written between 698 and 705, had advanced Cuthbert's cause considerably, and it was likely in response to this text that Stephen took up his quill to pen the life of his own patron. What ensued was a virtual 'pamphlet war' between the supporters of these two saints in which no less a figure than the Venerable Bede himself played an active and partisan role (he liked Cuthbert better).

The textual rivalry between Wilfrid and Cuthbert is but one example of the extent to which intellectuals in Britain and Ireland were already by the late seventh century turning to the written word not merely to describe but also to reshape the societies in which they lived. That Wilfrid should inspire such a frantic literary competition after his death was only suitable, as he had himself been during his lifetime one of the most document-using clerics of his day. More than half of his episcopacy was spent in exile writing letters soliciting support from anyone who might assist him in regaining the lands and ecclesiastical offices from which he so frequently found himself ejected. And many of the properties granted to his monastic houses during the sunnier moments of his career had been guaranteed by written charters, a type of documentation the value of which he was well aware. Indeed, the sermon he gave on the occasion of the formal dedication of Ripon consisted in substantial part of his reading aloud a list of his possessions compiled from these land grants—the sheer tediousness of which presentation may explain why the partying following upon the audience's release from this sermon lasted for several days. Twice during his lifetime Wilfrid travelled to Rome to petition the pope for assistance in his struggles with royal and archiepiscopal authority, in both cases substantiating his claims with a portfolio of written documentation. And twice he returned with documents containing papal judgements he believed—not entirely accurately, as it turned out—to express unambiguous support for his position. Texts mattered, both to Wilfrid and to those unfortunate enough to come into conflict with him—admittedly not a terribly select club by the end of his life, embracing as it did almost every prominent secular and ecclesiastical figure of the age.

And yet if Wilfrid's career bears testimony to the increasing prominence of this new technology of the word, it also provides an important reminder of the equally essential fact that the culture within which he lived was one in general oriented towards oral communication and display. People knew Wilfrid was powerful because of the lavish garments he wore and the fine foods to which he treated himself; they knew he was authoritative because of his consummate command of the spoken word. It was his skilful verbal argumentation that carried the day for the Roman dating of Easter at the synod of Whitby, and his fiery preaching (validated by a timely and commendably plentiful catch of fish) that won the hearts of the Frisian pagans. Time and again, accounts of his life stress the authority of his physical presence: presiding at Mass, ordaining priests, vanquishing pagans, sonorously condemning bishops and kings. It was as a living, breathing, speaking person that he was most difficult to ignore. Even death slowed him up only temporarily. Like all good saints, he is reported to have performed miracles on behalf of his communities after his passing, including a spectacular pure white rainbow that hovered over the church housing his tomb. Texts and performance were both very much part of Wilfrid's world: indeed, Stephen's Life probably gained its greatest currency in performance, by being publicly read aloud as part of the yearly liturgical commemorations with which Wilfrid's communities marked the death of their founder bishop.

That text and performance should intermingle in such a way may surprise us, given our modern predilection for the literate and our tendency to perceive written and oral as essentially opposites of one another. So often when thinking about world cultures, we tend to associate the reliance on the spoken word with the primitive, while (mis)taking the proliferation of paperwork as proof of civilization's advance. And, of course, writing *is* a particularly powerful tool. Authors are very much in command of the worlds they create: within the confines of their text, they can order relationships, establish hierarchies, and reconfigure the contours of past and present very much as they like. Moreover, their work endures. Unlike oral performance, which reacts primarily to the moment and to the community for and within which it is enacted, writing leaves traces. Texts can travel from one venue to another; they can survive from one decade to the next; they can be responded to, borrowed from, and altered almost ad infinitum.

Writing played a crucial role in helping to shape Insular culture in this period, and must therefore form an important topic for consideration in any history of early Britain and Ireland. But even in our appreciation for the power of the written word, we must remember that all forms of discourse, oral and written, have the ability to structure society and relationships in a particular way and, in so doing, persuade others of the validity of that way of seeing. The texts to which this chapter is largely devoted functioned within a sophisticated oral world. Even after the advent of writing, authority was and remained vested largely in the meaning communities attached to particular gestures, places, and actions. Texts became part of this oral environment; they participated in it, and they helped to shape and to change it. They did not, however, replace it.

# The sources

It is in the seventh century that we get, for the first time since the end of the Roman era, evidence for the wide-scale production of texts in Britain and Ireland. Genres deriving from, though not always formally dictated by, the Roman and Christian past were adopted and reworked to meet the needs of the hybrid cultures characteristic of the period. In addition to the biblical and liturgical writings so necessary to the Christian mission, a significant body of political and social literature began to appear: texts that described, and thereby consciously or unconsciously ordered and shaped, institutions and events within the society that produced them. Such works can be understood on their own, as instances of individual creative genius; they can also be taken as a group, as a response to the cultural diversity and shifting political boundaries of the age. For even apart from the political tumult engendered by the constant movement of

peoples, Christianity's claim to universal loyalty had introduced startling new ideas about power and identity, and about the present and
the past. What we see in the texts produced in this period is a literate
elite struggling with the reality of change, attempting to find some
common cultural ground within their society. They wrote not merely
to describe things as they actually were, but to persuade or command
the consent of others to a particular vision of how they ought to be.

So what are the texts that remain to us, and what problems do we
as historians face in gaining access to the meaning they had for the
societies that created them? As one might expect, documents from
this period display considerable variety in style and genre. Some
works are highly individual and have become famous as literary pro-
ductions in their own right. Bede's *Ecclesiastical History*, the cycle of
Welsh battle poems known as the *Gododdin*, St Patrick's poignant
*Confession*, and Adomnán's Life of Abbot Columba of Iona are excellent examples of texts that resonate as powerfully with modern
readers as they did with the medieval men and women who clustered
eagerly in hall and refectory to hear them. Likewise with the numerous tales, poems, and myths that survive in all three of the vernacular
languages, of which the Anglo-Saxon *Beowulf* and the Irish Ulster
Cycle tales are only the best-known examples. Other works might
strike the reader as less emotionally involving but are nonetheless
unique and important in their own particular ways. It would be
interesting to know, for example, whether the genres represented by
the Anglo-Saxon tribute list known as the *Tribal Hidage* and the
Scottish *Senchas Fer nAlban* might once have been more widespread
than they seem to us now.

Not surprisingly, it is these very special works—the unusual, the
imaginative, the artistic, the mysterious—that have attracted the
most attention among scholars and the educated public. They seem
to possess a remarkable power to reach across the centuries to inspire,
amuse, intrigue, or touch those who search them out. From the point
of view of understanding the impact of writing on Insular culture,
however, it may be that the most important texts to study are those
that appear on the surface the most mundane: those works which are,
in other words, less the exception than the rule. Texts of this sort are
frequently not easy to read: it is difficult to thrill to the cadence of a
genealogical pedigree, for example, or to get emotionally swept away
by the painstakingly prudent prose of a charter. And only a very

special person indeed would read breathlessly into the night in order to finish a law tract devoted to crimes committed by and against cows. But it is precisely these prosaic, everyday texts that people of the time would have seen, and felt, and experienced the effects of most directly. Ruinous ruminants may not stir the soul, but they mattered a great deal to the small, primarily agricultural communities of the period, and the act of writing about them mattered just as much. Mundane as they are, these texts contributed as much to the development of power and identity in early Britain and Ireland as did the writings of Bede, and it is important to give them their due.

Among the most important of these 'everyday' genres are the laws, which are extant in great numbers from Ireland, and survive also from England, albeit to a much more limited degree. The Irish lawbooks are one of the glories of the culture, as significant in their own way as the much admired illuminated Gospel books for which the Irish are so much better known. No fewer than seventy-seven vernacular tracts survive entirely or in part from the period before the ninth century; in addition, there are numerous Irish wisdom texts that bear obvious similarities to the lawbooks, as well as a considerable body of fragmentary legal material that cannot now be assigned with certainty to any particular tract. Many of these tracts were incorporated into lawbooks, the two most important of which are the *Senchas Már*, compiled somewhere in the eighth century in the midlands of Ireland, and the roughly contemporaneous *Bretha Nemed*, which seems to have originated in Munster. There are Latin tracts as well, the most significant of which is an eighth-century collection of canons on various ecclesiastical and secular subjects known as *Collectio Canonum Hibernensis*, certain provisions of which later made their way into the Welsh lawbooks of the high middle ages. The motives for the composition of these texts are unclear, but it is worth noting that the *Senchas Már* is thought by some historians to have been composed as a less overtly church-focused counterpart to the ecclesiastical *Collectio*. It is important to underscore how unique these texts are: no other early medieval western European culture produced a body of legal literature that even comes close to the Irish material in volume and sophistication.

And yet what is perhaps most remarkable about this material is its originality. Ireland was never occupied by Rome, and its law did not therefore derive from Roman tradition. Nor was it royal: the lawbooks were written by and for a self-consciously professional class of jurists, a group of specialists whose origins seem to have lain in the distant Celtic past. In no other contemporary European culture did such specialists exist. Professional jurists did not develop in England, for example, until the twelfth and thirteenth centuries. This is not to say that kings were irrelevant to justice in early Ireland. We know that kings sometimes issued edicts called *cánai* that legislated solutions to various secular and religious dilemmas, and that some of these at least took written form. Kings also sat in judgement, much as they did elsewhere in Europe. However, in Ireland authority in judicial matters did not rest ultimately in royal hands. When kings pronounced judgement on individual disputes, they did so in collaboration with, and on the advice of, these jurists—men trained in professional schools of law. Not surprisingly, the extant lawbooks reflect in their nature and content their origins in these schools. The law they contain is stylized, rhetorical, and greatly given to presenting idealized portraits of society and social relationships. It tends to be descriptive rather than prescriptive, and is more philosophical than legislative in tone. Some of it is even artistic: a significant portion of the corpus is written either in verse or in highly ornate prose. To judge from the extant texts, law in Ireland was a craft, an art, and a profession, rather than a body of legislation to be pronounced by a distant king.

Early English law appears from the extant sources to have been a very different kettle of fish. Considerably less of it survives from the earliest period. Only four vernacular law codes are extant from the seventh century—three from Kent and one from Wessex—and only one, Alfred's, from the ninth. There may once have been others: Alfred mentions that he drew in his work not merely on the work of his Kentish predecessors but on laws issued by the eighth-century Mercian King Offa. No code of Offa's is extant today, although it has been suggested that Alfred was here referring to the proceedings of a synod held under royal sponsorship in 786 which were said to have been read out both in Latin and in the vernacular. In nature and tone, the English laws could not be more different from those being produced in Ireland. Whereas the Irish codes are discursive and rhetorical, the early English codes are brief, blunt, prescriptive, and pragmatic. That this should be so is not surprising. In its structure and approach, Anglo-Saxon law follows closely the example set by contemporary Continental (particularly Frankish) law, which was itself heavily influenced by the model of Rome.

One of the most striking differences between the English codes and the Irish tracts is the role attributed to the king in their promulgation. The earliest of the English codes is usually associated with the great Kentish King Æthelberht, the target of Augustine's missionary efforts. In fact, the code is not actually attributed to Æthelberht in the body of the text itself, but the historian Bede had no doubt that it was issued under his authority, and this seems likely to be right. There are indications that in this very early period, the making of law may have been viewed as being as much a community as a royal venture, and indeed the participation of the nobles of the kingdom in the law-making process is a common theme in the prologues to all the early codes. Already by the late seventh century, however, we find Æthelberht's successors Hlothhere and Eadric claiming direct responsibility for the code issued under their names. Eadric's brother Wihtred's code is even localized to a specific royal council, and law-giving for Alfred was an essential part of what it meant to be king.

But to characterize this law as royal raises more questions than it answers. The Anglo-Saxon codes certainly look more similar to what we expect law ought to look like than do the Irish lawbooks: most of the clauses have either a prescriptive or compensatory aspect to them, and some passages appear to have been inspired by actual legal cases. The prohibition against holding a spear so carelessly that a person accidentally impales themselves on it, for example, is so detailed and peculiar that it would be hard to account for it in any other way. On the other hand, there is no sign of a sustained effort to keep the law on particular issues up to date, and no indication that many of the provisions contained in the codes originated in a particular legislative act.

Moreover, it would be a mistake to interpret any early medieval legal text in light of the practices of our own day. For us, written law serves both as a vehicle through which the state can communicate its legal standards to the communities it governs and as a basis on which charges can be brought and offenders prosecuted once those standards are violated. However, there is no indication in the evidence that the early English or Irish laws were ever used in such a manner. Irish law was not even the product of the state, as we have seen, and in any case was descriptive and artistic rather than legislative in character.

The Anglo-Saxon codes are more statutory in appearance, but they also do not seem to have functioned in the way our own cultural experiences might lead us to expect. None of the extant records of Anglo-Saxon lawsuits ever cites or even refers to the written laws as having played a role in the resolution of the dispute. And the laws themselves seem too selective, ill-organized, and contradictory to allow for use in an actual court case.

Indeed, the notion that underlies our own presumptions about the use of written law—such as that all individuals should be treated equally before the law, and that justice therefore consists of applying the same standards of proof and punishment equally to all persons—was foreign to early medieval peoples in general. In these cultures, a man's past behaviour and social status were regarded as quite relevant—and appropriately so—to his experiences in court. The idea of consulting a book to determine the proper penalty to be exacted for each particular type of case is one that would have seemed odd and inappropriate to those who composed the codes. The familiarity of the laws to the modern eye is thus more apparent than real. They may seem like sources the contours of which are recognizable to us still today, but in fact the presumptions governing their authorship and use were very different from our own.

But what function, then, did these laws serve, and how should we read them? This is an important question, and the answers are likely not the same for English as they are for Irish law. In some ways, the main function of the Anglo-Saxon codes was less what we might recognize as 'legal' than it was political. Roman, biblical, and indeed contemporary Frankish example both made clear that the giving of written law to a people was crucial to the definition of what it meant to be a ruler. In putting their customs into written form, and thus projecting themselves into the role of law-givers, early English rulers were asserting their kingship in circumstances where such things could not be taken for granted. For kingship was itself in this period an idea very much in the process of formation. All indications are that in the sixth and seventh centuries particularly, Britain was dotted with rulers—some, like Æthelberht, claiming to rule broadly over territories and peoples, and some people of much smaller stature, rulers whose jurisdiction may well have encompassed an area not much larger than today's average industrial park. The eighth century saw the question of 'what makes a king a king' grow increasingly urgent, as kings and would-be kings struggled to consolidate their holdings and distinguish themselves from the non-royal aristocrats by whom they were constantly surrounded. Law-giving played an important role in advancing such claims. Not all early English kings chose to issue written texts of law; on the other hand, after Æthelberht, most who did so were kings.

Much less familiar to us as a genre is another important type of early medieval text, the charter. Apart from the Bible, charters were probably the kind of writing with which medieval persons of all classes were most likely to come in contact. In essence, a charter is a written record of the transfer of rights in land or other property. However, the term can be used broadly to describe a wide variety of specific types of document, including legal deeds, diplomas (royal or, later, noble grants recording the transfer of land), writs (sealed royal letters informing or instructing local authorities regarding the disposition of land or other property), leases, *notitiae* (records of transactions or legal proceedings), *placita* (documents recording the final resolution of a lawsuit), and grants of immunity (a grant of exemption from fiscal demands by secular or ecclesiastical authorities).

Survival conditions of these documents vary considerably. Some are extant as single sheets; others were written into Gospel books, appended to saints' lives, or collected together later in the Middle Ages into volumes called cartularies. Often the manuscripts in which they are preserved are considerably later than the transaction to which they refer, which makes dating individual texts a somewhat tricky matter. Moreover, since forgery was an art much practised in early medieval monasteries, it is often difficult to distinguish what is real from what is not. In the period with which we are concerned, the charter was primarily a Latin genre, although vernacular charters became more common in the post-Viking age. The earliest mixed-language charter (which frequently takes the form of a grant in which the text of the donation is in Latin and the boundaries described in the vernacular) known from England dates to 814; a few possibly earlier examples are known from Wales and (in fragmentary form) from Ireland.

The charter derives from the late Roman private deed, and its history in the Celtic British-speaking parts of the island presumably began there, since our earliest extant charter from Wales dates to the late sixth century. The genre's history among the Anglo-Saxons seems to have begun somewhat later with the advent of the Church— perhaps with the original missionaries from Rome, perhaps with Theodore's arrival in 668. In the earliest period, clerics were universally the beneficiaries of the grants detailed in these charters. Charters survive from Wales almost entirely in clerical contexts, and indeed, the original function of the genre seems to have been to ensure that donations made to churches would remain secure. The usual procedure seems to have been for a record to be made—either retrospectively or at the actual time of the donation, and normally by the recipients themselves—of a particular grant or transaction, identifying the donor, recipient, and witnesses, detailing the nature of the donation, and invoking the protection of God upon the arrangement. This record, which was generally kept by the recipient of the land, could later be used as evidence in cases where his claim to the property was subsequently disputed. In Britain, the main function of charters was evidentiary rather than dispositive (that is, a charter did not constitute in and of itself the transfer of the ownership of the property). In other words, the making of a charter was not actually *necessary* to the validity of a given transaction: validity was vested instead in the community rituals traditionally governing such events, and in the witnesses present to record them. But though charters were not actually mandatory in this early period, they were certainly helpful. Already by the 730s in England, donors were reflecting that 'nothing would seem stronger to prove donations and to refute the man wishing to infringe donations than [charters] of donation strengthened by the hands of donors and witnesses'.[1]

Charters were often appended to or incorporated into a third type of text common in the period, saints' Lives. These were not simple biographies, but stories told from a particular point of view and for a specific purpose: to establish or confirm a cult by persuading others of the sanctity of the individual they described. In this period, no official canonization procedure existed by which holiness could be recognized and rewarded: indeed, not before the twelfth century did the papacy begin requiring documentation and subjecting potential candidates to any sort of real official scrutiny. Before this, saints became saints by virtue of others creating cults in their name after,

---

[1] *English Historical Documents* [*EHD*], vol. 1, No. 66.

and occasionally before, they had died. There were several significant steps in the process of cult creation. Perhaps the most important was the translation of the body of the saint, either from one church to another (often a new construction built precisely for the purpose) or from one locale in the church itself to another of greater sanctity, typically under or close by the central altar. The translation was a public and highly dramatic ritual that conjoined religious rites to formal processions and ceremonies of welcoming the saint to his or her new home.

Another important step was the writing of a saint's Life. These were often commissioned upon a decision to translate the saint, and may often have played a role in the rituals by which the translation itself was effected—a clear intersection of text and performance. Such texts resembled biographies in that they purported to detail the manner in which the saint had lived and died. However, insofar as their primary purpose was to assert the holiness of the individual they honoured and, frequently, provide historical validation for a given church's claim to the special connection of the saint, accuracy was not always their primary concern. Or, at least, not accuracy as we understand it: truth was always an important goal, but truth in the largest sense—the essential truth that was the holiness of the saint. To this end, stories were invented, traded, or borrowed back and forth between texts in ways that modern readers sometimes find troubling, but that seemed to medieval readers the ultimate proof of their saint's membership in a long and venerable tradition.

Hagiography was a genre deriving from the late antique past and was, as far as we can tell, common throughout Britain and Ireland. Unfortunately, we can say relatively little about the extent and nature of early Welsh hagiographical traditions. Apart from materials pertaining to the life of Germanus incorporated into the ninth-century *Historia Brittonum*, the Welsh Lives extant today date to the eleventh and twelfth centuries and later. It is possible, of course, that some of these later Lives incorporate earlier material: certainly it is striking that many of the saints these Lives purport to describe date to the pre-Viking period, and are very local in the extent of their cult. Certainly there is no real reason to doubt that the genre was common in Wales, just as it was elsewhere; and an early Breton text, the Life of Samson of Dol, may give us some insight into British hagiographical traditions in this period.

Scotland and Ireland are slightly better served in terms of extant texts. The monastery of Iona produced one of the most famous hagiographical texts of the age, the Life of Columba by Adomnán, the abbot of Iona who died in 704. A significant number of early Lives are extant also from Ireland proper, of which the best known are the seventh-century Lives of Patrick by Muirchú and Tírechán, and of Brigit by Cogitosus. And several survive also from eighth-century England, including the Life of Wilfrid with which this chapter opened, several Lives of St Cuthbert, and an intensely dramatic account of St Guthlac's spiritual and emotional struggles in the demon-infested fens of East Anglia. The Anglo-Saxons particularly were given to royal saints: Bede provides short Lives of several members of the royal families of the island in his *Ecclesiastical History*, including Kings Oswald of Northumbria and Sigeberht of East Anglia, Queen Æthelthryth (Etheldreda), who was one of four daughters of Anna, king of the East Angles, and Hild, not a queen herself but a close relative of King Edwin of Northumbria.

Saints' Lives frequently overlapped with another important genre of the period, genealogies. Genealogies also were more concerned with truth than with accuracy—although in this case the truths in question were political rather than religious. For whereas a pedigree might appear to express a simple biological relationship, the situation was frequently much more complicated than that. As a rule, genealogies reflect more the concerns of the period in which they are compiled than they do the period they purport to describe. The information they communicate about biological relationships in the past may indeed be accurate. Indeed, there is some evidence to suggest that one of the motives for keeping such records in societies in which the kindred was expected to participate in legal arrangements made by their relatives was to clarify the degree of relationship—and hence of obligation or compensation—of individual members. In societies that engaged in feud, for example, only relatives within a certain biological proximity to the victim (or the homicide) were entitled to receive (or pay) compensation for the death.

However, most genealogies of the period were royal, and another very clear motive for the construction of a genealogy was to validate a relatively new political arrangement by making it appear to have originated in the past and to have the authority of long usage. Kings and families who earned their power on the battlefield or by entering into a powerful alliance, for example, rather than by heredity, might seek to justify their newly acquired position by asserting a long-standing genealogical relationship with more established dynasties. Accordingly, it is not at all uncommon to see famous figures of the past sprouting without warning—or biological warrant—hitherto unknown brothers or cousins who then serve as ancestors for dynastic groups who have only recently come to prominence. And of course, the opposite process also takes place: just as visible in the sources is the posthumous purging of the (often biologically quite genuine) ancestors of peoples whose political prominence was either short-lived or nonexistent. This is not to say that genealogies are not genuine: one simply has to take the word 'genuine' in its broadest, and most politicized, sense.

Genealogies did not have to be written, of course. Indeed, they were probably usually oral—poems or pedigrees performed at court or in halls as a way of honouring the poet's patron of the moment. Later medieval sources suggest that royal inaugurations might also have been a frequent venue for such performances. With respect to written genealogies specifically, their frequency and importance seem to have varied from region to region in the British Isles. Relatively few survive from England; of those the most common are simple, single-line royal pedigrees tracing the kings of various dynasties back to pagan deities like Woden (the putative ancestor of the Anglian royal lines) or Seaxneat (the deity associated with the East Saxons). More are extant from Wales: the earliest genealogical collection dates to the mid-tenth century, but the historical credibility of some of the pedigrees contained within it has been shown to reach back into the sixth century. For the Welsh, legitimacy was conveyed through Rome rather than the gods. Ironically, the late Roman leader Magnus Maximus, who in 383 pulled the army out of Britain and took it to the Continent in what proved ultimately to be a doomed bid for the position of emperor—thereby setting up the conditions for the Saxon conquests—shows up as an ancestor figure (or authoritative in-law) in a number of British royal lines. So powerful, indeed, was the linking of the end of Roman rule with the beginnings of native independence that even those lines that do not name him as an ancestor will often correlate their ancestors' rise to prominence with the year of Maximus' death.

But by far the largest and most varied corpus of genealogical material survives from Ireland—some 13,000 names and counting. Not all of these are early: the main collection of pedigrees, branching lineages, regnal lists, and origin legends seems to have been put together sometime in the eighth century out of a variety of materials, some contemporaneous with the time of compilation and some considerably earlier. This collection, which is today extant principally in four high or late medieval manuscripts, was then revised continually over the years into the twelfth century and beyond. Interestingly, although kings and peoples are definitely the focus, not all the lines contained in this corpus are royal. Many of the names contained in the corpus are of non-royal individuals, and in addition to the main collection there are genealogical compilations focusing on saints and on women respectively.

One of the most notable characteristics of the vast Irish corpus is the wide variety of genealogical genres represented: not merely pedigrees, but elaborate branching collateral genealogies, regnal lists, and tribal origin legends. The latter can be quite elaborate, stretching over several pages and (in some cases) functioning as superbly entertaining stories in their own right. Indeed, one of the important aspects of these sources is the extent to which they overlap with, and therefore replicate or revise information found in, other literary sources of the period—not merely saints' Lives, but tales, poems, laws, and the massive account of Irish prehistory known as the *Lebor Gabála Érenn*, 'The Book of the Taking of Ireland.' Genealogies were in Ireland part and parcel of a vast pseudo-historical enterprise.

Another very important written source from the period are the annals—year-by-year accounts of important events. These likely emerged as a genre from the practice of adding yearly notations about notable occurrences to the Easter tables kept in medieval monasteries. These earliest annals were little more than notes; over time, however, they became quite elaborate, eventually becoming one of the major vehicles through which the literati rewrote the story of the past. In this guise, they frequently laid claim to historical knowledge they manifestly did not have. Both British and Irish sources claim, for example, to describe events in the fifth century (including, on the Irish side, the arrival and mission of St Patrick), even though they do not appear to have any direct information on the subject. As far as we can tell, it is not until the second half of the sixth century that Irish annals start to become contemporaneous with the events they describe. The earliest Welsh annals preserved in a tenth-century text from St Davids known as the *Annales Cambriae* do not contain entries from St Davids itself before the late eighth century; however, the text seems to have been drawing on earlier (probably seventh-century) annalistic material from the British north. The history of the genre in England is equally murky, although it seems extremely likely that Bede must have drawn on such Easter table notes in his writing of the *Ecclesiastical History*, and Bede was himself in any case a pioneer in a genre closely related to annals, the chronicle, a narrative account of events, often (but not necessarily) in annalistic form.

One significant written genre of the period that is often overlooked by all but specialists is that of the inscribed stones of Britain and Ireland, which vary from the (seemingly) simple memorial markers in Latin or ogham found in Ireland and Wales to the sophisticated Pictish Christian designs of the eighth and ninth centuries. Often these take the form of crosses, or of stones inscribed with a cross; sometimes they are ornamented by carved figures or scenes. Over 400 of these stones are known from Wales alone—some inscribed in Latin, and some both in Latin and ogham. Ireland also preserves more than 300 ogham inscribed stones, most from the southern counties of Kerry, Cork, and Waterford. And there are more than 200 Pictish symbol stones extant, twenty-seven of which bear inscriptions written in the ogham alphabet, but couched in a language we cannot today understand. Indeed, so mysterious are the Picts, and so few the writings they have left us, that they seem in historical and cultural terms the equivalent of the tree that falls in the forest with no one to hear it.

# Texts and contexts

Laws, charters, saints' Lives, genealogies, annals, inscribed stones—these are but a sampling of the genres extant from pre-Viking Britain and Ireland. One problem historians have in making use of these sources is understanding why certain types of text are extant from one region but not from another. It is possible that what remains today may reflect only a tiny percentage of what once existed. So many manuscripts have disappeared over the centuries that it is

difficult to know whether a gap in the evidence ought to be interpreted as a sign that the genre in question was never widespread in
that culture or, rather, as an indication that a large body of material
once in existence has subsequently been lost. Certainly, there are indications that the latter was a common occurrence, especially in
Celtic-speaking countries, where conditions for the preservation of
manuscripts were unusually poor.

England's preservation record is better, but there also the rate of
survival is an issue. Sometimes we know that texts are now missing
because others that are extant tell us of those that are not. One of the
best-known documents of the Anglo-Saxon period, for example, is an
account of an agreement reached at the synod of Clofesho in 798 over
a jurisdictional dispute already by that date several decades old. The
monastery of Cookham in Berkshire had been granted to Canterbury
by the reigning king of Mercia in the first half of the eighth century.
However, after the death of the archbishop of Canterbury, the deeds
recording the grant were stolen and given to Cynewulf, king of
Wessex at the time, who on this basis immediately appropriated the
monastery and its lands. Some years after that, the powerful Mercian
King Offa forcibly took possession of the monastery—though not its
charters—from Cynewulf. Cynewulf, professing a bitter, if conveni-
ently tardy, regret over his treatment of Canterbury's property, then
restored the missing deeds to the reigning archbishop. This had little
effect on Offa, who died possessed of the monastery, leaving it to his
heirs after him. After Offa's death, however, possession of the deeds
allowed Canterbury to claim the monastery back from the king's
heirs at Clofesho, fully a half century after the original donation. This
arrangement was confirmed in writing, and were it not for this text,
we would know nothing of the dispute—nor indeed of Cookham
itself—since none of the documents mentioned in the agreement,
nor indeed any other text mentioning the monastery by name,
survives.

A gap in the evidence need not, therefore, indicate a gap in what
once existed. Here's the catch, though: sometimes it does. It would be
perfectly possible to have a sophisticated culture that could use writing if it wished, but simply chose not to do so. Unfortunately, it is
nearly impossible to tell. The example of early Scotland is an excellent
one. The disappearance of whatever manuscript culture might once
have existed there is virtually complete, even though the complex

iconography of the Pictish inscribed stones implies the presence there at one time of a literate culture fully on a par with others of its day. Unquestionably, the Picts were familiar both with writing and with Latin script—indeed, they also invented—if recent interpretations of the symbol stones are correct—a writing 'system' of their own. Ought we then to understand the dearth of documentation as a sign that they knew how to write but preferred to express their own native culture in traditional oral-performative ways? Or are we dealing here with a culture that did produce manuscripts which, sadly, did not survive?

Similarly, no extended piece of legal writing has survived from Wales from the period before 1200. However, there are several high and late medieval lawbooks extant from Wales that claim to descend from a text compiled in the tenth century by the powerful King Hywel Dda. The thirteenth century saw a tremendous explosion of interest all across Europe in the writing down of law: virtually every European nation produced a lawbook in this period, including Spain and Iceland. Ought we thus to assume from the lack of early texts that law in pre-Conquest Wales was essentially an oral endeavour, and that the Welsh lawbooks of the thirteenth century reflect the general European trend toward written law in that period? Or ought we to interpret the thirteenth-century lawbooks as but the end product of a long tradition of legal writing in Wales, the early stages of which have disappeared over the centuries? The plain fact is that we just don't know: it is possible to make both cases well.

One of the very important things we do know is that the intellectual climates in which these texts were produced differed from region to region across the British Isles, and that these differences were likely reflected both in the assumptions these cultures made about the uses of writing and in the nature of the texts they produced. Perhaps the most significant of these differences was the fact that whereas most of Britain was occupied by the Romans, Ireland and northern Scotland were not. It is difficult to speak with certainty about continuity with Roman government and literate traditions in mainland Britain. We know very little about the institutions and habits of mind that might have survived the chaos of the Saxon conquests in Britain itself. However, it is clear that the Anglo-Saxons had close relations with their Frankish neighbours, who were intimately acquainted with Roman practices and priorities, and of course

Theodore's arrival from Rome (and earlier the highly cosmopolitan East) reintroduced to England a variety of Roman customs with regards to writing. In Wales, particularly in the more Romanized regions of the south-east, some knowledge of late Roman practices and genres seems to have remained long enough to shape textual production in the early Middle Ages. Indeed, the continuing existence of Latin as a prestige dialect among the Welsh and the association of the Latin language with the written word may have discouraged writing in the vernacular in a way it did not in Ireland—a fact that might help us to understand the relative paucity of extant vernacular texts.

The fact that Ireland and Scotland were never Romanized does not mean that these cultures had no knowledge of Roman intellectual concerns. However, they had no direct administrative or cultural legacy to contend with: what they knew of Roman ideas and practices was by and large filtered to them through Christian texts of the late antique and early medieval period. And with respect to Ireland specifically, the fact that the Roman armies never occupied the island mattered tremendously to its subsequent intellectual development. Gaelic was and remained a high-status language, not least because it had no native linguistic competitors. Moreover, the most striking difference between Ireland and the cultures of Continental Europe was the existence in the former of a native learned class that almost certainly would not have survived had the island been officially subsumed into the all-encompassing embrace of the Empire. A wide variety of intellectual specialties were represented within this learned class: poets, bards, druids, jurists (sometimes referred to as 'brehons', from Old Irish *brithemain*), genealogists, pseudo-historians, and shanachies (storytellers, historians). All were regarded as guardians of, and authorities within, their particular branches of native tradition, specialists whose charge it was not only to remember the past but to represent it, typically in oral performance.

The advent of Christianity in Ireland thus marked the coming together of two organized, long-standing intellectual traditions, one Christian and one pagan, each with their own histories, 'texts', and personnel. We know little about the early stages of this intersection of traditions, although it is probably right to imagine a wide variety of responses on the part of native intellectuals towards the newcomers, ranging from enthusiastic acceptance to hostile dismay. Undoubtedly significant intellectual exchange took place over time between the two groups: indeed, some historians have suggested that with the exception of the druids, whose special province of religion was not easily translatable into terms acceptable to the Church, these two traditions merged so completely with one another that it is impossible for us today to hope to recover anything truly 'native' in the texts they produced. Others believe, by contrast, that members of the Irish learned class used what they learnt from the Church—most notably, of course, writing—to construct and record what was for these scholars still essentially a native tradition visible in the extant sources. Whatever position one ultimately decides to adopt, what is unquestionable is the tremendous significance of the body of literature resulting from this fusion of native and Christian. It is no accident that Ireland preserves the most extensive vernacular tradition attested from anywhere in western Europe before the twelfth century. Native and ecclesiastical intellectuals alike grasped very quickly the idea that writing could play an important role in the transmission and preservation of *all* cultural material, vernacular and Latin.

The situation in Wales was likely quite similar, although this is difficult at this point to prove. Because we have so little demonstrably early material remaining to us, the evidence for the existence of a learned class of this sort in Wales lies mainly in the fact that when we do start to get texts from Wales in the twelfth and thirteenth centuries, the professions visible in the early Irish sources—lawyers, poets, storytellers, and the like—are already very much in evidence. Moreover, the literature they produce makes use of themes and symbols that look native, secular, and old in ways that imply the organized transmission over time of native culture. The situation in Pictland is even more difficult to assess because of the paucity of native written cultural material of any date. In Ireland and Wales, antiquarian scholars of the high and late Middle Ages played an enormous role in preserving early texts and traditions. However, Scotland was for historical reasons more attuned in the high medieval period to Anglo-Norman perceptions and priorities than to its own native past. The heirs of a native learned class survived in Scotland into the high medieval period, as they did in Ireland and Wales, but Scottish kings were less concerned with the preservation of the tradition from which they had sprung than with integrating Scotland within the greater European world.

There are, then, important differences separating the various learned traditions of Britain and Ireland. The peoples who became the Anglo-Saxons certainly had poets, and a vigorous vernacular that made its way into writing. However, they do not appear to have had anything truly comparable to the intellectual elites of Ireland and Wales. There were no professional jurists in England before the high medieval period, and no single class of individuals charged with the preservation of an identifiable body of native tradition. Indeed, given the mixed ethnic origins and affiliations of those who became the Anglo-Saxons, the idea of a specifically 'native' tradition is unlikely to have had much inherent resonance for some time after their arrival. As a result, most Anglo-Saxon texts show clear signs of connections either to Church or court. One of the most striking aspects of literature produced in England per se is its precocious concern with royal authority, and with writing as a means of advancing that authority. Under the influence of the Church, and of their Frankish neighbours, Anglo-Saxon literati turned the diversity of genres bequeathed to them by the Romans and early Christians towards the purposes of the kings they served. Whereas the Celtic-speaking countries by and large eschewed what has been called 'pragmatic literacy'—the use of writing for bureaucratic or administrative purposes—the Anglo-Saxons embraced it enthusiastically. Anglo-Saxon practices with respect to writing thus occupy something of a middle ground between those of their Celtic and Continental neighbours. Like their mainland European colleagues, they used writing for royal and administrative purposes; like other Insular cultures, they wrote in the vernacular as well as in Latin.

# Writing history

Power and identity are the bread-and-butter issues of any historian. How peoples of diverse backgrounds and interests come together into discernible political entities, how hierarchies and relationships of dominance are constructed within a given culture—these are among the most common questions historians confront in their work. Traditionally such matters have been conceptualized almost entirely in terms of the most obvious forms of institutionalized power—kings, armies, churchmen, bureaucrats. This is not wrong, but it is incomplete, as many historians are now beginning to realize. Over the past two decades, our eyes have been opened to entirely new definitions of 'power'—definitions that transcend the strictly institutional and focus instead on the authority implicit in the ordering of domestic and personal relations, for example, or the manipulation of language and cultural imagery. Only now are we beginning fully to realize the tremendous power implicit in the telling of stories.

This is an approach and a set of questions particularly appropriate to the study of the early British Isles. For there especially, the emergence of a distinctive cultural and political identity was a story not merely of rulers and their wars but of the manipulation of vital cultural traditions—native and Latin, written and oral. Precisely because of the paucity of soberly bureaucratic sources from the Celtic areas particularly, historians of Ireland, Scotland, and Wales have long been forced to rely heavily on pseudo-historical genres in their attempts to reconstruct the early political life of these regions. Now English historians also are beginning to see their sources in a different light. Classics like Bede's *Ecclesiastical History of the English People*, which used to be taken as more or less straightforward historical narrative, are now understood as works of purposeful construction. For in describing good kingship to a people with no long history of same, Bede's *Ecclesiastical History* helped to bring it about; in charting the coming together of the various cultures of the island into a single whole united in their common adherence to the Roman Church, it implicitly suggested the inevitability and historical 'rightness' of such a political entity. Cultural diversity Bede either suppresses or reconstructs as obstreperous dissent: what must have seemed to many living at the time completely acceptable varieties of Christianity, for example, he reimagines as a few pesky British and Irish holdouts whose evil days are numbered. Image is not reality, but the deliberate deployment of images is an important part of the process by which reality can come to be defined.

Not all texts are as partisan as is the *Ecclesiastical History*. And Bede is obviously an exceptional writer. But it is important to realize that even the most mundane of texts represents more than just the objective recording of events. The mere act of conceptualizing a given individual or set of relationships in a particular way can itself have the effect of guiding or forestalling other interpretative possibilities, even if it is not intended deliberately to mislead. A genealogy that identifies a given individual with a prominent kindred, for example, implicitly denies his links with another. An annalist who chooses to record a battle but not a peace silently shapes the events he purports to chronicle. A law code that describes the noble and freemen classes but completely omits the poor is creating an image of society completely at odds with reality. All texts remake the past—sometimes subtly, sometimes in a more overt fashion—and, in so doing, reshape the present. This is why, in order to understand the ways in which the advent of writing helped to redraw the cultural map of early Britain and Ireland, we must pay attention not only to the Bedes of the past but also to the less glamorous and largely anonymous authors whose voices so often seem muted in comparison.

With this in mind, let us turn now to some specific case studies—individual texts that are in some cases well known, at least to specialists, and in others, not. In the churchyard at Castelldwyran near Carmarthen in Wales a stone was found with two inscriptions. One, in Latin letters, reads MEMORIA VOTEPORIGIS PROTICTORIS, 'to the memory of Votepor Protector' the other, inscribed in ogham characters up the side of the stone, simply gives an Irish version of the name in the genitive: VOTECORIGAS. On top of the Latin inscription—actually smashed down right on top of the word *memoria*—is a type of cross within a circle known to archaeologists as a 'ring-cross'. This stone has received a great deal of scholarly attention because of the proximity of the name of the deceased to that of Vortipor, an early mid-sixth-century king of Dyfed denounced as a 'tyrant' by Gildas. Indeed, until only very recently most historians would with little hesitation have identified the two as the same man. However—and annoyingly for those historians who would prefer that their epigraphic sources match up with the extant narrative texts, which is probably all of us—there is the small problem of a 'missing R' here. Votepor is similar to Vortipor, but it is not, alas, the same.

Most discussions of the stone have centred on the issue of the identity of the man it was intended to commemorate. It is, of course, entirely possible that the missing 'R' was merely due to a stone carver's error and that the individual in question was in fact the Vortipor excoriated by Gildas. Or it could be another ruler altogether. It may seem unlikely that there would be two such rulers operating simultaneously in the same kingdom, but the two individuals involved could easily represent different generations or, since *protector* was a prestigious, but distinctly junior, title in the Roman army, its meaning in this context might have been something like 'deputy' or 'heir'. Other historians have suggested that, given the tendency of British ruling kindreds to give similar names to their members as a marker of familial identity (witness the seventh-century dynasty of Cadfan, Cadwallon, and Cadwaladr), the Votepor of the stone might even be a relative of the king mentioned by Gildas, or perhaps even a kindred ruler of an earlier generation.

All of these explanations are sensible, and it seems quite likely that one or more of them may also be right. However, what these readings all have in common is that they interpret the stone as a *record* of reality rather than as an attempt to shape or even subvert it. And yet texts can 'mean' in many different ways. They can function as objects, as symbols, and as languages in their own right: not merely passive vehicles for the transmission of ideas, but active cultural agents helping those ideas to come into being. The context in which they are composed and consumed matters very much to their impact on the society that produced them. An ogham stone that proclaims X to be the son of Y and descendant of Z, for example, may seem on one level simply to commemorate an individual and provide information about his biological descent. However, in the context in which the stone was actually commissioned, the message of such a stone may have been considerably less innocuous than it appears to us today: the assertion of a politically motivated claim to membership in a powerful kindred, for example, or the rendering permanently into stone of a particular version of a contested pedigree. Perhaps the stone was raised as an aggressive gesture—as a declaration of hostilities against a competing kindred, or as a boundary marker placed provocatively on lands in dispute. Or perhaps it was intended to communicate the defiant assertion of Irishness in the midst of a surrounding British population. The meaning of a text resides not merely in the words it contains, but in the movement of those words in time and space.

Bringing such perspectives to bear on the Votepor stone enlarges our possibilities for its interpretation. Memorials are raised by and for the living. They can be testimonials to grief, or assertions of a right to reorder political relations in the wake of a significant death, or a hundred things in between. We cannot simply assume, for example, that the use of the title *protector* on the stone indicates that this was an office occupied by the deceased during his lifetime. It may have been an office to which he and his heirs were attempting to lay claim, or a way of characterizing his authority to which not everyone who knew him would have consented. Similarly, in the proximity of the names Votepor and Vortipor we might be seeing the assertion of a claim to membership of a ruling dynasty rather than the record of a true biological relationship. And what of the purpose of the stone itself? Might the man commemorated have been a rival of the reigning king whose supporters raised the stone as a defiant gesture designed to rally support for his heir? Or might the stone have been set up by the reigning king himself as a way of appropriating unto himself the potentially politically explosive rites associated with the death of a powerful rival, or as a means of minimizing the authority of his heir by according the dead man a title—*protector*—associated with the junior ranks of the Roman army?

Similar questions could be asked of the ground on which the marker was originally raised. It was found in a churchyard, which at least raises the possibility that the land even then might have been associated with the Church and the stone itself a statement of the link between Christian, Roman, and the right to rule. Clearly the design on the stone is Christian—but again, it is difficult to say whether this symbol had meaning for the deceased himself, or only for those who came after him. Ring-crosses of this sort are known from catacombs in Rome from around the year 500: does this stone merely record recent contacts between Wales and the Mediterranean world, or is it a proud proclamation of the dynasty's links with the other cultures of Christendom?

And what of the Irish on the stone? Bilingual inscriptions are not uncommon in the area, and, as historians have frequently noted, there is good evidence to suggest the intrusion of Irish dynasts into the kingship of Dyfed in this period. And some of the bilingual stones in the area do in fact seem to commemorate Irishmen—or at least persons whose heirs in death laid claim to Irish names. But what of the Votepor stone? The name Votepor is British, and this is a language we assume that he would have spoken. Was the Irish on the stone also there because Votepor and his surviving kin spoke Irish, or was it intended to serve as a reminder of the dual ethnic heritage of the royal line of Dyfed? Or might it represent an assertion of the right to rule over an immigrant and subject Irish population, or a conciliatory gesture, a recognition of the mixed nature of the community?

Similar questions must be asked about the ogham script itself. Historians are generally agreed that ogham was originally invented as a vehicle through which to express the sounds of the Irish language, but there is considerably less consensus on its ideological implications. Some have seen in the choice of ogham and the vernacular a declaration of allegiance to native culture and an expression of hostility to Rome and Latin Christianity. Others have gone in another direction entirely, pointing to the Latin inscriptions that accompany many of the early British stones and taking even early ogham as primarily Christian in its associations. And of course there is no a priori reason for which one must envisage a single set of associations governing all of the contexts in which ogham occurs. Ogham, like Latin, or German, or cuneiform, or in fact any code, whether language or script, can come over time and space to communicate differently in the various contexts in which it is employed. Its interpretation may be as diverse as its distribution. What in eighth-century Pictland means native and noble might well be taken in sixth-century Wales as the sign of an individual completely *au fait* with contemporary ecclesiastical trends.

Indeed, perhaps the only certain message communicated by this stone is the infinite complexity of personal and political identity in western Britain in the sixth century. Here we have a memorial inscribed in Latin and Irish to a ruler in Britain, and yet British is the language that appears nowhere on the stone (other than in the name Votepor). It invokes in its inscription the Roman army title of *protector* in its characterization of the nature of the authority exercised by the deceased, and yet the man of whom that title is alleged lived in a Britain from which the last Roman troops had departed a century and a half earlier. Moreover, he lived in a Britain in which, to judge from Gildas himself, many aristocratic Britons not only identified themselves as British rather than as Roman, but regarded the Romans with something approaching hostility for having abandoned them to the ravening hordes of the period. To find a ruler of this period—or at least those who raised the stone—drawing on an imperial imagery in this manner is not something that can merely be taken for granted. It is a question in itself.

In a very real sense, then, the precise identity of the deceased is one of the less important questions to be asked about the stone. Of far greater import is what it implies about the manner in which texts like these literally inscribe meaning on the landscape they inhabit. They may assert things that are not true in order to make them happen; they may serve as the focus for political rebellion or, alternatively, constitute a performance of political unity. In some instances, they will form the physical backdrop for socially significant rituals we can no longer resurrect; in others, they will be moved, up-ended, or defaced as a gesture of dissent. Like all texts, they mean in context, and in performance—and of course they can change this meaning over time and from audience to audience. We are by definition excluded from any but the more contemporary of these perform-ances, but this does not mean that we should forgo any attempt to make sense of them. It merely suggests that we would do better to go beyond our natural tendency to read them as straightforward or uncomplicated records of what 'was' and see them instead for what they really were: important aspects of how that particular 'was' came into being.

Our second case study is an unusually complex text from Anglo-Saxon Wessex. Sometime between 670 and 676, Cenred, king of Wessex and (likely) father of the future West Saxon lawgiver Ine, granted several estates to one Abbot Bectun 'for the relief of my soul and the remission of my sins'. This grant was confirmed by charter. Some time afterwards, Bectun's successor Catwali gave 'for his money' one of these lands to Abbot Wintra of Tisbury. A new charter was then made recording the transaction that may have followed the wording of the original grant, but which naturally only made men-tion of the one estate given to Abbot Wintra instead of all of the estates listed in the original charter. Wintra preserved this new char-ter in his archives as proof of his monastery's title to the land. Abbot Catwali, for his part, kept Cenred's original charter of donation— with its enumeration of all the estates granted by Cenred, including the one he had since sold to Wintra—since it constituted his monas-tery's title to the other lands included in Cenred's original grant. Then, several decades after the transaction had taken place, when all the principals were dead and the details of the event had faded from memory, a dispute over the ownership of the estate sold by Catwali to Wintra arose between their successors, with the successors of Catwali offering as proof of their claim the original donation charter from Cenred, and the successors of Wintra offering the text of Catwali's grant to Wintra in response. Intricate negotiations ensued in which both the bishop of Winchester and the reigning king of Wessex were involved, and the matter was finally resolved by all parties in 759.

What remains to us today as a record of this protracted series of events is a text made by the bishop of Winchester in 759 detailing the long history of the dispute and its eventual resolution. The text is of more than ordinary interest in that, in addition to the bishop's own account of the agreement reached by the disputing parties, it contains a transcription of what appears to be the original charter of donation from Cenred to Bectun emended to reflect only upon the land at issue:

Wherefore I, Cenred . . . have decided to grant a certain small portion of land to the venerable man, Abbot Bectun, i.e. 30 hides north of the stream Font-mell by name. . . . Now I have placed for more complete security sods of the above-mentioned lands on the Gospels, so that from this day he may have in all things free and secure power of holding, having, possessing. (*EHD*, vol. 1, p. 481)

To this early charter is then attached the bishop's subscription of 759, which explains the confusion arising from the existence of the two conflicting charters and the means by which the dispute was finally settled:

Therefore I now, and our king, and the rest whose witness and subscription is noted below, have made a peaceful reconciliation between them, partly through the giving of money, partly through the performance of an oath, to the extent that hereafter the successors of Abbot Wintra, i.e. Ecgwold . . . are to have and possess forever . . . the land about which there long was a dispute . . . and I have given this writing to Abbot Ecgwold, with the witnesses named below consenting and confirming it, but rejecting other writings which have been drawn up about this land. (*EHD*, vol. 1, p. 482)

As the late subscription to the text makes clear, both king and bishop were instrumental in negotiating a peaceful settlement between the disputing parties. The charter is thus on one level a record of the authority exercised by these two figures within the community, and this is how historians have typically approached this and other similar texts.

However, as was the case with the Votepor stone, charters also were more than mere records of static realities. What we must do is attempt to understand the role texts of this sort may have played in helping to bring such royal and episcopal authority into being: to see them not merely as passive reflections, but as active agents, of the construction of power in early England. For until at least the mid-eighth century, the issuing of charters was a royal prerogative among the Anglo-Saxons; even after this point, when private deeds began to appear, they had still to be approved by kings. In a very real sense, in fact, the link between kingship and the written word is implicit in the charter genre, in that land granted by written charter or 'book'—termed 'bookland' in the early English sources—was thereby freed from various royal taxes and rents. In other words, the giving of a charter was itself an act of lordship, on a par with those other acts of munificence and expropriation through which those who claimed to be royal attempted to set themselves apart from those who aspired to that status. For in remitting dues, one implicitly claims the right to impose them; in making use of a literary form that only kings have the right to employ, one implicitly claims that status for oneself.

Understanding charters as active agents of authority instead of passive reflections of it helps us to make sense of some confusing aspects of other literature of the period. The link between charters and lordship may be why Bede, in his letter to Ecgberht, bishop, and later archbishop, of York, refers to charters as 'royal edicts': the difference between these two genres may not have been all that appreciable on the ground. That claims to royal status were not always accepted, and that indeed the granting of charters could function sometimes as a battleground on which conflicting claims might be fought out, is evident from another charter of 799, which describes an incident in which Offa, king of Mercia, revoked written grants issued by one Ecgberht and redistributed the lands in question. In his own eyes, Ecgberht was king of Kent and fully capable of making such grants on his own; in Offa's, he was merely a 'thegn' and not of sufficient status to undertake actions of this sort independently.

Charters helped to establish royal authority in other ways as well. The bishop's subscription makes clear that the mere fact of the document's existence as a physical object had a dramatic impact on the manner in which the dispute over the land sold by Catwali to Wintra proceeded to resolution. In an uniquely oral culture of the sort the Saxons would presumably have had in the days before literacy became widespread, both donations and disputes would have been inseparable from the community within which they were enacted. Authority in such a venue would have been vested in

performance: in the rites and rituals by which possession was transferred and ownership confirmed, and in the 'audience' of witnesses
before which they would have been enacted. Once transactions came
to be committed to writing, however, they became, in a very real
sense, portable. Their physical existence as documents permitted
them to be taken elsewhere for interpretation or judgement; similarly,
they could be altered, repudiated, or invalidated without reference to
the locality from within which they had emerged. Moreover, as texts,
they could remain to confuse or agitate generations far removed from
the original actors and spectators. Contradictions that in an oral
culture are quietly erased or elided through the natural processes by
which social memory is constructed and reconstructed over time
cannot be as easily overlooked once they take written form.

What we are seeing in the charters pertaining to the Catwali case
are two conflicting versions of the past, both of which are partial and
yet have also some claim to being 'true'. Had these versions of the
past never been written down, they might never have come into
conflict. It is only because the original land grant survived in the
archives—itself testimony to the relative speed with which churches
had come to see charters as crucial to their ability to prove title to
their lands—that questions over the ownership of land arose in the
first place. We do not know how the dispute came to the attention of
the king and bishop in whose name the charter resolving the matter
was issued. What we do know, however, is that the existence of
these conflicting texts provided an opportunity for these officials to
impose themselves and their authority in what might otherwise have
remained local ecclesiastical affairs. In adjudicating between the
claims presented to them, king and bishop established themselves and
their successors as the appropriate authorities to whom such questions ought to be submitted. Moreover, on issuing the written documents that finally laid the dispute to rest, they implicitly laid claim to
yet another important prerogative: the ability to rewrite the past in a
manner consistent with their own priorities.

Our final case study differs from the other two in that the text
under consideration is used primarily as a lens through which to
examine similar themes in related genres of the period. Of the composition of the text itself and of its impact as a physical object we can
say relatively little, since it is extant only in a context that obscures the
original context of its inscription and use. At issue is a fragment of

Irish legal verse incorporated into a medieval miscellany on the law of contract known as *Di Astud Chor*. The date of *Di Astud Chor* itself is uncertain; the language of the poem itself, however, suggests a composition date in the early eighth century:[2]

> The contract [made by] a legally competent person is not released
> Because of [parties to the arrangement] reflecting [on its terms] afterwards
>     with the wisdom of hindsight,
> As long as it be a legally competent person who is acting.
> Around Lucifer there has been fastened
> His [own] ill-advised, ignoble, disadvantageous contract
> For which he can not evade payment.

Readers not attuned to the pleasures of legal verse of this sort may require assurance that the passage in question is, in fact, a poem: the verse itself is of a type not uncommon in the literature, with internal (though haphazard) alliteration, tri- and monosyllabic endings for lines, and a (relatively simple) pattern of linking alliteration between short and long lines.

Many things will strike the reader immediately about this text, not least of which is the obvious distance between it and what an average person might expect a fragment of medieval law to look like. The principle at the heart of the poem is recognizable—barely—as legal in nature and import: persons who possess an appreciably normal level of mental, material, and legal competence cannot agree to a deal that they know to be disadvantageous to themselves and hope to get out of it later. Other passages in the miscellany add some qualifiers: if fraud has been involved, or if the items exchanged had defects hidden to the purchaser at the time of the transaction, adjustments can and will be made. Otherwise, those who in a moment of carelessness, haste, or injudicious goodwill towards their fellow man commit themselves to paying more for something than it is actually worth are just going to have to live with it. Nothing unusual in this per se: different formulations of the same legal principle (of which the Roman *caveat emptor* is only the most famous) are visible in any number of historical legal traditions. What is unusual, however, is the manner in which this tenet is expressed in the Irish tract—the alliteration and syllabic patterning, the allusions to Lucifer, the less

---

[2] N. McLeod, *Early Irish Contract Law* (Sydney, n.d.), pp. 138, § 13.

than crystalline clarity of the phrasing. Those familiar with the Irish original might note in addition the poem's frequent use or paraphrasing of phrases and expressions known from elsewhere in the legal literature: the third line of the poem is repeated verbatim in another verse found later in the miscellany; and the very last line is constructed around a *figura etymologica* that occurs in very similar form in another legal tract of the period.

What are we to make of this poem, and what does it tell us about the role of textual production in the construction of early Irish culture? As with so many of the texts we have examined, it can be read on a variety of levels. At its most basic level it is a statement of law, an attempt by one individual or entity to regulate the behaviour of another, and as such is inevitably bound up with the power politics of the period. However, it is also a statement about identity, and about the complex forms of cultural assimilation characteristic of the period. As mentioned above, there is today considerable controversy among Irish legal scholars as to the role played by ecclesiastical texts and personnel in the production of the Irish lawbooks that remain to us. Some argue that these texts essentially originated from within the Church—that the ecclesiastical impact on the extant lawbooks has been so great that it is simply not possible to speak in terms of a genuinely 'native' tradition. Others, by contrast, suggest instead that the lawbooks are the work of native legal professionals who made use of ecclesiastical techniques and texts (literacy and the Bible) in their efforts to preserve and extend native law, but whose perspective remained separable (and occasionally separate) from that of their ecclesiastical colleagues. The debate has been a fierce one, but regardless of the point of view one wishes to take on the matter, what seems absolutely clear is that the extant legal tracts represent a coming together of two great legal traditions: one a native, essentially oral and performative tradition thought to have originated as a branch of poetry, and the other a literate, book-centred tradition with ties to the ancient world.

Reflected in the poem, then, is something of the manner in which texts helped to facilitate this accommodation between traditions. The excerpt quite deliberately juxtaposes the two in a way designed to prove that they are compatible. There is no reason to believe that the principle expressed was anything but native in origin: the fact that Lucifer as an example of someone who made a disadvantageous contract with God is a bit of a stretch certainly suggests that the contractual principle in question pre-dated, rather than originated in, the biblical tale. On the other hand, the example offered as a precedent is taken from Christian theology rather than native mythology. In other words, native law is shown not only to be compatible with, but validated by, Christian belief.

But the accommodation between traditions asserted through the poem goes deeper than this. For while the excerpt itself is written, a type of communication originating in and associated with the Church, the passage itself is verse. Verse obviously does not have to be an oral genre, and since we know so little about this excerpt it is difficult to know whether it might ever have been performed orally or whether it was intended entirely for literate consumption. However, one of the most basic beliefs held by the Irish jurists about the origins of their tradition was that native law branched off as a discipline from poetry. Texts of the period almost invariably portray mythical jurists of the prehistoric era delivering their verdicts in verse, and there is a wonderful Irish tale that purports to explain how it was that poets historically lost jurisdiction in legal affairs (they insisted on speaking in incomprehensible verse and thus irritated everyone around them). In other words, the choice of verse as a medium in this passage itself constitutes an implicit reference to pre-Christian native tradition. Oral and written, native and biblical are deliberately juxtaposed as a means of asserting the essential compatibility and historical appropriateness of the melding of these two cultural traditions.

Other, more personal and professional forms of identity may also be in question. There are indications in other Irish sources that juristic authority was grounded not merely in a knowledge of the law, but in a knowledge of how to 'speak' it as well. Law may still have been a performative genre at the time the lawbooks were written; certainly the ability to speak in obscure, poetic, or rhetorically distinctive ways is frequently presented in the tracts as a sign of legitimacy. Moreover, the use of deliberately arcane, even obscurantist language in written law seems to have been used as a way to restrict intervention in legal matters to those suitably trained in the discipline—a discipline in which language was as important as legal knowledge per se. By phrasing this passage in verse, one of the culturally authoritative forms of speech recognized in Irish tradition, and by employing phrases and expressions known from elsewhere in the native legal tradition, the author (and speaker, if any) establishes his own authority as a member of the legally educated elite.

Identity—cultural and professional—is thus the issue at the heart of this rather mundane-looking text. Indeed, a case can be made that while Irish law differs considerably from other legal texts composed in the early British Isles in its manner of formulation and non-royal origins, similar concerns with identity and cultural assimilation lie behind all of the laws of the period. Written law was certainly one of the ways Anglo-Saxon kings found to introduce themselves and their peoples into the narratives of classical and Christian history. Whatever the customs of their Continental homeland, the people of Kent became, through the production of Æthelberht's code, participants in a tradition larger than themselves. Like other early Germanic peoples, the Anglo-Saxons found particular appeal in the stories of the Old Testament Israelites, whose hazardous journey out of superstition and unbelief seemed so closely to parallel their own. And for the Israelites, law was the essence of the covenant between God and his chosen people—that which celebrated and defined the special relationship existing between them, and established the rules necessary for a properly spiritual life. Small wonder, then, that with pagan Vikings threatening on all sides, King Alfred of Wessex chose not only to issue a law code, but to preface his laws with the Ten Commandments and excerpts from Exodus. This was not luxury or useless symbolism, but the invocation of an affiliation with the suffering of the past: in other words, pragmatism at its height.

Law likely also played an important role in helping the various peoples of early England begin to see themselves as a single folk. Bede tells us that those who settled the island included Angles, Saxons, and Jutes, and although we have little trace of them in our records, some British-speaking individuals must also have remained within the territories occupied by the Germanic invaders. It is unclear at what point these various groups came to see themselves as members of a single people, although efforts by the *literati* (not least, of course, Bede himself) to construct them as such began very early. Law was another of the venues in which such ideas about identity were articulated and explored. Æthelberht and his successors legislated as kings of the people of Kent, and Ine issued his code in the name of the West Saxons over whom he reigned as king. However, already by Ine's time there seems to be evidence of an incipient 'national' consciousness rooted in language and stretching across the boundaries of individual kingdoms. Ine's code terms the English-speaking subjects of his kingdom (differentiating them from the subordinate Welsh with whom his code also deals) *Engliscm[e]n*, literally, 'persons of the Angles'—despite the fact that he was himself a Saxon. And Alfred actually draws in his code on the laws of previous Anglo-Saxon-speaking kings, including Offa of Mercia and Æthelberht, whom he terms the king 'who first among the English (*Angelcynne*) accepted baptism'. No reference is made in his code to his having drawn on contemporary Irish or Welsh law as a model, and this despite the fact that at least one custom incorporated into the code is demonstrably Welsh in origin. Alfred was concerned with the laws of the people he saw as his own—a people defined both by their possession of a common language and their position as a latter-day Israel.

Indeed, the matter of the language of the laws itself speaks very directly to the issues of identity and assimilation that are such visible concerns in the Irish legal material. Æthelberht's code established a precedent that those who came after him faithfully followed. Not only did he put the customs of his people into written form, he put them into the vernacular instead of Latin. This use of the vernacular sets the Anglo-Saxon laws apart from all contemporary Continental codes—including those of the Franks on which we believe Æthelberht's own laws to have been modelled. That other early Germanic codes should be written in Latin, the language of late antique law and administration, is not in the least surprising—indeed, the early Continental codes are usually regarded as one of the great achievements of the late Roman senatorial aristocracy, members of which served in administrative and advisory functions to the Germanic kings settling on the lands of the former Empire. The issue of why the English kings alone would have chosen English rather than Latin as a medium for their laws is therefore a vexed one. Several suggestions have been made. Some have argued that there was no one in the English kingdom capable of bridging the gap between Germanic custom and the Latin language. Others have pointed to the fact that there seems to have been less direct administrative continuity with the Empire in England than there was elsewhere.

However, there are other possibilities also—ones more in keeping with the idea of thinking of documents as active constructors of hierarchies and relationships rather than as passive mirrors of events.

Perhaps it might be fruitful to think not about why the English would have been unable to use Latin but about why they might deliberately have chosen to employ the vernacular. We know that Frankish kings had exercised—or at least claimed—jurisdiction over Kent at a point not that far removed from Æthelberht's day. Might it be that Æthelberht and his advisers, in choosing English as the medium for their laws, were deliberately seeking to distance themselves from those early days by asserting their independence and separateness in the face of their powerful Frankish neighbours? Whatever the king's initial reasoning, the choice, once made, proved critical for subsequent English law-making. Linguistically and syntactically, Æthelberht's is the most primitive of the early English codes. Already in his laws, however, one can see the beginnings of a specialized legal vocabulary and approach on which Anglo-Saxon kings proceeded to draw for the next several centuries. In defining English as the language of law, Æthelberht helped to set the terms by which the English as a whole would come ultimately to imagine themselves as a common legal entity.

The laws may also have played a role in constructing relationships between individual English-speaking kingdoms, and between powerful groups within those kingdoms. One of the early Kentish codes is ascribed jointly to Hlothhere and his nephew Eadric, even though the former was killed in a battle brought against him by the latter. Since we have no record of the two kings having ever reigned as joint monarchs, might Eadric have reissued under both names a code previously associated only with Hlothhere in an effort to secure the support of his uncle's adherents? Adopting a saint's cult associated with a people one had defeated was a common way of laying claim to the loyalties of the supporters of the previous regime—perhaps the reissuing of a law code under both names functioned in a similar manner. At the very least, such a move might have functioned as a reassurance to nobles on the losing side that their prerogatives would be respected under the new regime. Similarly, the laws of Wihtred of Kent date to 695, one year after the Anglo-Saxon chronicle tells us that peace was made between his kingdom and that of Ine. One of Wihtred's laws is virtually identical with one of Ine's: might Wihtred's borrowing of that law from Ine's code be not merely a reflection of the good relations obtaining now between the two peoples but an active expression of alliance?

These are all speculations, of course. However, one thing above all is clear: the texts with which this chapter is concerned were not merely passive vehicles for the transmission of ideas, but active cultural agents helping those ideas to come into being. They had meaning not only as forms of communication, but as objects, symbols, and languages in and of themselves. Through their words, their movements in time and space—indeed, their very existence as texts—they constructed a vision of the past that spoke directly to contemporary concerns. They did not stand apart from the oral performance culture of their day, but were part and parcel of it. The Votepor stone functioned both as a text and a venue for ritual; Cenred ensured the validity of his donation not only by issuing a charter, but by publicly placing sods from the land in question on the written text of the Bible; literate and oral authority were both implicit in the legal poem from *Di Astud Chor*. Text was but one of the elements helping to shape the peoples and cultures of early Britain and Ireland into what they would become. Like Wilfrid himself, texts moved easily across the boundary between the written and the performed. That we cannot today define with precision their contribution to the whole is testimony to the richness of the world they helped to create.

**Figure 7.1** The Kilnasaggart inscription, Co. Armagh. This inscription, effectively a charter on stone, records a grant by Ternóc son of Cérán (Ciarán) who died in 716. It invokes the patronage of St Peter and uses the term *loc*, from Latin *locus* 'place'; on both points it may be compared with the Whithorn inscription illustrated in figure 3.1(b).

# Conclusion

## Thomas Charles-Edwards

Well before 800, scholars had begun to construct an image of a glorious Christian past for the British Isles. The most influential was Bede's *Ecclesiastical History of the English People*. In spite of the title, the work included information about the Irish, the Britons, and even the Picts, as well as the English. The Irish and the Britons played opposite roles in the conversion of the English: the Britons refused to preach the Gospel to their neighbours, whereas the Irish, although more distant geographically, proved far more willing to bring salvation to the English. Bede, developing Gildas's idea of the moral unity of a nation—that a nation might have duties to God and to other nations—went on to imply that the Irish mission had created a debt that was eventually discharged when Ecgberht, a Northumbrian *peregrinus* in Ireland, persuaded the community of Iona to adopt the Roman Easter in 716. When Bede was writing in 731, however, most of the Britons remained adherents of the Celtic Easter; there was thus, in his eyes, a moral symmetry between the giving and counter-giving that ruled, with the odd exception, between the Irish and the English, and the hostility, expressed as much in the sphere of religion as in warfare, between the English and the Britons. Alongside the debt to the Irish there was also the immense and overriding debt to papal Rome, a debt shared by the Irish and the English: Bede knew of Palladius but apparently not of Patrick the Briton. For both conversions, of the Irish and of the English, the initiation of an organized mission came from the popes, Celestine for the Irish, Gregory the Great for the English. This was a debt which had never been discharged and which could only be met by continued loyalty as of children to their father.

Bede thus had a unified tale to tell, the core of which ran from 597 to 716; and within that tale certain characters were presented as exemplary models. Among the major figures from Northumbrian history accorded this treatment were Aidan, a model bishop, Cuthbert, a model holy man, and Oswald, a model king. Bede's anxiety to do full justice to their virtues was deepened by his belief, conveyed most urgently in the letter he wrote to another Ecgberht, bishop of York, in 734, that the Northumbria of his day had fallen away from earlier virtues and was incurring divine wrath, just as the Britons castigated by Gildas had merited God's punishment in their own day. Reform in 734 needed the cooperation of king and bishop, as in the days of Oswald and Aidan.

In a rather different form, a similar argument was pursued in Ireland later in the eighth century. On 7 July 792 Máel Ruain, founder and first abbot of Tallaght, 'bishop and soldier of Christ, slept in peace'. He is best known through a text, *The Monastery of Tallaght*, which is a collection of sayings of Máel Ruain and other like-minded monks about the ascetic life together with notes on the customs observed at their monasteries. The model for the text was the body of ascetic literature about the monks of the Egyptian desert. To write this text was to align Máel Ruain with such Egyptian holy men as Arsenius or Paphnutius. Yet the text also insinuated a proposition which was controversial, not least in Máel Ruain's day—that a fully ascetic life needed no physical desert, only a thoroughgoing self-denial and separation from the world. Máel Ruain's Tallaght was situated in one of the most fertile regions of early medieval Ireland, 'the Plain of Liffey'; it was not in any physical way a desert, even in the transferred sense in which islands in the sea such as Skellig Michael or Inishmurray performed that role. Yet the idea that a desert might exist as an enclave within a much-peopled and fertile landscape prevailed in Ireland, Wales, and Scotland, as shown by the scatter of place names, Irish and Scottish Gaelic Díseart (Anglicized as Dysart), Welsh Diserth, all from Latin *desertum*, 'desert'. *The Monastery of Tallaght* was written in Irish and was thus intended for a purely Irish readership; yet the full implications of the way of life it recommended would only have been apparent to those readers who could read Latin and thus knew its ancient forerunners.

Appropriately, one of the concerns of Máel Ruain's disciples was the commemoration of past Irish ascetics. To this end they used a copy of the standard martyrology—a list of saints arranged under their feast days—derived from Iona, and before that from Northumbria. The monks of Iona had added Irish saints according to the day of their death, and those of Tallaght added more. Three British saints, David, Beuno, and Daniel, were included, not counting those Britons who ended their days in Ireland, such as Patrick and Cairnech of Dulane. Since the text came to Tallaght from Iona, it is not surprising that Irish saints who lived in Britain were also included, such as Columba of Iona and Aidan of Lindisfarne; there were also a few non-Irish saints from North Britain, such as Blaan of Dunblane and Kingarth. In addition, a few names crept in of persons who were by no stretch of the imagination saints, such as Ecgfrith, king of Northumbria, probably included because he was buried on Iona after his death in battle against the Picts. By and large, however, what *The Martyrology of Tallaght* presents is a combination of two distinct assemblages of the holy: universal saints, acknowledged as potential heavenly patrons available for all Christians still living in a sinful world, and those saints proper to one nation, the Irish. When a nation has a recognized representation in heaven, it is indeed a nation; and not just the Irish but also the Britons and the English were gathering together their national saints: to perform this task for the English was a principal function of Bede's *Ecclesiastical History*; the unity of the Britons and the Bretons was displayed even in the later Middle Ages by their saints.

## Universal and national

A thoughtful churchman of AD 800, probably wherever he was in the British Isles, was ready to think on different planes—universal, national, provincial, and local. The tension between the claims of a universal Church and national traditions had been an issue ever since the Easter question became acute in Ireland about 630: the Irish Church split between 'Romans' and 'Hibernians'. Saints' cults also exemplify the same tension. Adomnán wrote at the end of his Life of Columba:

This too is no small favour conferred by God on the man of blessed memory, that one who dwelt in this little island [Iona] on the edge of the ocean should have earned a reputation that is famous not only in our own Ireland and in Britain, the largest of ocean's islands, but has also reached the three corners of Spain and Gaul and Italy beyond the Alps, and even Rome itself, the chief of all cities.

Here Adomnán moves from the local and even peripheral (Iona) to the Insular (Ireland and Britain), to the adjacent countries of Continental Christendom (Gaul, Spain, and Italy), and finally to Rome, the chief of all cities. The historian of the British Isles between 400 and 800 must display an equal fleetness of foot.

The period saw both the triumph within the British Isles of a universal religion, Christianity, and the emergence of a new array of nations. The two were already in creative tension in the work of Gildas, for whom the Britons, as a Christian nation, were fit subjects for that whole battery of prophetic denunciation of sins past and present contained in the Old Testament and levelled at the Chosen Nation, Israel. Of course the whole Christian Church was the primary counterpart under the New Covenant of Israel under the Old Covenant; yet a single Christian nation was also a counterpart.

The tension was also present in the combination of two languages, written as well as spoken. In the West, Latin was the language of the universal Church, the language of its liturgy, of its Bible, and of indispensable commentators on the Bible. Although there was some interest in Greek, the other universal language of the Roman Empire—especially in the Canterbury school of Theodore and Hadrian but also as early as Columba's Iona—and even in Hebrew, the last of 'the Three Sacred Languages', the normal linguistic medium of the universal intellectual culture of the Church in the British Isles, as elsewhere in the West, was Latin. In sixth-century Gaul, although most Franks were still speakers of their variety of Germanic, the Church recruited clergy overwhelmingly from a Gallo-Roman and thus Latin-speaking population. In sixth-century Britain and Ireland, this was not a viable policy: there were still Latin-speakers among the Britons, but they were a diminishing minority, and there was no Latin-speaking population in Ireland or in Pictland. Out of plain necessity, therefore, the Church in Britain and Ireland needed schools; and when the English became Christian in the seventh century, the same need was as inescapable for them as it had been earlier for the British, the Irish, and the Picts. One of Bede's anxieties displayed in the Letter to Ecgberht concerned 'idiot' priests—idiots, 'unskilled persons', that is, in the sense defined by Bede for the benefit of the bishop of York, namely persons who knew only their mother tongue. In this context, even some priests were idiots because they did not know Latin; Bede had attempted to mitigate their ignorance by giving them the Creed and the Lord's Prayer translated into English.

The schools of the fourth-century Empire were not Christian. A very few teachers were funded by the Empire itself, but to have teachers who were paid by the parents of the boys who attended was considered desirable for a *civitas*: the local political units of the Empire should sustain the Empire's culture. In neighbouring Frankish Gaul this system decayed rapidly in the fifth and sixth centuries; and the Church, in general, had no need to step into its place, provided it could obtain sufficiently literate recruits. In the British Isles, however, the Church did need schools; the question was, therefore, how they should be run and what they should teach.

There is just enough evidence to show that the Britons and the Irish had largely the same pattern of education. For Ireland the evidence as a whole is richer than for the Britons, so that what follows is mainly based on Irish evidence. We may begin, however, with the implications of Gildas, who is important not just for himself but because he was admired and imitated by Columbanus: the two sixth-century Insular writers whose intellectual procedures and prose styles are still well known were themselves connected by a literary debt. The first implication stems from Gildas's ability to write a grammatically correct Latin: even though spoken British Latin had some conservative features, it shared in those developments in Late Latin which were to transform the grammar of the language. If Gildas learnt Latin at his mother's knee, that was not the form of the language in which he wrote. Secondly, he wrote in a highly rhetorical, carefully crafted style; thirdly, he wrote in deadly earnest, hoping to save his people from the divine vengeance which their sins amply merited. Gildas's *On the Ruin of Britain* was not a playful verbal exercise nor was it directed primarily at scholars: he had to persuade kings, bishops, priests, and teachers—the elite of a Christian nation. There is evidence within the text that the style was not inappropriate to the intended readership. The most powerful of the kings addressed, Maglocunus, king of Gwynedd, had received instruction from 'the refined master of almost all Britain'. The adjective used here, *elegans*, 'refined', had the specific function of praising a person's Latin style.

Early Irish churches gained in status through having within their communities persons who themselves had high status. Early Irish society was notably hierarchical, and this applied as much to the Church as to lay society. Within the Church, however, there were two distinct hierarchies: the ordinary grades of the Church, bishop, priest, deacon, and the rest, and also the hierarchy of ecclesiastical scholars. An individual church gained in status if it currently had or even had had a bishop; it also gained in status if it had a leading scholar. Churches, therefore, had a direct interest in maintaining scholars. There was also a further incentive: both among the Britons and among the Irish, leading scholars as well as bishops and the abbots of major monasteries had the right to participate in synods as full members. Synods were an essential part of the government of the British and Irish Churches. An important church without a leading scholar had a reduced influence. A clear corollary of all this is that it was very much in the interests of a major church to be a centre of ecclesiastical education. The British and Irish Churches had not just taken over the role of providing education from the *civitas* but had made it into an intrinsically important aspect of their entire organization.

At a more personal level, the practice of fosterage also played a major part. It was normal for Irish and British (but not English) children to be fostered in the homes of people who were not their parents; and elements of education (not necessarily literate) were part of the standard duties of a foster-parent. An institution whose primary role was probably to strengthen alliances between families was easily adapted to the needs of the Church. In the second half of the sixth century, Columba of Iona was fostered by a priest called Cruithnechán, before going on to study the Bible with a teacher in Leinster called Gemmán. Both with fosterage and with the status of scholars, the Irish Church, and to some extent the British, employed aspects of secular society to sustain Latin culture.

The curriculum was derived from the traditional arrangements of the Empire but with major changes to make it thoroughly Christian. After an elementary education (essentially the three Rs), an individual went on to a school in which were taught the techniques of explaining a text and of writing a persuasive and refined Latin. The culminating stage was a close study of the Bible, the central text of the culture. When Bede described Englishmen as crossing to Ireland in the seventh century to study in the schools of Irish teachers, it was primarily this third level of which he was thinking, although the second level was probably not excluded. If he was right in claiming that English students in Ireland received free teaching and maintenance, it is perhaps as much a testament to the secure economic condition of major Irish churches as of their generosity to their English pupils. If there was a precedent within Irish society it was probably 'the fosterage of love' by which someone might foster a child not, as normal, for a payment but for free.

The British Isles were a cultural province in the post-Roman centuries essentially because they shared the one need—to provide a clergy educated in a language, Latin, which they learnt at school, not at home—and because they also conferred upon the vernacular languages the privilege of being written. Irish at least received the even higher prestige of being subject to grammatical analysis in the manner of Latin. The Insular Churches needed to invest heavily in Latin, and some of the cultural values which they recognized in Latin they transferred to the vernacular. This is the reason why vernacular literature flourished in the British Isles centuries before it acquired any great significance in the rest of Christendom.

The essential need was present in all the Insular countries, but the driving force conferred by the presence, before Christianity, of a learned order with high rank—and hence a precedent for attaching high status to scholars and to the churches which supported them—was strongest in Ireland, much weaker among the Britons, and probably not present at all among the English. Again, while both the Irish and the Britons admitted scholars to synods, the English, at least after 664, admitted only bishops to full participation. This may be a reason why, as Chapter 5 has made plain, the Latin culture of eighth-century England lacked strength in numbers: it had brilliant individual scholars, especially Bede and Alcuin, but once the few had been attracted abroad to the German mission field or to Carolingian courts, it was hard to replace them.

# The unity of the British Isles

In 800 the British Isles were far more unified than in 400. The principal reasons have been discussed in previous chapters: the end of the Roman frontier, the extension of Christianity—in large part through a circular movement from post-Roman Britain to Ireland, from Ireland to Northern Britain, and from Northern Britain to England—and the sharing of all the peoples of the British Isles in one Latin Christian culture. The links were strongest in the north, where the North Channel connecting the Irish Sea with the Atlantic is as little as thirteen miles wide. The shape of the kingdom of Dál Riata, on both sides of the North Channel and so connecting north-eastern Antrim with Argyll, demonstrates that communications could be maintained; and this was in spite of the fierce tidal flows. A prerequisite of the influence of Iona was the presence within its community of skilled sailors, probably mainly *manaig*, monastic clients. Before 800 the closest relations across the North Channel were, therefore, with the western Highlands and the Hebrides. Yet in the ecclesiastical and cultural spheres, and even to some extent in the political, the great mountain zone known in Irish as Druimm Alban, 'the Ridge (or "Back") of Britain', was no obstacle. Eastwards, the long-standing Irish influence on Pictland would lead, in the novel conditions created by Viking attacks, to outright conquest by an Irish dynasty *c.*842, and then to the emergence *c.*900 of a kingdom known to the English as Scotland but to its inhabitants as Alba.

A further influence favourable to the unity of the British Isles was the prominence of kingdoms and churches in the northern half of Ireland and Britain. In the tenth century, all this would change, first with the creation of a kingdom of England based upon Wessex, and then with the rise of Dál Cais in the Shannon basin, initially to power in Munster but by the end of the century in Ireland as a whole. In the pre-Viking period, however, Northumbria among the English and the Uí Néill among the Irish for long had the greater power. The seventh century, especially, was a period in which the northern halves of Britain and Ireland seemed to have the initiative—and not just because Bede was a Northumbrian. Men visualized this northern world in terms of the greater islands, Ireland and Britain, and also of their satellites: the Orkneys, the Hebrides, the Isle of Man, and the other smaller islands off both Ireland and Britain. When, at a synod in Rome in 679, Wilfrid 'confessed the true and catholic faith for all the northern part of Britain and Ireland, and for the islands which were settled by the peoples of the English and the Britons and also of the Irish and the Picts', he was meticulous in including all the islands—and rightly so, for they included Iona and Lindisfarne. The geography of the world written by the Irish scholar Dícuil for the Emperor Louis the Pious in 825 describes the northern world as he knew it when he was himself living in the Hebrides, thirty years before, when the Viking attacks were just beginning. His description is of many islands, from the Hebrides themselves to the Faeroes and even as far as southern Iceland. The extension of Christianity in the northern seas is traced by crosses, from the great high crosses of the Iona school in the southern Hebrides to rough crosses incised on rock in the isolated islands of the North Atlantic, St Kilda, and North Rona. Yet by 850 even the southern Hebrides would be part of Insi Gall, the Islands of the Norsemen; and the same Norsemen pushed further south into the Irish Sea to found Dublin and to conquer the Isle of Man. The many islands of the north passed under alien control as power in mainland Britain and Ireland was shifting southwards.

Yet there were also ways in which the different parts of the British Isles were sharply distinct. These do not include uniquely close ties with Francia and with Rome, for no country within the British Isles was isolated from Continental Europe. True, the strength of such ties varied in nature and in strength. There was a considerable strengthening at the end of the sixth century through the mission of Augustine to Kent and the ascetic exile of Columbanus in Burgundy, but even in the north, in Pictland, the St Andrews Sarcophagus, perhaps of the mid-eighth century, reveals artistic links with Mercia within Britain, and with the Continent. Links with Scandinavia are, however, a different matter. These were strong in the material culture of England, especially north of the Thames, and they are still present in the poem *Beowulf*, set in Denmark and southern Sweden. For the English the North Sea was surrounded by kindred peoples; and it was this kinship across the sea which would drive the Anglo-Saxon missions to Frisia and to central Germany—an enterprise conceived in Ireland by the same Northumbrian Ecgberht who persuaded the monks of Iona of the superior merits of the Roman Easter. The mission was launched as trade with Frisia and Francia was expanding, a trade largely channelled through the *emporia* or wics of south-eastern England.

The organization of agriculture was different in Ireland and in Britain. Here the division was not so much between the English and the Celtic peoples as between those regions which had been within the Roman Empire and those which had not. Much remains obscure about the history of rural society—that is, of almost the entire society—of England and Wales before the Vikings—even though (as Chapter 2 has shown) archaeology can reveal which crops were sown, patterns of consumption, and the layout of settlements. There is more written evidence for Ireland, especially in the laws. A distinction needs to be drawn between the widespread obligation to deliver food-renders and the basis on which those food-renders were demanded. The food-renders themselves were similar across the British Isles as far as the evidence will take us—not surprisingly, since they supplied a royal or aristocratic diet. They consisted of fixed quantities of alcoholic drink, of bread, and of an 'accompaniment' to the bread, varying according to the season, since more meat was available in the winter, more dairy produce in the summer. In much of Wales, land seems to have been defined in terms of how much ale it ought to provide; once that was known, the corresponding quantities of bread and accompaniment in the render would also be determined.

What differed was the basis of the obligation to deliver food-renders to lords. In England and Wales this seems to have been on one basis for the king, on another for a lord. The king required to be fed by his people because he was their king; their food-renders were tax or tribute. But for a lord and especially a church, the obligation was on the basis that the land belonged to the lord or church. In early eighth-century England many nobles appear to have obtained royal charters to enable them to found minsters—churches staffed by communities and headed by abbots. They did so in large numbers partly because it strengthened their hold on estates, partly because it lightened the public burdens normally placed on those estates, and partly also, no doubt, because the ideals that came in the wake of conversion were by then having a major impact on the aristocracy. On the one hand there was 'extensive lordship'—the relatively occasional tribute from a local district to an itinerant king, whose household could only consume so many casks of ale, loaves of bread, flitches of bacon, and cheeses, and only when they visited a local royal centre; and on the other hand, there was the permanent obligation to support a static religious community with its attendant groups of craftsmen; the latter is likely to have intensified the demands made on the peasantry. In turn it may have encouraged a division between 'inland', in which there were concentrations of slaves and small-holders supplying labour on directly administered land, and 'war-land', where relatively free peasants owed food-renders and light services. The natural size for the estates of kings, sub-kings, the greater nobles, and minsters was, however, large: a local district rather than a single village or hamlet. There was a gradation from the most extensive lordship of the king through that of sub-kings, 'royal leaders', and the greatest noblemen down to something more like the local *gesithas* of the Tweed basin attested in the Lives of St Cuthbert, great men in a village or hamlet. With this gradation, tribute gradually changed into rent, from the food-renders of a people to a king all the way down to the food-renders owed to a local noble by his peasants.

In Ireland most lay lords gained their positions more through their wealth in cattle than through possession of land. Of the three factors of production—land, labour, and capital—capital consisted largely of livestock; and among livestock cattle took pride of place. The lord's wealth in cattle was, however, matched by his client's poverty: although the normal freeman inherited land, he must have needed to seek cattle from a lord. The assumption was that free laymen were divided into lords and clients, no room apparently being left for any great class of independent peasants; both lord and client possessed inherited land, but only the lord inherited sufficient cattle. Indeed, as the client inherited too little in the way of cattle, the lord inherited too much for his own farm: the need of the one and the superfluity of the other were supposed to balance. What seems to make sense of this situation is that a lord could demand food-renders and hospitality which, year by year, reduced the initial capital stock he had himself granted to his client and augmented the stock he controlled. Only in this way would there be any expectation that the heirs of a client would themselves have needed to become clients by receiving further grants of cattle from lords. The economic nature of lordship thus differed radically in Ireland from the pattern in Wales and England. In this respect, at least, the old Roman frontier still endured.

The unity of the British Isles was strongest at the level of religion and of high culture, unsurprisingly weakest in the organization of agriculture. Yet even in the latter there were broad similarities across wide territories: the Irish pattern of clientship appears to have prevailed across the entire island and in Scottish Dál Riata, while 'extensive lordship' was characteristic of eastern Scotland as well as of England and Wales. The pressures on local agrarian society of providing for static religious communities were common to the entire British Isles.

In the end, however, what matters most about this period in the history of the British Isles was the creation of a local form of Christian civilization. Within Insular Christianity there were many tensions, often creative, sometimes destructive. Sometimes they are simplified by scholars into a single opposition between Iona and Canterbury, between a local loyalty to the holy founder of an island monastery and the English city designed by Augustine and his companions to be an Insular Rome. Such a simple opposition is seriously misleading, essentially because tensions between local traditions and those of the wider Church were present everywhere, and also because it was possible to reconcile the two. The Lindisfarne Gospels were one such reconciliation, Adomnán's Life of Columba, with its portrait of the saint as an Irish St Benedict, was another. An explicit attempt to define and to reconcile differences about how one should live was 'the Irish Collection of Canons', *Collectio Canonum Hibernensis*. This was a work of theology as much as of canon law, begun in the aftermath of the adoption of the Roman Easter by the monks of Iona in 716. Disagreements between 'the Hibernians', *Hibernenses*, and the Roman party within Ireland, *Romani*, were only one kind of tension encompassed by this work of two scholars, Cú Chuimne from Iona and Ruben from Dairinis in Munster. The greatest and the most creative tension within Insular culture was between two languages, Latin and the vernacular, whether that vernacular was Irish, British, or English; out of this tension came the first vernacular literatures of Europe; and it was a tension and an achievement which Insular Christianity would bequeath to medieval Europe.

# Further reading

### General works of reference

Fryde, E. B., Greenway, D. E., Porter, S., and Roy, I. (eds.), *Handbook of British Chronology*, 3rd edn. (London, 1986); the lists of kings and bishops are especially useful.

Kenney, J. F., *Sources for the Early History of Ireland: Ecclesiastical* (New York, 1929; repr. Blackrock, Co. Dublin, 1993).

Hill, D., *An Atlas of Anglo-Saxon England* (Oxford, 1981).

Keynes, S. D., *Anglo-Saxon England: A Bibliographical Handbook for Students of Anglo-Saxon History*, 2nd edn. (Cambridge, 2001).

Lapidge M., and Sharpe, R., *A Bibliography of Celtic-Latin Literature, 400–1200* (Dublin, 1985).

Moody, T. W., Martin, F. X., and Byrne, F. J. (eds.), *A New History of Ireland*, ix: *Maps, Genealogies, Lists* (Oxford, 1984).

Ordnance Survey of Great Britain, *Map of Britain in the Dark Ages*, 2nd edn. (Chessington, 1966).

Ordnance Survey of Ireland, *Map of Monastic Ireland*, 2nd edn. (Dublin, 1964).


### Main primary sources (in translation)

*Anglo-Saxon*

(*Note*: 'HE' in the text refers to Bede's *Historia Ecclesiastica Gentis Anglorum*: see McClure and Collins below.)

Crossley-Holland, K., *An Anglo-Saxon Anthology*, Oxford World Classics (Oxford, 1984). Includes *Beowulf* and the *Dream of the Rood*.

Farmer, D. H., and Webb, J. F., *The Age of Bede*, Penguin Classics (Harmondsworth, 1983).

Heaney, S., *Beowulf* (London, 1999).

McClure, J., and Collins, R., *Bede's Ecclesiastical History of the English People*, World's Classics (Oxford, 1994); and see also J. M. Wallace-Hadrill, *Bede's Ecclesiastical History of the English People: A Historical Commentary*, Oxford Medieval Texts (Oxford, 1998).

Whitelock, D., *English Historical Documents, c.500–1042*, English Historical Documents, gen. ed. D. C. Douglas, i, 2nd edn. (London, 1979).

## Irish and British

Koch, J. T., and Carey, J., *The Celtic Heroic Age: Literary Sources for Ancient Celtic Europe and Early Ireland and Wales* (Andover, Mass., 1997).

## Irish

*The Annals of Ulster (to A.D. 1131)*, ed. S. Mac Airt and G. Mac Niocaill (Dublin, 1983).

*Audacht Morainn*, ed. and trans. F. Kelly (Dublin, 1976).

*Cáin Adomnáin*, trans. M. Ní Dhonnchadha, 'The Law of Adomnán: A Translation', in T. O'Loughlin (ed.), *Adomnán at Birr, AD 697* (Dublin, 2001), 53–68.

Carey, J., *King of Mysteries: Early Irish Religious Writings* (Dublin, 1998).

Clancy, T. O., and Márkus, G., *Iona: The Earliest Poetry of a Celtic Monastery* (Edinburgh, 1995).

*Críth Gablach*, trans. E. MacNeill, *Proc. Royal Irish Acad.*, 36 C (1923), 265–316 (Legal tract of the early eighth century on status, but with a long section on kingship).

*The Patrician Texts in the Book of Armagh*, ed. and trans. L. Bieler (Dublin, 1977).

Patrick, *Confession* and *Letter to the Soldiers of Coroticus*, trans. D. R. Howlett, *The Book of Letters of Saint Patrick the Bishop* (Blackrock, Co. Dublin, 1994). Also in L. de Paor, *Saint Patrick's World* (Blackrock, Co. Dublin, 1993).

Sharpe, R., (trans.), *Adomnán of Iona: Life of St Columba*, Penguin Classics (Harmondsworth, 1995).

## British

Gildas, *De Excidio Britanniae*, ed. and trans. M. Winterbottom, in *Gildas: The Ruin of Britain and Other Documents* (London and Chichester, 1978).

Jarman, A. O. H., *Aneirin: Y Gododdin. Britain's Oldest Heroic Poem*, The Welsh Classics, 3 (Llandysul, 1988).

Nash-Williams, V. E., *The Early Christian Monuments of Wales* (Cardiff, 1950).

*Nennius: British History and the Welsh Annals*, ed. and trans. J. Morris (Chichester, 1980).

## Northern Britain

Allen, J. R., and Anderson, J., *The Early Christian Monuments of Scotland* (Edinburgh, 1903; repr. Balgavies, Angus, 1993).

General surveys covering the entire British Isles in this period are noticeable by their absence.

For Scotland (including the Northern Britons), a good starting point is:

Foster, S. M., *Picts, Gaels and Scots* (London, 1996).

Crawford, B. (ed.), *Scotland in Early Medieval Europe* (St Andrews, 1994).

—— (ed.), *Scotland in Early Medieval Britain* (St Andrews, 1996).

Duncan, A. A. M., *Scotland: The Making of the Kingdom* (Edinburgh, 1975).

Henderson, I., *The Picts* (London, 1967).

Nicoll, E. H. (ed.), *A Pictish Panorama, and a Pictish Bibliography* (Balgavies, Angus, 1995).

Ritchie, A., *Picts* (Edinburgh, 1989).

Smyth, A. P., *Warlords and Holy Men* (London, 1984).

For Irish history, a good place to start is with two good rapid introductions with different outlooks: K. Hughes's introductory chapter to A. J. Otway-Ruthven, *A History of Medieval Ireland* (London, 1968), repr. in K. Hughes, *Church and Society in Ireland, A.D. 400–1200*, Variorum Reprints (London, 1987), ch. 1, and D. Ó Corráin, 'Prehistoric and Early Christian Ireland', in R. F. Foster (ed.), *The Oxford Illustrated History of Ireland* (Oxford, 1989). A introductory survey of middling length is D. Ó Cróinín, *Early Medieval Ireland, 400–1200* (London, 1995); T. M. Charles-Edwards, *Early Christian Ireland* (Cambridge, 2000) covers a shorter period, generally in greater detail. K. Hughes, *Early Christian Ireland: Introduction to the Sources* (London, 1972), is an admirably clear account.

Ó Corráin, D., 'A Handlist of Publications on Early Irish History', *Historical Studies*, 10 (1976), 172–203.

For Anglo-Saxon England, the best starting point is J. Campbell (ed.), *The Anglo-Saxons* (Oxford, 1982; also in Penguin paperback). F. M. Stenton, *Anglo-Saxon England* (Oxford, 1943 etc.; now an OUP paperback) remains the classic account.

## Wales

Davies, W., *Wales in the Early Middle Ages* (Leicester, 1982).

—— *Patterns of Power in Early Wales* (Oxford, 1990).

Edwards, N. (ed.), *Landscape and Settlement in Medieval Wales* (Oxford, 1997).

Hughes, K., *Celtic Britain in the Early Middle Ages: Studies in Scottish and Welsh Sources*, Studies in Celtic History (Woodbridge, 1980).

## Introduction

Cleary, A. S. E., *The Ending of Roman Britain* (London, 1989).

Dark, K. R., *Civitas to Kingdom: British Political Continuity 300–800* (Leicester, 1994).

Redknap, M., *The Christian Celts* (National Museum of Wales, Cardiff, 1991). Has some excellent photographs and useful text (notably on Llangors).

Stafford, P. A., *The East Midlands in the Early Middle Ages* (Leicester, 1985).

Ward-Perkins, B., 'Why Did the Anglo-Saxons Not Become More British?', *English Historical Review*, 115 (2000), 513–33.

## Chapter 1

Bassett, S. (ed.), *The Origins of Anglo-Saxon Kingdoms*, Studies in the Early History of Britain (London, 1989).

Bhreathnach, E., *Tara: A Select Bibliography*, Discovery Programme Reports, iii (Dublin, 1995).

—— 'Temoria: Caput Scotorum?', *Ériu*, 47 (1996), 67–88.

Binchy, D. A., 'The Fair of Tailtiu and the Feast of Tara', *Ériu*, 18 (1958), 44–54.

—— *Celtic and Anglo-Saxon Kingship* (Oxford, 1970).

Blair, P. Hunter, *Anglo-Saxon Northumbria*, ed. M. Lapidge and P. Hunter-Blair (London, 1984).

Brooks, N. P., *Anglo-Saxon Myths, State and Church, 400–1066* (London, 2000).

Brown, M. P., and Farr, C. A. (eds.), *Mercia: An Anglo-Saxon Kingdom in Europe* (London, 2001).

Byrne, F. J., *Irish Kings and High-Kings* (London, 1973).

Campbell, J., *Essays in Anglo-Saxon History* (London, 1986).

Charles-Edwards, T. M., 'A Contract between King and People? *Críth Gablach* on Kingship', *Peritia*, 8 (1994), 107–19.

Dumville, D. N., *Britons and Anglo-Saxons in the Early Middle Ages*, Variorum (Aldershot, 1993).

Gelling, M., *The West Midlands in the Early Middle Ages* (Leicester, 1992).

—— 'Why Aren't We Speaking Welsh?', in W. Filmer-Sankey (ed.), *Anglo-Studies in Archaeology and History*, 6 (1993), 51–6.

Hope-Taylor, B., *Yeavering: An Anglo-British Centre of Early Northumbria* (London, 1977).

Kelly, S. E., 'Trading Privileges from Eighth Century England', *Early Medieval Europe*, 1 (1992), 3–28.

Kirby, D. P., *The Earliest English Kings* (London, 1990).

Ó Corráin, D., 'Nationality and Kingship in Pre-Norman Ireland', in T. W. Moody (ed.), *Nationality and the Pursuit of National Independence = Historical Studies*, 12 (Belfast, 1978), 1–35.

Stacey, R. Chapman, *The Road to Judgment: From Custom to Court in Medieval Ireland and Wales* (Philadelphia, 1994).

Thacker, A., 'Some Terms for Noblemen in Anglo-Saxon England, c.650–900', *Anglo-Saxon Studies in Archaeology and History*, 2, ed. D. Brown, J. Campbell and S. C. Hawkes, BAR, Brit. Ser., 92 (Oxford, 1981), 201–36.

Wood, I. N., 'The Fall of the Western Empire and the End of Roman Britain', *Britannia*, 18 (1987), 251–62.

Wormald, P., 'Bede, Bretwaldas and the Origins of the Gens Anglorum', in *Ideal and Reality*, ed. P. Wormald et al., 99–129.

Yorke, B., *Kings and Kingdoms of Early Anglo-Saxon England* (London, 1990).

—— *Wessex in the Early Middle Ages* (London, 1995).

## Chapter 2

Alcock, L., *Arthur's Britain* (London, 1971).

—— *Economy, Society and Warfare among the Britons and Saxons* (Cardiff, 1987).

Arnold, C. J., *An Archaeology of the Early Anglo-Saxon Kingdoms*, 2nd edn. (London, 1997).

Bammesberger, A., and Wollmann, A. (eds.), *Britain 400–600: Language and History* (Heidelberg, 1990).

Carver, M. O. H. (ed.), *The Age of Sutton Hoo* (Woodbridge, 1992).

Charles-Edwards, T. M., 'Language and Society among the Insular Celts', in M. Green (ed.), *The Celtic World* (London, 1995), 703–36.

Dark, K. R. (ed.), *External Contacts and the Economy of Late Roman and Post-Roman Britain* (Woodbridge, 1996).

Davies, W., *Wales in the Early Middle Ages* (Leicester, 1982).

Edwards, N., *The Archaeology of Early Medieval Ireland* (London, 1990).

Foster, S. M., *Picts, Gaels and Scots* (London, 1996).

Hines, J., 'The Becoming of the English: Identity, Material Culture and Language in Early Anglo-Saxon England', *Anglo-Saxon Studies in Archaeology and History*, 7 (1994), 49–59.

—— (ed.), *The Anglo-Saxons from the Migration Period to the Eighth Century: An Ethnographic Perspective* (Woodbridge, 1997).

Hinton, D. A., *Archaeology, Economy and Society: England from the Fifth to the Fifteenth Century* (London, 1990).

Hooke, D., *The Landscape of Anglo-Saxon England* (London, 1998).

Kelly, F., *Early Irish Farming* (Dublin, 1997).

Laing, Ll., *The Archaeology of Late Celtic Britain and Ireland, c.400–1200 AD* (London, 1975).

Nielsen, H. F., *The Continental Backgrounds of English and its Insular Development until 1154* (Odense, 1998).

Rackham, J. (ed.), *Environment and Economy in Anglo-Saxon England* (York, 1994).

Southworth, E. (ed.), *Anglo-Saxon Cemeteries: A Re-appraisal* (Stroud, 1990).

Thomas, A. C., *The Early Christian Archaeology of North Britain* (Oxford, 1971).

Welch, M. G., *Anglo-Saxon England* (London, 1992).

## Chapter 3

Binchy, D. A., 'Patrick and his Biographers: Ancient and Modern', *Studia Hibernica*, 2 (1962), 7–173.

Blair, J., and Sharpe, R. (eds.), *Pastoral Care before the Parish* (Leicester, 1992).

Bonner, G. (ed.), *Famulus Christi: Essays in Commemoration of the Thirteenth Centenary of the Birth of the Venerable Bede* (London, 1976).

——Rollason, D., and Stancliffe, C. (eds.), *St. Cuthbert, his Cult and his Community to AD 1200* (Woodbridge, 1989).

Brooks, N., *The Early History of the Church of Canterbury* (Leicester, 1984).

Charles-Edwards, T. M., 'The Social Background to Irish *Peregrinatio*', *Celtica*, 11 (1976), 43–59.

Crawford, B. E. (ed.), *Conversion and Christianity in the North Sea World* (St Andrews, 1998).

Dumville, D. N. et al., *Saint Patrick, A.D. 493–1993* (Woodbridge, 1993).

Doherty, C., 'The Cult of St Patrick and the Politics of Armagh in the Seventh Century', in J.-M. Picard (ed.), *Ireland and Northern France AD 600–850* (Dublin, 1991), 53–94.

Edwards, N., and Lane, A. (eds.), *The Early Church in Wales and the West* (Oxford, 1992).

Etchingham, C., 'Bishops in the Early Irish Church: A Re-assessment', *Studia Hibernica*, 28 (1994), 35–62.

Gameson, R. (ed.), *St Augustine and the Conversion of England* (Stroud, 1999).

Geake, H., *The Use of Grave Goods in Conversion-Period England, c.600–c.850*, BAR Brit. Ser. 261 (Oxford, 1997).

Gelling, M., 'Place-Names and Anglo-Saxon Paganism', *University of Birmingham Historical Journal*, 8 (1961–2), 7–25.

Herbert, M., *Iona, Kells, and Derry: The History and Hagiography of the Monastic Familia of Columba* (Oxford, 1988; repr. Blackrock, Co. Dublin, 1996).

Hughes, K., *The Church in Early Irish Society* (London, 1966).

Levison, W., *England and the Continent in the Eighth Century* (Oxford, 1946).

Mayr-Harting, H. M. R. E., *The Coming of Christianity to Anglo-Saxon England*, 3rd edn. (London, 1991).

—— *Two Conversions to Christianity: The Bulgarians and the Anglo-Saxons* (Reading, 1994).

Sharpe, R., 'Some Problems concerning the Organization of the Church in Early Medieval Ireland', *Peritia*, 3 (1984), 230–70.

—— 'Armagh and Rome in the Seventh Century', in P. Ní Catháin and M. Richter (eds.), *Ireland und Europa: Die Kirche im Frühmittelalter* (Stuttgart, 1984), 58–72.

Sims-Williams, P., *Religion and Literature in Western England, 600–800* (Cambridge, 1990).

Stancliffe, C., 'Kings and Conversion: Some Comparisons between the Roman Mission to England and Patrick's to Ireland', *Frühmittelalterliche Studien*, 14 (1980), 59–94.

—— and Cambridge, E., (eds.), *Oswald: Northumbrian King to European Saint* (Stamford, 1995).

Thacker, A., and Sharpe, R. (eds.), *Local Saints and Local Churches in the Early Medieval West* (Oxford, 2002).

Thomas, [A.] C., *Christianity in Roman Britain to A.D. 500* (London, 1981).

Wood, I. N., 'The Mission of Augustine of Canterbury', *Speculum*, 69 (1994), 1–17.

Wormald, P., 'Bede, "Beowulf" and the Conversion of the Anglo-Saxon Aristocracy', in R. T. Farrell (ed.), *Bede and Anglo-Saxon England: Papers in Honour of the 1300th Anniversary of the Birth of Bede, given at Cornell University in 1973 and 1974*, British Archaeological Reports, 46 (Oxford, 1978), 32–95.

—— *Bede and the Conversion of England: The Charter Evidence*, Jarrow Lecture, 1984.

## Chapter 4

Alexander, J. J. G. (ed.), *Insular Manuscripts, 6th to 9th Century* (London, 1978). Catalogue.

Backhouse, J., *The Lindisfarne Gospels* (Oxford, 1981).

Bailey, R., *England's Earliest Sculptors* (Toronto, 1996).

Brown, M. P., *The Lindisfarne Gospels: Society, Spirituality and the Scribe* (London, 2003).

Farr, C., *The Book of Kells, its Function and Audience* (London and Toronto, 1997).

Harbison, P., *The Golden Age of Irish Art* (London, 1999).

Henderson, G., *From Durrow to Kells: the Insular Gospel-books* (London, 1987).

Henry, F., *The Book of Kells* (London, 1974).

Meehan, B., *The Book of Durrow* (Dublin, 1996).

Nees, L., *Early Medieval Art* (Oxford, 2002).

Nordenfalk, C., *Celtic and Anglo-Saxon Painting* (London, 1977).

Ó Carragáin, É., *The City of Rome and the World of Bede*, Jarrow Lecture 1994.

O'Reilly, J., 'Patristic and Insular Traditions of the Evangelists: Exegesis and Iconography', in A. M. Luiselli and E. Ó Carragáin (eds.), *Le Isole Britanniche e Roma in età romanobarbarica* (Rome, 1998), 49–94.

Royal Commission on the Ancient and Historical Monuments of Scotland, *Pictish Symbol Stones: An Illustrated Gazetteer* (Edinburgh, 1999).

Conference Proceedings (papers on Insular metalwork, sculpture, manuscripts and their contexts):

Bourke, C. (ed.), *From the Isles of the North: Early Medieval Art in Ireland and Britain* (Belfast, 1995).

Foster, S. M. (ed.), *The St Andrews Sarcophagus: A Pictish Masterpiece and its International Connections* (Dublin, 1998).

Hawkes, J., and Mills, S. (eds.), *Northumbria's Golden Age* (Stroud, 1999).

Karkov, C., Farrell, R. T., Ryan, M. (eds.), *The Insular Tradition* (New York, 1997).

O'Mahony, F. (ed.), *The Book of Kells* (Aldershot, 1994).

Redknap, M., Edwards, N., Youngs, S., Lane, A., Knight, J. K. (eds.), *Pattern and Purpose in Insular Art* (Oxford, 2001).

Ryan, M. (ed.), *Ireland and Insular Art 500–1200* (Dublin 1987).

Spearman, R. M., and Higgitt, J. (eds.), *The Age of Migrating Ideas: Early Medieval Art in Northern Britain and Ireland* (Edinburgh 1993).

Exhibition catalogues:

Webster, L., and Backhouse, J. (eds.), *The Making of England: Anglo-Saxon Art and Culture A.D. 600–900* (London and Toronto, 1991).

——and Brown, Michelle (eds.), *The Transformation of the Roman World, 400–900* (London, 1997).

Youngs, S. (ed.), *The Work of Angels: Masterpieces of Celtic Metalwork, 6th to 9th Centuries A.D.* (London, 1989).

## Chapter 5

Binchy, D. A., 'The Background to Early Irish Literature', *Studia Hibernica*, 1 (1961), 7–18.

Bromwich R., and Jones, R. B. (eds.), *Astudiaethau ar yr Hengerdd* (Cardiff, 1978).

Charles-Edwards, T. M., 'Language and Society among the Insular Celts AD 400–1000', in M. Green (ed.), *The Celtic World*, ed. Miranda Green (London, 1995), 703–36.

Dumville, D. N., *Three Men in a Boat: Scribe, Language, and Culture in the Church of Viking-Age Europe* (Cambridge, 1996).

Green, D. H., *Language and History in the Early Germanic World* (Cambridge, 1998).

Harvey, A., 'Latin, Literacy, and the Celtic Vernaculars around the Year AD 500', in C. C. J. Byrne, M. Harry, and P. Ó Siadhail (eds.), *Celtic Languages and Celtic Peoples: Proceedings of the Second North American Congress of Celtic Studies, Halifax, 1989* (Halifax, NS, 1992), 11–26.

Herren, M. W. (ed.), *Insular Latin Studies: Papers on Latin Texts and Manuscripts of the British Isles: 550–1066*, Papers in Mediaeval Studies 1 (Toronto, 1981).

Houwen, L. A. J. R., and MacDonald, A. A. (eds.), *Alcuin of York*, Germania Latina 3 (Groningen, 1998).

Koch, J. T., 'When Was Welsh Literature First Written Down?', *Studia Celtica*, 20/21 (1985–6), 43–66.

Lapidge, M., *Anglo-Latin Literature, 600–899* (London, 1996).

—— and Godden, M. (eds.), *The Cambridge Companion to Old English Literature* (Cambridge, 1991).

—— and R. Sharpe, *A Bibliography of Celtic-Latin Literature, 400–1200* (Dublin, 1985).

McManus, D., *A Guide to Ogam* (Maynooth, 1991).

Ó Corráin, D., 'The Historical and Cultural Background of the Book of Kells', in F. O'Mahony (ed.), *The Book of Kells* (Aldershot, 1994), 1–32.

Orchard, A. 'After Aldhelm: The Teaching and Transmission of the Anglo-Latin Hexameter', *Journal of Medieval Latin*, 2 (1992), 96–133.

—— *A Critical Companion to 'Beowulf'* (Cambridge, 2002).

Page, R. I., *Runes and Runic Inscriptions* (Woodbridge, 1995).

Plummer, C., 'On the Colophons and Marginalia of Irish Scribes', *Proceedings of the British Academy*, 12 (1926), 11–44.

Pryce, H. (ed.), *Literacy in Medieval Celtic Societies*, Cambridge Studies in Medieval Literature 33 (Cambridge, 1998).

Roberts, B. F. (ed.), *Early Welsh Poetry: Studies in the Book of Aneirin* (Aberystwyth, 1988).

Rowland, J., *Early Welsh Saga Poetry* (Cambridge, 1990).

Sims-Williams, P., 'The Five Languages of Wales in the Pre-Norman Inscriptions', *Cambrian Medieval Celtic Studies*, 44 (winter 2002), 1–36.

*Thesaurus Palaeohibernicus: A Collection of Old-Irish Glosses, Scholia, Prose and Verse*, ed. and trans. W. Stokes and J. Strachan, 2nd edn. (2 vols., Dublin, 1975).

## Chapter 6

Bateley, J., 'English Prose Before and During the Reign of Alfred', *Anglo-Saxon England*, 17 (1988), 93–138.

Charles-Edwards, T. M., *The Welsh Laws* (Cardiff, 1989).

Dumville, D. N., 'Kingship, Genealogies and Regnal Lists', in P. H. Sawyer and I. N. Wood (eds.), *Early Medieval Kingship* (Leeds, 1977), 72–104.

Higgitt, J., 'Early Medieval Inscriptions in Britain and Ireland and their Audiences', in D. Henry (ed.), *The Worm, the Germ, and the Thorn: Pictish and Related Studies presented to Isabel Henderson* (Balgavies, Angus, 1997), 67–78.

Kelly, F., *A Guide to Early Irish Law* (Dublin, 1988).

McCone, K., *Pagan Past and Christian Present in Early Irish Literature*, Maynooth Monographs, iii (Maynooth, 1990).

McKitterick, R. (ed.), *The Uses of Literacy in Early Mediaeval Europe* (Cambridge, 1990).

McLeod, N., *Early Irish Contract Law* (Sydney, n.d.).

Pryce, H. (ed.), *Literacy in Medieval Celtic Societies* (Cambridge, 1998).

Stacey, R. Chapman, *The Road to Judgment: From Custom to Court in Medieval Ireland and Wales* (Philadelphia, 1994).

Wormald, P., *The Making of English Law: King Alfred to the Twelfth Century*, i: *Legislation and Its Limits* (Oxford, 1999).

—— *Legal Culture in the Early Medieval West: Law as Text, Image, and Experience* (London, 1999).

## Conclusion

Brooks, N., 'Canterbury, Rome and the Construction of English Identity', in J. M. H. Smith (ed.), *Early Medieval Rome and the Christian West: Essays in Honour of Donald A. Bullough* (Leiden, 2000), 221–47.

Charles-Edwards, T. M., *Early Irish and Welsh Kinship* (Oxford, 1993).

Davies, W., '*Unciae*: Land Measurement in the *Liber Landavensis*', *Agricultural History Review*, 21/2 (1973), 111–21.

——*An Early Welsh Microcosm* (London, 1978).

——'Land and Power in Early Medieval Wales', *Past & Present*, 81 (1978), 3–23.

Dillon, M., *Early Irish Literature* (Chicago, 1948).

Faith, R. J., *The English Peasantry and the Growth of Lordship* (London, 1997).

Fisher, I., *Early Medieval Sculpture in the West Highlands and Islands*, RCAHMS and Society of Antiquaries of Scotland, Monograph Ser. 1 (Edinburgh, 2001).

Forsyth, K., *Language in Pictland* (Utrecht, 1997).

Hamlin, A., and Lynn, C. J. (eds.), *Pieces of the Past: Archaeological Excavations by the Dept. of the Environment for Northern Ireland 1970–1986* (Belfast, 1988).

Hughes, K., and Hamlin, A., *The Modern Traveller to the Early Irish Church* (London, 1977; repr. Dublin, 1997).

Ó Riain, P., *Anglo-Saxon Ireland: The Evidence of the Martyrology of Tallaght*, H. M. Chadwick Memorial Lecture (Cambridge, 1993).

Sharpe, R., 'Hiberno-Latin *Laicus*, Irish *Láech* and the Devil's Men', *Ériu*, 30 (1979), 75–92.

Thacker, A., and Sharpe, R. (eds.), *Local Saints and Local Churches in the Early Medieval West* (Oxford, 2002).

Wallace-Hadrill, J. M., *Early Medieval History* (Oxford, 1975).

Wormald, P., 'Bede and Benedict Biscop', in G. Bonner (ed.), *Famulus Christi*, 141–69.

——'The Uses of Literacy in Anglo-Saxon England and its Neighbours', *TRHS* 5th Ser., 27 (1977), 95–114.

# Chronology

446 × 452    Letter of the Britons to Aetius, the leading Roman general: 'The barbarians push us back to the sea, the sea pushes us back to the barbarians' (Gildas)

449 × 455    Date of the 'Arrival of the English in Britain' according to Bede (before 456, his date for the death of Marcian); but this was dependent on an error by Gildas

450–500    Period within which Patrick's mission in Ireland probably lies

461    Subscriptions to the Council of Tours (AD 461) included: 'Mansuetus, bishop of the Britons'

469    British army under King Riothamus, and part of the Emperor Anthemius' anti-Gothic coalition intended to defend Aquitania Prima, is betrayed by the Prefect Arvandus, defeated by Euric's Visigoths at Bourg-de-Déols in Berry, and driven to take refuge with the Burgundians, then in alliance with the Empire

482–511    Reign of Clovis, who unites the Franks under his rule and makes them the most powerful people in Gaul; he was said to have subjugated the Bretons

c.490–535    The ancestors of the Uí Néill conquer the Irish midlands

c.500    Battle of Mount Badon leads to a respite of some forty-four years in the wars between the Britons and the English. The year of Mount Badon was also the year of Gildas's birth

530 × 540    Franks establish their dominion over all of Gaul (apart from the far south-west), Liguria (around Genoa) and the far north-east of Italy (around Trento); they also enforce an overlordship over what is now Germany between the Rhine and the Elbe and around the upper Danube; their most powerful king, Theudebert I, claims authority over some of the inhabitants of Britain

534    The army of the Emperor Justinian recovers the province of Africa from the Vandals and then (535) goes on to retake Sicily and (from 536) much of Italy from the Ostrogoths

c.540    Gildas writes his book *On the Destruction of Britain*

540s    Plague crosses the Near East and Europe

547    Bede's date for the beginning of the reign of Ida (547–59), the first king of Bernicia; to his reign the *Historia Brittonum* attached its notice of five distinguished poets, Talhaearn 'Father of Inspiration', (A)neirin, Taliesin, Blwchbardd, and Cian, 'who is called "Wheat of Poetry" '

554–84    Thirty-year reign of Bridius son of Meilochon as the

|     |     |
| --- | --- |
|     | leading king of the Picts; Columba's mission to the Picts probably makes major progress in the last twenty years before his death |
| 555 | Foundation by Comgall of the monastery of Bangor (Co. Down) |
| 563 | Columba comes to Britain in *peregrinatio* and founds Iona |
| 565 × 566 | Approximate date of the first Irish vernacular poem to survive, composed by Colmán mac Lénéni, founder and patron saint of Cloyne, Co. Cork, when he was still a professional poet |
| 570 | Death of Gildas (Irish annals) |
| 573–9 | Reign of Theodric as king of Bernicia, according to the *Historia Brittonum*, a period during which Urien of Rheged was the leading king in Northern Britain in opposition to the Bernicians |
| 574–606 (or 576–608?) | Reign of Áedán mac Gabráin as king of Dál Riata |
| 586–92 | The reign of Hussa as king of the Bernicians; according to the *Historia Brittonum*, four British kings, Urien, Rhydderch Hen (of Dumbarton), Gwallog, and Morgan, fought against him |
| 590–604 | Gregory the Great (Gregory I) is pope |
| 591 | Columbanus, formerly a monk of Bangor (Co. Down), founds the monastery of Annegray in the Frankish kingdom of Burgundy; this is followed by the foundation of his main monastery at the nearby Luxeuil |
| 592–616 | Reign of Æthelfrith, 592–604 solely in Bernicia, 604–16 also in Deira |
| 596 | Pope Gregory the Great sends Augustine and his companions to preach Christianity to the English |
| 597 | Augustine and his companions arrive in Kent and are given royal protection by King Æthelberht |
|     | Death of Columba: the second dated Irish vernacular poem, the *Amrae Choluim Chille* ('The Wonders of Columba'), is a lament on his death |
| 597 × 600 | King Æthelberht baptized |
| 603 | The battle of Degsastan in which Áedán mac Gabráin is defeated by Æthelfrith of Bernicia |
| c.604 | Æthelfrith of Bernicia takes control of Deira (Bernicia with |

Deira made up the later Northumbria) and drives Edwin, native contender for the Deiran throne, into exile

610        Columbanus expelled from Burgundy by King Theuderic

611        Death of Colmán Elo, founder and patron saint of Lynally (Lann Elo) in Mide, to whom 'the Alphabet of Piety', perhaps the earliest Irish vernacular text in both prose and verse, is (perhaps incorrectly) attributed

613        Chlothar II defeats the forces of Brunhild and destroys the rival branch of the Merovingians; Columbanus leaves Switzerland for Italy, where he is welcomed at the Lombard court at Pavia and founds the monastery of Bobbio

613 × 615    The battle of Chester, in which Æthelfrith, king of the Northumbrians, defeats and kills Selyf ap Cynan, 'king of the Britons' (later associated with Powys)

614        Council of Paris summoned by Chlothar II, now ruler of all the Franks, at which the bishop of Rochester and the abbot of St Peter's, Canterbury, attend

614 × 616    Possible date of the Laws of Æthelberht, promulgated on royal authority and written in the vernacular

615        Columbanus dies at Bobbio

616        Death of Æthelberht, king of Kent, is followed by a brief pagan revival in Kent led by his son and heir, Eadbald

            The battle of the River Idle in which Æthelfrith is defeated and killed by Rædwald, king of the East Anglians, and patron of the subsequent king of Northumbria, Edwin

616–33     Edwin rules over both Deira and Bernicia

c.625      Death of Rædwald, king of the East Angles

625–38     Honorius I is pope, a supporter of the policies of Gregory the Great and correspondingly interested in Britain and Ireland

626 × 627    The Synod of Mâcon: the probable occasion on which Luxeuil abandons the Celtic Easter

627        Edwin baptized at Easter

627 × 628    Earpwald, king of the East Anglians, baptized, and shortly afterwards killed

628        Honorius I issues a privilege in favour of Bobbio freeing it from episcopal control; Bobbio charged with championing, among the Lombards, the cause of orthodoxy against Arianism; probably at the same time Honorius sends a letter to the Irish on the Easter question

630 × 631   Succession of Sigeberht to East Anglia after he had been converted and baptized when an exile in Gaul driven out by Rædwald; Sigeberht receives a bishop from Burgundy (perhaps from Columbanian circles) called Felix

631   Irish legates in Rome to make further enquiries on the Easter question

632 × 633   Cummian writes the Letter on the Paschal Controversy to Ségéne, abbot of Iona, and the hermit Béccán; he argues in favour of the Easter rules of Victorius of Aquitaine, recently adopted by the southern Irish churches at a Synod

633   Cadwallon, king of Gwynedd, in alliance with Penda, of the Mercian royal kindred, rebels against the overlordship of Edwin, king of the Northumbrians; Edwin killed by them in the battle of Hatfield, 12 October 633; Osric, Edwin's first cousin, succeeds to Deira but Eanfrith son of Æthelfrith to Bernicia

634   Cadwallon kills Osric in the summer and Eanfrith in the autumn or early winter, only to be himself killed by Oswald, Eanfrith's brother, in the battle of Denisesburna or Heavenfield, near Hexham

635   The foundation of Lindisfarne and the beginning of the thirty-year 'episcopate of the Irish' in Northumbria, during which its bishops, Aidan, Fínán, and Colmán, were sent from Iona

637   Domnall mac Áeda defeats and kills Congal Cáech (the last known king of Tara who was not of the Uí Néill until Brian Bóraime at the end of the tenth century) in the battle of Mag Rath (Moira, Co. Down)

637 × 640   'Siege of Edinburgh' (Annals of Ulster) may signal the final fall of the kingdom of the Gododdin

?late 630s   Fursa comes to East Anglia, probably from Louth, while Sigberht was still king, and founded a monastery at *Cnobheresburg* (Burgh Castle?)

642   Oswald killed in the battle of Maserfelth, 5 August; Cynegils, king of the West Saxons, dies and his son Cenwalh succeeds; in December, Domnall Brecc, king of Dál Riata, is killed in the battle of Srath Caruin (Strath Carron) by Owain, king of Dumbarton; the power of Dál Riata is now in decline in Ireland and in Northern Britain

642–695   Síl nÁeda Sláne (the branch of the Uí Néill that ruled Brega) monopolizes the kingship of Tara for most of this period

| 644 | Oswine becomes king of Deira: Northumbria divided until 651 |
|---|---|
| 645 | Cenwalh expelled by Penda (ASC) and takes refuge with Anna, king of East Angles |
| 648 | Cenwalh restored |
| c.648 | Fursa goes to Francia, where he receives the patronage of Erchinoald, mayor of the palace and founds the monastery of Lagny. |
| c.649 | Death of Fursa, who is laid to rest in a chapel of a Church on Erchinoald's own estate at Péronne. This becomes the principal monastery associated with Fursa rather than Lagny. Even in the ninth-century Péronne remained closely tied to Irish monasteries in the eastern midlands, Slane and Louth. |
| 650 | Agilbert, a Frank who had been studying in Ireland, becomes bishop of the West Saxons (ASC) |
| 651 | Oswine killed 20 August; Aidan died 31 August |
| 653 | Peada, sub-king of the Middle Angles is baptized; mission sent to the Middle Angles; late in the year Cedd is withdrawn from the Middle Angles and sent to Essex; death of Honorius, bishop of Canterbury, 30 September |
| 654 | Cedd consecrated bishop for the East Saxons |
| 655 | Lastingham founded in Lent by Cedd at the command of Œthelwald, king of Deira |
|  | Penda's last campaign against Northumbria, with an army including 'thirty royal leaders', among them, Œthelwald son of Oswald, king of Deira: *Atbret Iudeu*, 'The Restitution of *Iudeu*', by which, according to the *Historia Brittonum*, Oswiu is forced by Penda to hand over the treasures in the fortress of *Iudeu* (probably Stirling); these Penda then distributes to the kings of the Britons; battle of the Winwæd (near Leeds and thus in Deira), in which Penda is defeated by Oswiu on his way south and killed, 15 November |
| 658 | Mercians rebel against Oswiu and recover their independence; Wulfhere made king of the Mercians |
| 664 | Synod of Whitby; Colmán, the last bishop of the Northumbrians sent from Iona, leaves: the end of 'the episcopate of the Irish' in Northumbria (635–64) Bubonic plague: deaths of Diarmait and Blaímac (Blathmac), kings of Tara, and Deusdedit, bishop of Canterbury, Tuda, bishop of the Northumbrians |

| | |
|---|---|
| *c.*666 | Letter of Pope Vitalian to Oswiu, king of the Northumbrians; the pope welcomes what seems to have been Oswiu's statement that he would use Northumbrian military power to enforce orthodoxy in Northern Britain and its adjacent islands |
| 668 | Theodore of Tarsus consecrated by Pope Vitalian with the title archbishop of the island of Britain |
| 669 | Theodore arrives at Canterbury 27 May and soon afterwards goes on a visitation of the English kingdoms; removes Chad from the bishopric of York and installs Wilfrid in his place |
| | Wulfhere asks Theodore for a bishop to replace Jaruman, recently dead, and Theodore asks Oswiu to send Chad from his monastery at Lastingham (N. Yorks.) to Mercia |
| 670 | Oswiu dies 15 February |
| 673 | Synod of Hertford, presided over by Theodore |
| 674 | Foundation of Wearmouth by Benedict Biscop |
| 675 | Wulfhere dies; between 675 and 679 the power of Ecgfrith, king of the Northumbrians, reaches its peak |
| *c.*675 | Cogitosus writes his Life of Brigit |
| 678 | Expulsion of Wilfrid from Northumbria; his diocese divided by Archbishop Theodore into three (Bernicia, Deira, and Lindsey) |
| 679 | Æthelred, king of the Mercians, defeats Ecgfrith, king of the Northumbrians, in the battle of the Trent; Ælfwine, Ecgfrith's brother and joint king, is killed; and Lindsey is lost to Mercian overlordship; the Synod of Hatfield is summoned by Theodore, 'archbishop of the island of Britain and of Canterbury', to declare the English Church's Trinitarian faith |
| 680 | Hild, abbess of Whitby, dies |
| 681 | Foundation of the monastery of Jarrow by Benedict Biscop, aided by Ceolfrith who becomes its abbot |
| 684 | A Northumbrian army sent to invade Brega; it ravages the country and returns with captives (hostages?); Synod of Adtuifyrdi: Bede, *HE* iv. 28/26 |
| 685 | Dedication of the Church of Jarrow; Bridei son of Derilei, king of Fortriu, defeats and kills Ecgfrith, king of the Northumbrians, 20 May, at Dunnichen near Forfar (Nechtanesmere); Ecgfrith is probably buried on Iona; the end of Northumbrian overlordship over the Picts |

678 × 687     (perhaps *c*.685) Armagh goes over to the Roman Easter; the Book of the Angel was written shortly after this change

686     The first visit to Northumbria of Adomnán, abbot of Iona

686–8     Cædwalla king of the West Saxons; by him the kingdom of the Isle of Wight is conquered and permanently annexed to Wessex

687     Cuthbert dies 20 March and is buried in the Church at Lindisfarne; Wilfrid, recalled from exile, rules Lindisfarne for one year, but his rule causes great distress to the community

688     Adomnán's second visit to Northumbria; perhaps the visit on which he meets Ceolfrith, who became abbot of Wearmouth–Jarrow on 12 May; perhaps also the occasion on which Adomnán is persuaded to change to the Roman Easter, although he is unable to secure the agreement of the monks on Iona; Sigfrith, abbot of Wearmouth, resigns by 12 May, and dies on 22 August; Eadberht consecrated bishop of Lindisfarne, ending Wilfrid's year of authority over Lindisfarne

688 × 689     The probable date of the negotiations leading to the Testament of Áed of Sleaty, when Bishop Áed subjects his Church and his kindred to the bishop of Armagh

688 × 693     Tírechán writes his *Collectanea*

688 × 694     Ine, king of the West Saxons, promulgates his laws

689     Benedict Biscop dies 12 January

690     Death of Archbishop Theodore

692     Wilfrid again expelled from Northumbria

695     Fínsnechtae Fledach, king of Tara, killed in battle; succeeded by Loingsech mac Óengussa of Cenél Conaill

    Laws of Wihtred, king of Kent, promulgated

*c*.695     Muirchú writes his Life of St Patrick

696     Œthelwald, hermit of Farne, buried 'next to the bodies of the aforesaid bishops [Aidan and Cuthbert] in the Church of the blessed apostle Peter' (Bede, *HE* v. 1)

697     Adomnán arranges for the Law of the Innocents (the Law of Adomnán) to be promulgated at Birr (Co. Offaly, on the border between Munster and Mide) by a joint lay–ecclesiastical assembly (which Adomnán himself describes as a synod)

    Adomnán may also have been writing his Life of Columba in response to the centenary of the saint's death in 697 (it was not completed until after the promulgation of the Law of the Innocents)

698      Elevation of Cuthbert's body 20 March; Eadberht, bishop of Lindisfarne, dies 5 May (*HE* iv. 30)

A proposed date for the Lindisfarne Gospels

'A royal leader of the Northumbrians', Berhtred son of Beornhæth, who had been the leader of the army which invaded Brega in 684, is defeated in battle and killed by the Picts

704/5      Adomnán, abbot of Iona, dies

705      Aldfrith, king of the Northumbrians, dies

706      Synod at the River Nidd; Wilfrid restored to Ripon and Hexham

709      Death of Wilfrid; Acca consecrated as bishop of Hexham

711      Picts defeated by the Northumbrians in the Plain of Manaw, 'between the Avon and the Carron' (near Falkirk)

Britons of Dumbarton defeated by Dál Riata

?711 × 716      Envoys of Naiton (Nechtan), king of the Picts, come to Ceolfrith, abbot of Wearmouth–Jarrow, because Naiton seeks his help in adopting the Roman Easter and tonsure, and also in building a stone Church

715      Death of Cellach Cualann, the last Uí Máil king of Leinster

716      The monks of Iona adopted the Roman Easter, persuaded by, among others, the English *peregrinus* Ecgberht

Ceolfrith resigns the abbacy of Wearmouth–Jarrow and goes on pilgrimage to Rome, taking with him the Codex Amiatinus but dying on the way at Langres, 25 September

Osred, king of the Northumbrians, killed and the monopoly of the descendants of Æthelfrith on the kingship of Northumbria broken

Æthelbald succeeded Ceolred as king of the Mercians; Mercia ceases to be dominated by the descendants of Penda

717      'The expulsion of the community of Iona across Druimm Alban by King Nechtan' of the Picts (Annals of Ulster)

718      The community of Iona adopt the Petrine tonsure

722      The battle of Allen, in which Fergal mac Máele Dúin, king of Tara, is killed when attempting to enforce the tribute owed by Leinster

725      Death of Wihtred, king of Kent, after which the kingdom is

firmly under the overlordship of Æthelbald, king of the Mercians

731     Bede completes his *Ecclesiastical History of the English People*

734     Flaithbertach mac Loingsig, the last king of Tara from Cenél Conaill, is driven from the kingship by Áed Allán of Cenél nÉogain

Bede's *Letter to Ecgberht*, bishop of York, written on 5 November

735     Death of Bede; Ecgberht, bishop of York, receives the pallium from Pope Gregory III and the right to call himself archbishop; the archbishops of Canterbury cease to be, as Theodore, Berhtwald, and Tatwine had all been, archbishops of all Britain

The battle of Fochart, in which Áed Allán defeats and kills Áed Rón, king of the Ulstermen; the kingdom of Conailli Muirthemne (most of Co. Louth) passes under Cenél nÉogain overlordship

737     'The Law of Patrick came into force throughout Ireland' (Annals of Ulster) Æthelbald, king of the Mercians, ravages Northumbria

738     The battle of Áth Senaig, in which the Uí Néill resoundingly defeated the Leinstermen and killed their king

741     'The hammering of Dál Riata by Óengus son of Forggus', king of the Picts (Annals of Ulster)

743     The battle of Serethmag, in which Áed Allán, king of Tara, was killed, Domnall mac Murchada was victorious, and succeeded as king of Tara

750     The battle of *Catohic* between the Britons (of Dumbarton) and the Picts, in which the Picts were defeated and Óengus's brother, Talorgan, was killed. 'The ebbing of the power of Óengus', king of the Picts (Annals of Ulster). 'Cuthred, king of the West Saxons, rose against Æthelbald and Óengus' (Continuation of Bede)

757     Æthelbald, king of the Mercians, killed by his own retinue; Beornred was the immediate successor but was killed in the same year by Offa

763     Death of Domnall mac Murchada, king of Tara (Cland Cholmáin), succeeded as king of Mide by his son, Donnchad, and as king of Tara by Niall son of Áed (Niall Frossach) of Cenél nÉogain

| 768 | The Britons (of Wales) adopt the Roman Easter under the leadership of Elfoddw |
|---|---|
| 770 | Donnchad mac Domnaill leads 'the army of the Uí Néill' into Leinster, encamps for three days at the Iron-Age site and traditional 'seat of kingship' at Knockaulin, and enforces his overlordship over Leinster |
| 775 | Donnchad sends an army of the Uí Néill to harry Munster; he enforces his control of the monastery of Clonard, in Mide but close to the Leinster border |
| 776 | The relics of Uinniau of Clonard taken on circuit |
| | An Uí Néill army again defeats the Munstermen |
| | The battle of Otford, after which Kent for a time passes out of Offa's dominion |
| 777 | Donnchad begins to attack Síl nÁeda Sláne (the Uí Néill of Brega) |
| 778 | Donnchad defeats and kills the king of Northern Brega; Donnchad, with Bresal, abbot of Iona, then proceeds to promulgate the Law of Columba Niall Frossach, Donnchad's predecessor as king of Tara, who had earlier abdicated, dies on Iona |
| | Offa ravages south Wales |
| 780 | Donnchad again attacks Leinster |
| | 'An assembly of the synods (or "elders"?) of the Uí Néill and the Leinstermen in the *oppidum* of Tara, where there were many anchorites and *scribae*, whose leader was Dublitter' (Annals of Ulster) |
| 786 | Separate legatine councils for the provinces of Canterbury (Southern English) and York (Northumbrians) |
| | Donnchad defeats the Uí Néill of Brega and kills several members of Síl nÁeda Sláne |
| 787 | Council of Chelsea, which accepts Offa's demand that Lichfield be elevated to an archbishopric; Ecgfrith consecrated as king of the Mercians during his father's reign |
| 793 | Sack of Lindisfarne 'by heathens' |
| 794 | 'All the islands of Britain were harried by heathens' (Annals of Ulster) |
| | Æthelberht, king of the East Anglians, executed by the command of King Offa |
| 795 | 'The burning of Rechrann by Gentiles and Skye was overwhelmed and laid waste' (Annals of Ulster) |

| | |
|---|---|
| 796 | Death of Offa; his son Ecgfrith killed at the end of the same year to be succeeded by Cenwulf; Kentishmen revolt against Mercian overlordship under Eadberht Præn |
| 797 | Death of Donnchad mac Domnaill, king of Tara (Cland Cholmáin); Áed Oirdnide (Cenél nÉogain) defeats and kills two brothers of Donnchad and another Uí Néill ruler in Mide at Druim Ríg, close to Tara; he thereby enforces his succession to Donnchad as king of Tara |
| 798 | Eadberht Præn deposed and mutilated by Cenwulf, king of the Mercians Caradog, king of Gwynedd, is slain by the English |
| 806 | Sixty-eight of the community of Iona killed by Vikings |
| 807–14 | Cellach, abbot of Iona, builds 'the new city of Columba at Kells' |
| 809 | Elfoddw 'archbishop of the kingdom of Gwynedd' dies (*Annales Cambriae*) |
| 816 | The English invade Snowdonia and the kingdom of Rhufoniog |
| 818 | Cenwulf lays waste the lands of the men of Dyfed |
| 819 | Áed Oirdnide, king of Tara, dies |
| 821 | Death of Cenwulf, king of the Mercians |
| 822 | The fortress of Degannwy is destroyed by the Mercians and they take under their power the kingdom of Powys |
| 825 | Beornwulf, king of the Mercians, defeated by Ecgberht, king of the West Saxons, at Ellendun, after which Ecgberht takes control of Sussex, Surrey, Kent, and Essex; Beornwulf is killed later the same year by the East Angles. Death of Hywel, king of Gwynedd, after whom Merfyn Frych, from the Isle of Man, takes power in Gwynedd and establishes a dynasty which would last until 1282 |

# Genealogies

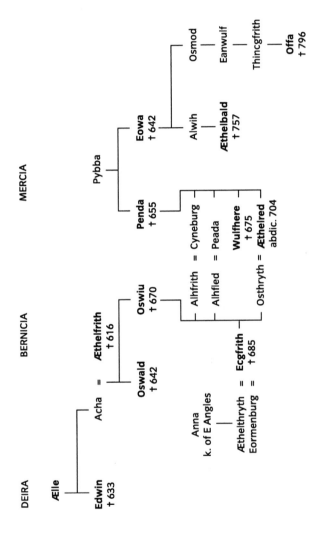

Genealogy 1  Three English dynasties: the marriages of enemies.

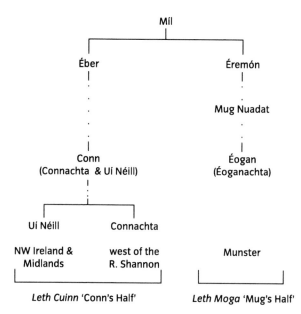

**Genealogy 2** The Milesian legend: a genealogical scheme for the domination of the *Féni*.

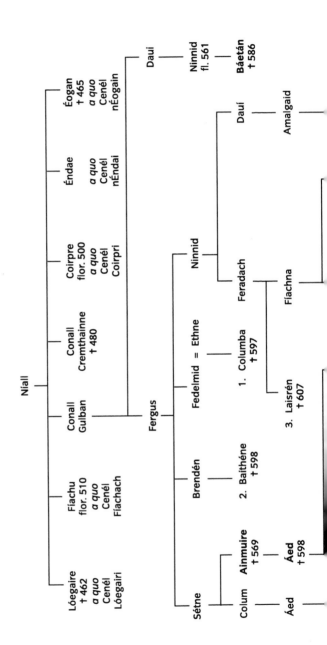

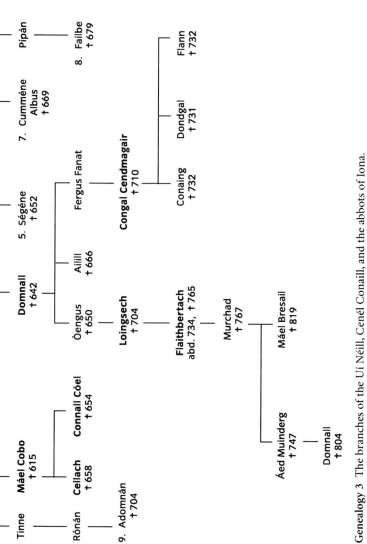

**Genealogy 3** The branches of the Uí Néill, Cenél Conaill, and the abbots of Iona.
(Numbers refer to the succession to the abbacy of Iona; names in bold are those of kings of Tara.)

# Glossary

**Adomnán:** ninth abbot of Iona (679–704/5), author of the Life of St Columba, completed in or after 697, and of an earlier work, *De Locis Sanctis*, 'On the Holy Places', about the sacred sites of Palestine. He was also the architect of *Cáin Adomnáin*, 'The Law of Adomnán', promulgated at a great mixed secular and ecclesiastical assembly at Birr, Co. Offaly, in 697, and designed to give physical protection to non-combatants, women, children, and clerics.

**Aetius:** the victor at the battle of the Catalaunian Fields in 451 against Attila's Huns. As the most powerful Roman general in the west, he was the recipient of an appeal by the Britons for help against victorious barbarians (446 × 452). With his murder at the hands of the Emperor Valentinian in 454, the Roman Empire was fatally weakened in the west.

**Alba, Albu:** the Irish name for Britain. From 900 used for the new kingdom of the Scots.

**Angles:** one of the peoples said by Bede to have invaded and colonized Britain. They came from Angeln, now Schleswig-Holstein at the base of the Jutland peninsula.

**annals:** a form of chronicle in which the information is entered under a sequence of years.

**annonae** (Latin plural): a form of taxation in food and other supplies for the Roman army (see **epimenia**).

**archbishop:** a term first securely attested in the British Isles with Theodore, archbishop of the Island of Britain and of Canterbury, who arrived in England in 669 and died in 690. His successors, Berhtwald and Tatwine, inherited his position, but in 735 Ecgberht was made archbishop of York, while Nothelm, Tatwine's successor, became archbishop just of the province of Canterbury; the settlement of 735 created the situation which endured, with some adjustments, to the present day. The terminology of this settlement, which Bede greatly desired to be put in place, was used by him for the period before Theodore. He therefore termed Augustine an archbishop, whereas in the contemporary letters of Gregory the Great he was only entitled a metropolitan bishop. The title of archbishop was claimed in Ireland, probably first by Kildare and then by Armagh; both claimed jurisdiction over the island of Ireland, and this makes it likely that their claim imitated the authority given to Theodore over the whole of Britain.

**Bede:** the greatest scholar of the English in the Anglo-Saxon period, born in 672 or 673 within the lands of Wearmouth, died in 735. He was given by his parents to Benedict Biscop, founder and first abbot of Wearmouth, at the age of 7 to be educated, and then to Ceolfrith, presumably at or after the foundation of Jarrow in 680. He saw himself primarily as an interpreter of the Bible, but he is most often remembered today as the author of *The Ecclesiastical History of the English People*, completed in 731.

**Brega:** the fertile region north of Dublin and south of the River Dee in Co. Louth, bounded on the east by the Irish Sea and on the West by Mide (Meath). Brega included major royal sites, notably Tara and Tailtiu. From the seventh century it was ruled by the descendants of Áed Sláne, Síl nÁeda Sláne, one of the principal branches of the Uí Néill (q.v.).

**Britain:** the name appears in three senses in the early Middle Ages, each overlapping with the others. The first is geographical: the island, together with those small islands attached to it. In this sense, Iona was said by Bede to belong to Britain. The second was derived from late Roman government: Britain was then a 'diocese', a super-province, of the Empire, with constituent provinces, such as *Britannia Prima*, 'The First Britain'; often the plural was used, *Britanniae*, 'the Britains', namely the British provinces. This usage continued in Latin scholarly writing long after the end of formal Roman rule. The third sense was ethnic: lands inhabited by Britons. In this sense, *Britannia* was used for Brittany, because it was settled by Britons. By the end of the ninth-century at least, and probably already in the eighth century, 'Britain' could also be used for those parts of the parent island inhabited by Britons. These overlapping senses also had historical significance: Theodore was archbishop of Britain, very possibly because, in the Eastern Empire, archbishops might preside over 'dioceses' and Britain had been a diocese; yet he claimed to be archbishop of the entire island of Britain, namely Britain in the first sense.

**British (language):** the Celtic language spoken by the Britons, from which Welsh, Cornish, and Breton are derived. British was subject to strong influence from Latin in the Roman and post-Roman period, and this was one influence which caused it to diverge from Pictish.

**Brittonic, Brythonic:** an overarching term for the language spoken by the Britons before the Roman conquest and all its daughter languages: Pictish, Welsh, Cumbric (the Brittonic language of southern Scotland), Cornish, and Breton. Brittonic languages belong, together with the Goidelic languages, to the Insular group within Celtic; but it is a matter of dispute whether affinities within this group, as opposed to the ancient Celtic languages of the Continent, arose from an original common parentage or from the influence of geographical proximity at a later period.

**Celtic:** one family within the broader Indo-European family of languages (others being, for example, Germanic and Italic, the latter including Latin, the former English). The Celtic languages were widespread in Europe in antiquity, but had all died out on the Continent by the end of the Roman period or shortly afterwards, apart from British, introduced into Brittany by immigrants. From this period on, the two families of Celtic languages were the Brittonic and the Goidelic (or Gaelic).

**cemetery:** an area set aside for human burials. These might take the form of cremation or inhumation. The broad trend was towards inhumation, with the body laid on its back and the legs extended ('extended supine inhumation' as opposed to 'crouched inhumation' and other forms). These extended inhumations were also increasingly orientated, with the head to the West and the feet to the east, even before conversion to Christianity.

**cenél** (Irish): 'kindred', common in the names of royal dynasties. An Irish example is the kindred to which St Columba and most early abbots of Iona belonged, Cenél Conaill. Its kingdom came to be known as Tír Conaill, 'the Land of Conall'. Similarly, its neighbour to the east was called Cenél nÉogain, 'the Kindred of Éogan'; its earliest territory was Inis Éogain, 'Inishowen', in the north-east of Co. Donegal; later lands were Tír Eóghain, Tyrone. These *cenéla* were patrilineal kindreds: one was a member if one could trace one's descent in the male line from the common ancestor, Conall or Éogan.

**civitas** (Latin): the etymological meaning is 'the community of fellow citizens', *cives*. It was used for Gaulish and British tribes or peoples, such as the Cantii of Kent, but by the late Roman period more often of the city which was the political centre of the tribal territory. In the post-Roman period it is found in Ireland used of major churches, because a fourth-century *civitas* was expected to have its bishop, so that, by reverse reasoning, a church with a bishop must be a *civitas*. Then this sense might be extended to major churches which were not episcopal.

**cland, clann** (Irish): 'offspring' and thus 'kindred' as in Cland Cholmáin, 'the Offsping of Colmán', the principal royal dynasty of Mide. This was the term which gave English 'clan', but it was derived from a Romano-British slang use of Latin *planta*, 'plant' for children (hence Welsh *plant*).

**cóiced** (Irish): 'a fifth' (the fraction); the term was used for the major provinces of Ireland, so that Leinster, Munster, the Ulaid etc. were 'fifths'; in the early Irish annals it is used only for the province of Ulster, but in the laws for all the principal provinces.

**Cymry** (plural, singular **Cymro**) is the principal word used by the medieval British to refer to themselves; similarly, the Welsh language is *Cymraeg* (the suffix -*eg* was used for languages, as in *Saesneg*, English, and *Gwyddeleg*, Irish). In the early medieval period, the Cymry were the Britons as a whole rather than the Welsh in particular; this wider sense was preserved in Cumberland and Cumbria. The English, however, seem to have used *Wealas* for the Britons of Wales and Cornwall (and earlier parts of what became England), but *Cumbras* only for the northern Britons, perhaps because many of the latter had lived beyond the formal Roman frontier on Hadrian's Wall and were thus not *Wealas* in the sense of Roman provincials. In origin *Cymry* means 'people of the same district' (*bro*). This produces a problem: how did a people whose territories stretched from the Forth to the Channel think of themselves as 'fellow locals', *bro* being a word for a local district, not some extended territory? A possible answer is that the term was originally linguistic, *Cymraeg* (*Combrogica*) being a word for the local vernacular as opposed to the official language of the Empire, Latin. As it happened, the local vernacular was the same language from the Forth to the Channel. Another term for the Britons was *Brython*, Latin *Brittones*, a variant of *Britanni*, introduced into Britain, along with *Britannia*, by the Romans (see under **Prydain**).

diocese: in the late Roman Empire a diocese was a form of super-province; thus Britain in the fourth century was a diocese divided into four provinces; see under **Britain**.

domnach (Irish), **dominicum** (Latin): early Latin terms for a church, in the sense of a building, as opposed to a community of believers. Its literal meaning was 'the Lord's place', from *dominus* 'lord'; it was the early Christian Latin word corresponding to the Greek *kuriakon*, the latter being the origin of English 'Church'. The Latin term, and then the Irish *domnach*, went out of use at an early date, probably *c.*500. For this reason there are no examples of *domnach* recorded from Gaelic Scotland. The distribution of *domnach* names thus becomes crucial evidence for assessing the progress of Christianity among the Irish before the end of the fifth century.

Ecgberht (1): the first Ecgberht took a vow to be a **peregrinus**, when he was studying in Ireland in the monastery of Ráith Máelsigi in 664 and was in danger of death from the plague. From his base in Ireland, he was the initiator of the English mission to Frisia, of which the principal figure was Willibrord, later bishop of Utrecht. Later he moved to Iona, where, in 716, he played a major part in persuading the monks to change to the Roman Easter. He died on Iona at Easter in 729, and the notice of his death acts as the culmination of Bede's *Ecclesiastical History*.

Ecgberht (2): the second Ecgberht was from 732 bishop and then, from 735 to 766, archbishop of York. He was of the Northumbrian royal dynasty and brother to the most effective of the eighth-century kings of Northumbria, Eadberht (737–58). Ecgberht was the recipient in 734 of a detailed letter from Bede about church reform, which is a key to understanding his *Ecclesiastical History*, and a key also to understanding the development of the Northumbrian church in the eighth century.

**epimenia** (Latin, from Greek, plural): literally 'monthly supplies'. This is a term used by Gildas, alongside *annona*, for the supplies given by 'the proud tyrant' and the councillors of the Britons to the Saxon army, when it undertook to fight against the Picts and the Irish. It is striking that Gildas knew the correct technical terms used in the late Roman Empire for such supplies. The situation—a barbarian army maintained by the supply system originally intended for the Roman army—was a common way in which barbarian peoples were able to gain access to, and mobility within, the Empire.

**Franks**: much the most powerful Continental neighbours of the inhabitants of Britain and Ireland. They became Catholic Christians *c.*500 and broke the tendency of Germanic barbarian Christians to be Arians; this form of conversion ensured that there was no religious divide between the Franks and their Gallo-Roman subjects, and that there was a natural link with the Eastern Roman Empire, whose formal authority the Franks still recognized for much of the sixth century. On the other hand, in correspondence with the Empire the Franks were also anxious to claim overlordship over their neighbours to the north and east, including some, at least, of the English. Even in the seventh century Hadrian, on his way from Rome to Canterbury, was detained by the Franks in 669 on suspicion of being a secret East Roman envoy to 'the kings of Britain', charged with a mission hostile to the Franks.

**Frisians**: north-eastern neighbours of the Franks around the mouths of the Rhine and one of the Germanic peoples said by Bede to have participated in the Anglo-Saxon settlement in Britain. Of all the Continental Germanic languages, Frisian is the closest to English. They built up a position as major middlemen in the trade routes which came up from the Mediterranean, along the Rhine and the Meuse, and so over the North Sea to England. From *c.*690 they were the objects of an Anglo-Saxon mission.

**Gael, Gaelic**: see **Goidelic**.

**Gaul, Gaulish, Gallic**: the Gauls were the Celtic people of Gaul, and thus neighbours of the Britons. Unlike the Britons they gradually abandoned their Celtic language, Gaulish, in favour of Latin. By the sixth century they seem to have considered themselves to be as much Romans as Gauls (hence the modern historians' term 'Gallo-Romans'). The Latin language spoken in northern Gaul eventually developed to become French. From no later than the fifth century Britons were established in large numbers in the north-west of Gaul; they kept their British language (hence Breton) and were thus felt by the Gallo-Romans to be a barbarian, non-Roman people, even though they were as much ex-Roman provincials as were the Gallo-Romans themselves.

**gens** (Latin): 'people', a term used by Bede for the English as a whole but also for the peoples of the principal English kingdoms, such as Northumbria. Almost always, Bede avoided using the term for the two constituent English peoples of Northumbria, the Bernicians and the Deirans. Adomnán uses *gens* for a group denoted by the Irish terms *dál, corcu,* and *rige*. It was sometimes perceived as a form of kindred, but its precise nature is not fully understood.

**Germania, Germanic:** Germania is a useful scholarly term for the area of Continental Europe, including Scandinavia, occupied in antiquity by speakers of the different Germanic languages. The latter formed one of the daughter families of Indo-European (alongside Celtic, Slavonic, Greek, etc.): English, Dutch, German, Swedish are examples of modern Germanic languages; Gothic was a major language in late antiquity but is now extinct.

**Gildas:** a Briton and the author of the *De Excidio Britanniae*, 'On the Ruin of Britain', probably written between *c.*530 and 545; he is also said to be the author of a Penitential and some fragments of letters. The *De Excidio* is of exceptional importance because no other written text survives from Britain in the sixth century (leaving aside inscriptions on stones or bone).

**Goidelic:** a family of Celtic languages including three which survived into the twentieth century, Modern Irish, Manx, and Scottish Gaelic. These all descend from Old Irish. With the Brittonic languages (q.v.), they form the Insular Celtic group. The scholarly term Goidelic is derived from Old Irish Goídelc, itself very probably a borrowing from Welsh Gwyddeleg; from Goídelc come Modern Irish Gaeilge, Scottish Gaelic Gáidhlig (and the English borrowing Gaelic).

**Gwynedd:** the British kingdom of north-west Wales, including Anglesey.

**Ireland, Irish:** throughout the pre-Viking period, the Irish had a strongly linguistic and cultural sense of their identity. Although more than one Celtic language may have been spoken in Ireland in the Iron Age, only Irish appears to have survived by 500. The colonies on the West coast of Britain, from Cornwall to Argyll, all brought Irish into Britain, but only the one in Argyll endured: this colonial branch of Irish is the origin of Scottish Gaelic. In Wales, Irish may not have continued beyond the seventh century. Some Englishmen learnt Irish in the seventh century, through exile, as with Oswald and Oswiu, kings of the Northumbrians, or by periods of study in Ireland, as with Cedd and Chad. The period of greatest Irish influence on the English thus followed the decline of Irish among the Britons.

**long-cist cemetery**: a type of inhumation cemetery in which graves were lined with stone slabs; there are numerous examples up the east coast of Scotland both in Lothian, a British area, and north of the Forth in Pictland.

**metropolitan bishop**: the bishop who presided over a provincial synod and was expected to participate in the consecration of other bishops within his province. The province in question was not, in origin, an ecclesiastical unit but was taken over from the late Roman Empire.

**ogham**: an alphabet developed to fit Irish as it was before the major changes which swept over north-western European languages in the fifth and sixth centuries. Although it was adapted to suit Irish, the inventor almost certainly knew Latin and probably a formal grammar of Latin. It was used for inscriptions, most often in a belt across southern Ireland from West Kerry (where it is densest in the Corkaguiney Peninsula) to Co. Waterford and into Co. Carlow. It was also used in the Irish settlements in western Britain, though hardly at all in the most successful of them, Argyll; curiously, it is better attested in eastern Scotland, among the Picts, than among the Irish in the West.

**pallium**: a piece of woollen cloth worn by a bishop celebrating mass. A custom arose by which popes gave a pallium to certain bishops. By Bede's time this was associated with the status of an archbishop; so, when Ecgberht received a pallium at the end of Bede's life, in 735, he also acquired the rank of archbishop. This connection was not yet in existence in the time of Gregory the Great; he granted the pallium to bishops who were not even metropolitans.

**Pict, Pictish**: the people of eastern Scotland north of the Forth, and probably also of western Scotland north of Ardnamurchan. They are first attested in the late third century and were evidently a federation of distinct peoples, such as the Verturiones, whose name continued through the post-Roman period as Fortriu, and the Caledonians, whose name is preserved in place names such as Dunkeld and Schiehallion. In the early Romano-British period Tacitus called the Caledonians and their allies Britons, and there is a strong argument for seeing the Picts as essentially those Britons who remained outside the Empire. This implies, however, that the British peoples of southern Scotland, such as the Gododdin, the ancient Votadini, were sufficiently closely allied with Rome that, even though they were beyond Hadrian's Wall, they did not ultimately become part of the Pictish federation. The effect was that the line between the Britons, allied with

Rome, and the Britons who remained beyond Rome's political orbit was drawn roughly along the Antonine Wall, even though that particular frontier line was held for relatively short periods. By the eighth century, Bede could regard Pictish as a quite distinct language from British; and the scanty records of Pictish suggest that he was right.

**Prydain, Prydyn:** Prydain was the normal medieval and later Welsh word for Britain; Prydyn was used for the Picts; yet even long after the Picts had become a distinct people with a distinct language, the two words, Prydyn and Prydain, were sometimes confused. The Irish cognate of Prydyn, Cruthin, was sometimes used for the people normally known as the Cruithni, situated in Antrim (apart from the north-east) and West Down. But that is not a strong reason for positing any close relationship between them, even in the prehistoric period, since different Celtic peoples sometimes bore the same name (for example, the British people of East Yorkshire were the Parisii, who may or may not have had something to do with the Parisii of the Paris region).

**Romance:** see **Latin**.

**runes:** an alphabet devised for Germanic dialects. It was used, but not exclusively, for inscriptions (just as ogham survives predominantly in the form of stone inscriptions but may have had other uses). It was brought to Britain by the Anglo-Saxon settlers in the fifth century. In Britain it tended to be associated with the English language as opposed to Latin: on the Ruthwell Cross the quotations from the Old English poem, the Dream of the Rood, are in runes, while Latin text is in the Roman alphabet.

**Saxons:** one of the peoples from whom, according to Bede, the Anglo-Saxon settlers derived. This appears to have been the case, even though late Roman writers tended to use 'Saxons' for sea-borne raiders, some of whom were probably not Saxons. The Welsh and Irish terms for 'the English' remain to this day 'Saxons' (Welsh *Saeson*, Old Irish *Saxan*). Gildas, like other writers in Latin, termed the Germanic settlers in Britain Saxons. It is thus something of a puzzle why Gregory the Great termed them English, a usage which prevailed.

**tuath** (Irish): 'people' and thus both 'the people of a minor kingdom' and 'the laity' as opposed to the Church. The king of a *tuath*, *rí tuaithe*, was the lowest grade of Irish king.

**Uí** (Irish): 'grandsons' and, more generally, 'descendants'. The term was commonly used in the names of royal dynasties, such as Uí Néill, Uí Chernaig.

**Ulaid, Ulster:** a people of north-eastern Ireland. Their own kingdoms were in the east of Co. Down, including the Ards Peninsula; they usually provided the over-king of the entire province, approximately the modern counties of Antrim and Down and also, at least until 735, much of Louth. However, they had to share the over-kingship of the province with the Cruithni (or Cruthin), who occupied most of Co. Antrim and the West of Co. Down.

**Venedotian:** see **Gwynedd** (Venedotia is the Latin version of the name Gwynedd).

**Welsh (Wealas, Walas, Wilisc):** by the end of the fifth century the Germanic settlers within the Empire, both in northern Gaul and in Britain, used the plural term *Walas* (of which *Wealas* is a variant) for the Roman provincial population. It was a term used by others, not by the provincials themselves, and it went along with the political and social superiority of the Germanic settlers as opposed to the Romano-British or Gallo-Roman populations. In Britain it was used of the Britons, who had belonged to the Empire, but not of the Picts or the Irish, who had not. It was not, therefore, by this stage, a general word for a foreigner. It also gained a strong linguistic dimension as the distinction between Britons and English became more linguistic; hence the term for an interpreter, already used as a name for a contemporary of Bede, a bishop, significantly, of Hereford, was *wealhstod*. During the Anglo-Saxon period the association between Britishness and servile status became firmer, so that *wealh* could be used simply of an unfree person. For the British terms for themselves, see **Cymry**.

# Maps

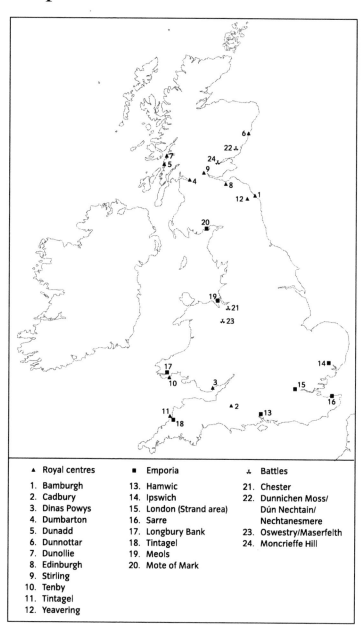

| ▲ Royal centres | ■ Emporia | ⏀ Battles |
|---|---|---|
| 1. Bamburgh | 13. Hamwic | 21. Chester |
| 2. Cadbury | 14. Ipswich | 22. Dunnichen Moss/ |
| 3. Dinas Powys | 15. London (Strand area) | Dún Nechtain/ |
| 4. Dumbarton | 16. Sarre | Nechtanesmere |
| 5. Dunadd | 17. Longbury Bank | 23. Oswestry/Maserfelth |
| 6. Dunnottar | 18. Tintagel | 24. Moncrieffe Hill |
| 7. Dunollie | 19. Meols | |
| 8. Edinburgh | 20. Mote of Mark | |
| 9. Stirling | | |
| 10. Tenby | | |
| 11. Tintagel | | |
| 12. Yeavering | | |

**Map 11** Britain: emporia, royal centres, battles.

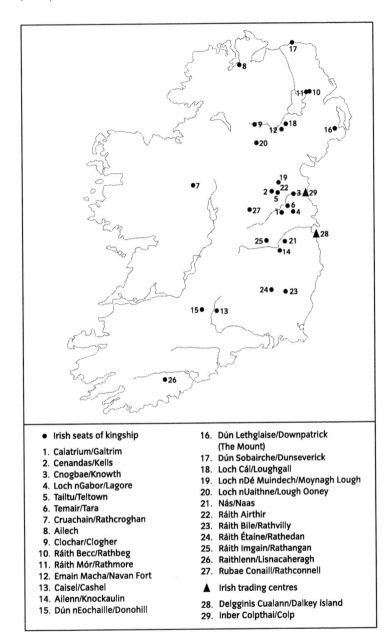

**Map 12** Irish seats of kingship and trading centres.

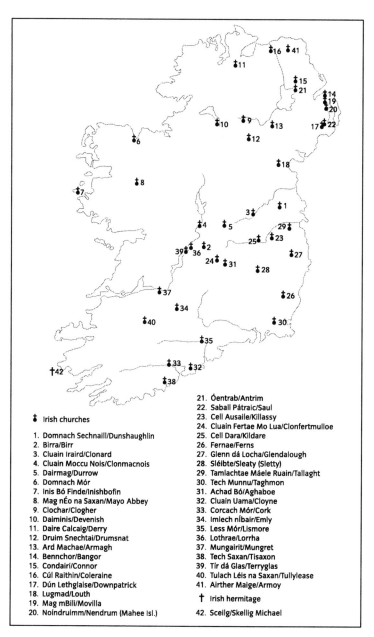

21. Óentrab/Antrim
22. Saball Pátraic/Saul
23. Cell Ausaile/Killassy
24. Cluain Fertae Mo Lua/Clonfertmulloe

**ᛏ Irish churches**

1. Domnach Sechnaill/Dunshaughlin
2. Birra/Birr
3. Cluain Iraird/Clonard
4. Cluain Moccu Nois/Clonmacnois
5. Dairmag/Durrow
6. Domnach Mór
7. Inis Bó Finde/Inishbofin
8. Mag nÉo na Saxan/Mayo Abbey
9. Clochar/Clogher
10. Daiminis/Devenish
11. Daire Calcaig/Derry
12. Druim Snechtai/Drumsnat
13. Ard Machae/Armagh
14. Bennchor/Bangor
15. Condairi/Connor
16. Cúl Raithin/Coleraine
17. Dún Lethglaise/Downpatrick
18. Lugmad/Louth
19. Mag mBili/Movilla
20. Noíndruimm/Nendrum (Mahee Isl.)

25. Cell Dara/Kildare
26. Fernae/Ferns
27. Glenn dá Locha/Glendalough
28. Sléibte/Sleaty (Sletty)
29. Tamlachtae Máele Ruain/Tallaght
30. Tech Munnu/Taghmon
31. Achad Bó/Aghaboe
32. Cluain Uama/Cloyne
33. Corcach Mór/Cork
34. Imlech nÍbair/Emly
35. Less Mór/Lismore
36. Lothrae/Lorrha
37. Mungairit/Mungret
38. Tech Saxan/Tisaxon
39. Tír dá Glas/Terryglas
40. Tulach Léis na Saxan/Tullylease
41. Airther Maige/Armoy

**ᛏ Irish hermitage**

42. Sceilg/Skellig Michael

Map 13  Irish churches and hermitages.

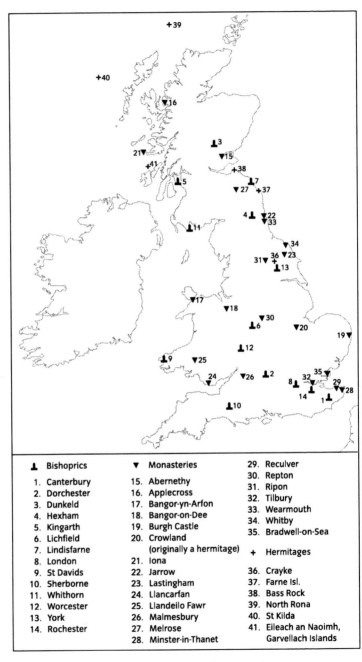

**Map 14** Britain: hermitages, bishoprics, and monasteries.

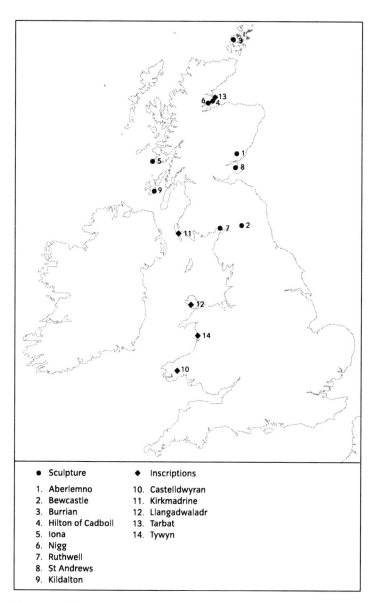

Map 15  Britain: inscriptions and sculpture.

# Index

For the sequence of the alphabet Old English *æ* is treated as *ae*; likewise Welsh *dd*, *ll*, and *rh* are not treated as separate letters (e.g. *ll* is placed as if it were a pair of *ls*). Irish 'nasalization' is ignored in the alphabetic sequence.

Lightning Source UK Ltd.
Milton Keynes UK
UKOW021656091211

183501UK00002B/1/P